Are Small Firms Important?
Their Role and Impact

Are Small Firms Important? Their Role and Impact

edited by

Zoltan J. Acs
University of Baltimore and
U.S. Bureau of the Census

Published in association with

U.S. Small Business Administration
SBA

Springer Science+Business Media, LLC

Library of Congress Cataloging-in-Publication Data

Are small firms important? : their role and impact / edited by Zoltan J. Acs.
p. cm.
Includes bibliographical references and index.
ISBN 978-1-4613-7356-8 ISBN 978-1-4615-5173-7 (eBook)
DOI 10.1007/978-1-4615-5173-7
1. Small business—United States. 2. New business enterprises—United States. 3. Small business—Government policy—United States. I. Acs, Zoltan J.
HD2346.U5A844 1999
338.6'42'0973—dc21 98-51488
CIP

Originally published by Kluwer Academic Publishers in 1999
Softcover reprint of the hardcover 1st edition 1999

Printed on acid-free paper.

This printing is a digital duplication of the original edition.

CONTENTS

CONTRIBUTORS

Zoltan J. Acs
U.S. Bureau of the Census and
University of Baltimore
Baltimore, MD

Paul Almeida
Georgetown University
Washington, DC

David B. Audretsch
Indiana University
Bloomington, IN

John R. Baldwin
Statistics Canada
Ottawa, Ontario, Canada

Candida Brush
Boston University
Boston, MA

John Sibley Butler
University of Texas
Austin, TX

Bo Carlsson
Case Western Reserve University
Cleveland, OH

Jere W. Glover
U.S. Small Business Administration
Washington, DC

Patricia Gene Green
University of Missouri
Kansas City, MO

John Haltiwanger,
U.S. Bureau of the Census and
University of Maryland
College Park, MD

Robert D. Hisrich
Case Western Reserve University
Cleveland, OH

Joanne Johnson
Statistics Canada
Ottawa, Ontario, Canada

C.J. Krizan
U.S. Bureau of the Census
Washington D.C.

Joshua Lerner
National Bureau of Economics Research and
Harvard University
Boston, MA

Randal Morck
University of Alberta
Edmonton, Alberta, Canada

Bernard Yeung
University of Michigan,
Ann Arbor, MI

PREFACE

Americans have strong feelings about individual and political freedoms and are quick to defend them if they are threatened. But what about economic freedoms? Are there essential elements worth defending? Those looking for an answer would do well to observe the stream of visitors to the United States from countries struggling to get their economic feet on the ground. What do they want to know about? The remarkable phenomenon of small business and entrepreneurship—and why it thrives in the United States.

Looking back from the end of the 20th century, it now seems clear that small business has been America's great economic strength all along. But that recognition was slow in coming to public policy consciousness. Less than one-quarter century ago, little or no attention was given to small business in the world of government statistics gathering or policymaking.

Then in 1976, with Public Law 94-305, the U.S. Congress created within the U.S. Small Business Administration an Office of Advocacy with a mandate to, among other things:

> examine the role of small business in the American economy and the contribution which small business can make in improving competition, encouraging economic and social mobility for all citizens, restraining inflation, spurring production, expanding employment opportunities, increasing productivity, promoting exports, stimulating innovation and entrepreneurship, and providing an avenue through which new and untested products and services can be brought to the marketplace.

In more than 20 years of existence, the Office of Advocacy has taken a long look at small firms—their contributions to the economy as well as their problems and public policy concerns. Clearly, there is much more to learn, and while the available data are imperfect, Advocacy's Office of Economic Research continues to work with other agencies to develop and mine new data bases. Along the way, the Office of Advocacy has picked up additional responsibilities, including, under the Regulatory Flexibility Act, monitoring federal agencies' analysis of the small business effects of proposed new regulations. The regulatory analysis process has brought new urgency to the practical application of small business research.

The collection of studies assembled in this book represents recent research and the best thinking of top economists on small business' economic contributions. The report was compiled by the SBA Office of Advocacy's Chief Economic Advisor Zoltan J. Acs in conjunction with Chief Economist Fred A. Tarpley and Office of Economic Research Director Bruce D. Phillips.

The impressive performance of the U.S. economy over the last six years contrasts with rather lackluster performance in both Europe and Asia. During the Clinton Administration, while employment has remained virtually unchanged in the European Union, it has increased by at least 14 million in the United States. What accounts for the disparity in performance between the United States and its trading partners? Differences in competition, entrepreneurship and new firm startups are a major factor.

Throughout most of this century, observers looked at what amounted to a still photograph of the American economy, saw that bigness had distinct advantages in producing standardized products at lower cost, and concluded that big business drove the economy. But the American economy is not a still photograph—it's a motion picture that changes before our eyes. Looked at from the perspective of process, change, and evolution, small firms make at least two indispensable contributions to the American economy:

- As sources of constant experimentation and innovation, they are an integral part of the renewal process that defines market economies. They have a crucial role as leaders of technological change and productivity growth. In short, they change market structure.
- By creating opportunities for women, minorities, and immigrants, they are an essential mechanism by which millions enter the economic and social mainstream.

In short, the crucial barometer for economic and social well-being is the continued high level of creation of new and small firms in all sectors of the economy by all segments of society. It should be the role of government policy to facilitate that process by eliminating barriers to entry, lowering transaction costs, and minimizing monopoly profits by large firms. And it is the job of the U.S. Small Business Administration's Office of Advocacy to measure the contributions of small firms and to ensure that small business concerns get a fair hearing in government legislative and regulatory processes.

I have the hope that this book will shed much additional light on the role of small firms in the American economy. It is possible that the various papers assembled herein would make a useful collection of supplementary readings for students of small business and entrepreneurship.

The Office of Advocacy appreciates the support of the small business community in its research efforts. Those interested in knowing more may write the Office of Economic Research, Office of Advocacy, U.S. Small Business Administration, 409 3rd Street, S.W., Washington, D.C. 20416, visit the Internet site at *http://www.sba.gov/ADVO/* or call at (202) 205-6530.

Jere W. Glover
Chief Counsel for Advocacy

1. THE NEW AMERICAN EVOLUTION

ZOLTAN J. ACS

U.S. Burean of the Census and University of Baltimore, Baltimore, MD

THE MACROECONOMY IN THE 1990s

A quiet evolution has revolutionized the American economy. At the time of the 1992 presidential election one of the main issues in the public debate was competitiveness. A common perception was that U.S. industry was losing the global economic race and that if government didn't respond, living standards would suffer. In that recession year, Under-Secretary of Commerce Jeffrey E. Garten summed up the conventional economic thinking about our state of affairs (1992, p. 221): "Relative to Japan and Germany, our economic prospects are poor and our political influence is waning. Their economic underpinnings—trends in investment, productivity, market share in high technology, education, and training—are stronger. Their banks and industry are in better shape; their social problems are far less severe than ours" (see also Tyson, 1992; Thurow, 1992).

By 1996 it had become apparent to experts and laypeople alike that profound changes had occurred and that the economic anxiety of four years earlier was no longer widespread in the electorate. After a quarter century of painful ups and downs, the U.S. economy was doing extraordinarily well. According to Lawrence H. Summers, Deputy Treasury Secretary, "The economy seems better balanced than at any time in my professional lifetime" ("U.S. Sails," 1996, p. 1). Unemployment in 1998 was just under 5 percent, the economy was growing at 3 percent a year, inflation was at bay, manufacturing productivity was rising by 4 percent a year, the dollar was strong, and the Dow Jones Industrial Average was breaking records almost as a matter of course. The U.S. economy seemed to have restructured, moving from an industrial economy to an information one, and made the transition to the twenty-first century.

The impressive performance of the U.S. economy in the last few years may be contrasted with the rather lackluster performance of the economies of both Europe and Japan, where GNP has grown at less than 1.5 percent per annum in the last five years. In the European Union (EU) the unemployment rate has remained stubbornly in double digits, and in Japan the stock market has been stagnant since the early 1990s at half its previous level.

But a comparison of only the last few years may be heavily influenced by cyclical elements that may distort more long-term developments. It is instructive, therefore, to compare the macroeconomic experience in Europe and the United States over the last few decades. In the period 1960 to 1984, GNP grew at almost identical rates in Europe and the United States: it rose by 3.3 percent annually in the EU and 3.1 percent in the United States. But beneath this superficial similarity lie some fundamental differences. While the total employment in the EU was virtually unchanged, it increased by 33 million in the United States. (Another 25 million were added between 1983 and 1996.) At the same time, the capital stock increased by 3.5 percent per year in the EC and by 2.4 percent in the United States (De Jong, 1989). As a result, labor productivity rose much more rapidly in Europe than in the United States—but so did unemployment. The unemployment rate hovered around 5 percent in the United States from 1960 to 1975 while it stayed below 3 percent in the European Union. By 1982 it rose rapidly on both sides of the Atlantic to around 10 percent. The unemployment rate has remained around 10 percent in Europe while it has been cut in half, to less than 5 percent, in the United States.

What explains this divergent macroeconomic behavior? While a number of factors can be cited, one of the contributing factors is certainly differences in competition, entrepreneurship, and new firm startups. The U.S. economy has had an extremely strong performance by new firms. Between 1960 and 1983, the number of corporations and partnerships in the United States more than doubled (from 2.0 million to 4.5 million) while the number of companies in Europe stagnated.[1] It declined in Sweden, Denmark, the Netherlands, and Britain and increased only slightly in West Germany, France, Switzerland, and Italy (De Jong, 1989). Between 1990 and 1996 this trend has continued in the United States. The number of corporations and partnerships increased from 5.271 million in 1990 to 6.631 million in 1996. The number of sole proprietorships has also increased from 14.783 million to 16.664 millions or 3.1 percent a year. The difference in business formation rates, in turn, reflects a number of other economic factors, such as consistently higher return on investment in the United States than in Europe, higher productivity, and lower unit labor costs. Other institutional factors such as less rigid labor and capital markets, freer competition, and lower industrial subsidies also play a role. According to Gary S. Becker (1998, p. 20), the 1992 Nobel laureate, "Europe's regulatory roadblocks and onerous taxation keep the job growth enjoyed by the United States out of reach."

How did the U.S. economy reinvent itself? It did so by fostering and promoting entrepreneurial activity (Hebert and Link, 1989). There are at least three entrepreneurial stories to the U.S. success. First, large firms that existed in mature industries have adapted, downsized, restructured, and reinvented themselves during the 1980s and 1990s and are now thriving. Large businesses have adopted and learned from smaller firms as they have downsized. As large firms have become leaner, their sales and profits have increased sharply. For example, General Electric cut its workforce by 40 percent, from over 400,000 twenty years ago to less than 240,000 in 1996, while sales increased fourfold, from less than $20 billion to nearly $80 billion (Harrison, 1994).

Second, while these large companies have been transforming themselves, new and small startup companies have been blossoming. Twenty years ago, Nucor Steel was a small steel manufacturer that had a few hundred employees and that embraced a new technology called *thin-slab casting*, allowing it to thrive while other steel companies were stumbling. In 1995, Nucor had 59,000 employees, sales of $3.4 billion, and a net income of $274 million. In fact, according to Lynch and Rothchild (1996), twenty-five companies, some of which did not exist in 1975, have created 1.4 million jobs.

Third, thousands of smaller firms have been founded by women, minorities, and immigrants. These new companies have come from every sector of the economy and every part of the country. Together these small firms also make a formidable contribution to the economy as each firm hires one or two employees. The cumulative effect of this new-firm formation was evident in the recovery from the 1991 recession when firms with fewer than five employees together created over 1 million jobs. The last two entrepreneurial success stories overlap with the role of new and small firms in the economy.

The purpose of this book is to examine a fundamental question: "Are small firms important?" This question can be understood only if it is recognized that change in our economy by definition is a dynamic process. This was pointed out by J.A. Schumpeter (1942) more than half a century ago in his classic work on capitalism, which is now being reconsidered. In order to understand this question one needs to take an evolutionary view. The static view misses the point completely by asking the wrong question or asking the question wrongly. When viewed through an evolutionary lens, small firms make two indispensable contributions to the American economy.

First, they are an integral part of the renewal process that pervades and defines market economies. New and small firms play a crucial role in experimentation and innovation that leads to technological change and productivity growth. *In short, small firms are about change and competition because they change market structure.* The U.S. economy is a dynamic organization that is always in the process of becoming rather than an established one that has arrived.

Second, small firms are the essential mechanism by which millions enter the economic and social mainstream of American society. Small business is the vehicle by which millions access the American dream because it creates opportunities for women, minorities, and immigrants. In this evolutionary process, community plays the crucial and indispensable role of providing the social glue and networking that binds together small firms in both high-tech and Main Street activities. The American economy is a democratic system, as well as an economic system, that invites change and participation.

After this introductory section, we present a theoretical framework for understanding the role of small firms in the economy.[2] In the third section we document the impact of small businesses on innovation, new firm startups, and job creation. The fourth section shows how small firms interact with the very fabric of American society by creating opportunities for women, minorities, and immigrants. Finally, we explain how community and the evolutionary process jointly connect us to the global economy.[3]

THE HISTORICAL BACKGROUND

With a few notable exceptions, for the better part of the history of the profession, economists have not spent much time studying small firms.[4] However, this has begun to change in the last twenty years. The twin oil shocks during the 1970s triggered an unexpected reappraisal of the role and importance of small and medium-sized enterprises. A surprising finding has been that small firms and entrepreneurship play a much more important role in economic growth than had been acknowledged previously.[5]

The view that the cornerstone of the modern economy is the large firm dates back to the onset of the industrial revolution. The concept of scale economies was proposed by Adam Smith (1776) with the famous passage on the pin factory. The classical economist's approach to industrial competition was dominated by an environment where technology was constantly increasing the minimum average plant size in a static context. Unfortunately, it reached its zenith in the late nineteenth century with the dominance of the trusts in steel, oil, and automobiles. The subsequent passage of the Sherman AntiTrust Act (1890) was intended to stem the growth of monopoly power.

In this view, which has prevailed for most of this century, small firms were not seen to play an important role in the economy, and furthermore, their role was expected to diminish in the future (Galbraith, 1956). This has been the case especially in the manufacturing sector, where large and even giant firms dominated Western economies throughout most of the twentieth century. As E.F. Schumacher pointed out (1973, p. 64): "I was brought up on the theory of economies of scale." In country after country, official policies favored large units of production and mechanisms of ownership. These goals were pursued in free-market and planned economies alike, as well as in developed and developing countries. *Thus, for the better part of two centuries, there was a convergence of opinion on the relevance of firm size, economies of scale, and their importance for economic growth.*[6]

Readers interested in documenting the role of small firms in the 1970s found much talk but few facts. For years the small-firm sector remained ignored and poorly understood even though a lot of people worked for small firms. However, all that has begun to change as powerful computers and large data sets have enabled researchers to assemble a far better understanding of the economic role of small firms.

In the first authoritative book on small businesses, *Small Business Economics*, Brock and Evans (1986) examined the changes in small businesses over time.[7] Between 1958 and 1980, the number of businesses in the U.S. economy increased from 10.7 million to 16.8 million. But the relative economic importance of small business in the overall economy declined over this period. Between 1958 and 1977 the share of employment accounted for by firms with fewer than 500 employees decreased from 55.5 percent to 52.5 percent. Between 1958 and 1979 the share of business receipts obtained by companies with less than $5 million in receipts declined from 51.5 percent to 28.7 percent (in part because the real value of the dollar declined). Between 1958 and 1977 the share of value added contributed by firms with 500 or fewer employees decreased from 57 percent to 52 percent. These trends are summarized in Table 1.1. The decline in the small-business share of value added was due to a shift in the small-business share of value added within industries. In other words, firms were getting bigger, and therefore the share of small firms was being reduced.[8]

However, by the early 1970s "cracks" had begun to appear in the structure of the manufacturing sector in some developed countries, including some of the most important firms and industries. At the same time, casual evidence began to suggest that small firms in several countries were outperforming their larger counterparts. One example of this was the U.S. steel industry—where new firms entered in the form of "minimills" (for example, Nucor), small-firm employment expanded, and the incumbent large companies shut down plants and reduced employment in a number of countries. Other examples are found in industries characterized by rapid product innovation, such as electronics and software. This development following

Table 1.1. Changes in the Small-Business Share of Employment, Sales, and Gross Product Originating (percent)

	Employment[a] (1958–1977)	Business Receipts (1958–1979)	Gross Product Originating (1958–1977)
Total change	−6%	−23%	−4%
Change due to shifts in industry composition[b]	+4	−2	+3
Change due to shifts in small business share within industries[c]	−9	−21	−7

Source: Brock and Evans (1986, p. 21, table 2.11).

Note: Small businesses are those with fewer than 500 employees for the employment and value-added measures and those with sales of under $5 million in 1958 dollars for the sales measure.

[a] Excludes the construction industry.

[b] Calculated under the assumption that each industry's share of total employment, sales, or value added, respectively, remained constant over the time period under consideration.

[c] Calculated under the assumption that small businesses' share of employment, sales, or value added, respectively, remained constant for each industry over the time period under consideration.

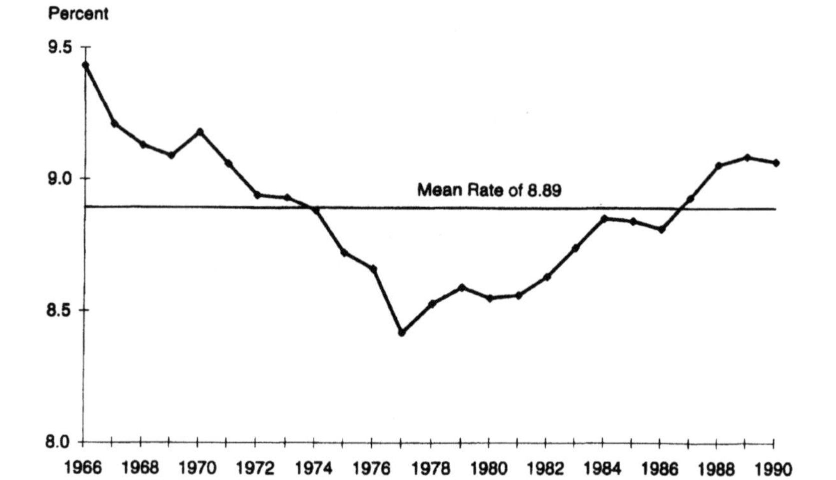

Figure 1.1. Self-Employment Rate in the OECD Countries.

the twin oil shocks triggered an unexpected reappraisal of the role and importance of small manufacturing firms, resulting in a divergence of opinion on the importance of firm size (Acs, 1984).[9]

In fact, several lines of research have found that something happened to the centuries-old trend toward larger business: depending on the measure of business size examined, the trend decelerated, ceased, or reversed itself sometime between the late 1960s and late 1970s. Contrary to the conventional wisdom at the time, Birch (1981, p. 8) found that "whatever else they are doing, large firms are no longer the major providers of new jobs for Americans." Davis (1990) showed that the typical nonfarm private-sector employee worked at increasingly larger establishments during the 1950s and 1960s but at increasingly smaller establishments in the late 1960s and 1970s. Brock and Evans (1989) showed that the average gross national product per firm increased from $150,000 in 1947 to $245,000 in 1980 but then decreased to $210,000 in 1986. Loveman and Sengenberger (1991) reported that average firm and establishment size began to decrease in most of the countries they examined in the 1970s after having increased from at least the end of World War II. Acs and Audretsch (1993) showed that the small-firm share of manufacturing employment increased in most OECD countries in the 1980s. Acs and Evans (1995) found that the increase in the self-employment rate after 1975 in most OECD countries was due to structural change (see Figure 1.1).

Between 1982 and 1992, the small-firm share of value added in the U.S. economy stabilized at 51 percent, peaking at 52 percent between 1985 and 1987, as shown in Table 1.2. This result is quite remarkable in light of the megamergers and consolidation in retail trade during the 1980s and the growth of giant global business service firms during the 1990s. The significant expansion of the service sector—and the role of growing small firms in it—helped end the decline in the small-firm share of value added. If the industrial makeup of the U.S. economy had remained constant at its 1982 distribution, the small-business share of value added would have declined from 51 percent in 1982 to 48 percent in 1992. Therefore, small service firms—many of them new startups—contributed to maintaining the aggregate small-business output share during the 1980s and early 1990s. The output share gains in some sectors during the past ten years were counterbalanced by relative declines in other sectors. In construction, for example, small-business value added rose from 78 percent to 88 percent of the industry total during the 1982 to 1992 period. Meanwhile, the small-firm share of value added in manufacturing and mining rose from 23 percent to 25 percent.

According to Piore and Sabel (1984), the economic crisis of the 1970s resulted from the inability of firms and policymakers to maintain the conditions necessary to preserve mass production and the stability of markets. Their claim is that the deterioration in economic performance in the 1980s resulted from the limits of the model of industrial development that is found in mass production: the use of special-purpose machines and of semiskilled workers to produce standardized products. In fact, if the Great Depression represented a macroeconomic crisis, the economic problems of 1970 to the 1990s were essentially microeconomic in that the focus was on the choice of technologies, organization of firms and industries, and markets. *As we move toward the twenty-first century, the emerging conventional wisdom seems to suggest that small firms and entrepreneurship are both necessary for macroeconomic prosperity (OECD, 1996).*

Table 1.2. Small-Business Share of Private Nonfarm Gross Product, 1982 to 1992 (percent)

	1982	1983	1984	1985	1986	1987	1988	1989	1990	1991	1992
Total private business	51	51	51	52	52	52	51	51	51	51	51
Mining and manufacturing	23	23	24	25	25	25	24	24	24	25	25
Construction	78	81	83	84	86	87	88	88	88	88	88
Transportation communications, and public utilities	22	21	22	23	23	23	23	23	24	24	24
Trade	70	69	68	67	66	65	64	64	63	61	62
Finance, insurance, and real estate	62	60	60	58	56	55	54	52	51	50	51
Services	81	81	80	79	78	77	76	76	75	74	74

Source: Joel Popkin and Company (1997, p. 2, table 1).

SMALL FIRMS IN ECONOMIC THEORY

In thinking about the economic role of small firms, the obvious starting point is the theory of the firm. The field of economics that focuses the most on links between the organization of firms in industries and the resulting economic performance has been industrial organization. It is the task of industrial organization scholars to sort out the perceived tradeoff between economic efficiency, on the one hand, and political and economic decentralization, on the other (You, 1995). Two disparate views about the impact of small firms on economic efficiency have emerged in the economic literature: (1) static theory suggests that large firms are efficient because it focuses on the status quo, and (2) dynamic theory suggests that small firms are efficient because it focuses on change.

The Static View

One of the most striking findings emerging in the static view of industrial organization is that small firms generally operate at a level of output that is too small to sufficiently exhaust scale economies, even when the standard definition of a small firm employing fewer than 500 employees is applied. The importance of scale economies in the typical manufacturing industry relegated most small firms to being classified as suboptimal. As shown in Figure 1.2, 47 percent of firms in 1995 had fewer than ten employees. Static theory would argue for reducing the share of firms that are suboptimal to increase efficiency.

Static analysis takes a snapshot of the economy at two different time periods and then compares different equilibrium points. Static theory assumes prompt adjustment to changes in the economic environment. It is not concerned with the time required for changes to take place or with the organizational and managerial structure needed for the change. Static theory is concerned with determining the direction in which economic variables move in response to other variables. These two pictures are then compared, and an assumption is made about the role of small or large firms, monopoly profits, market structure, or market efficiency.

Static theory favors large firms in the old raw-material-based economy because of economies of scale. For example, in the electric utility industry, if you doubled the size of a coal-fired utility plant, the output of electricity doubled while the cost of building the plant went up only 70 percent. The building of larger and larger plants contributed to cheaper electricity rates.

What are the economic welfare implications? Within this static theory, the existence of small suboptimal firms represented a loss in economic efficiency. Seen through the static lens provided by traditional industrial organization and labor economics, the economic-welfare implication of the recent shift in economic activity away from large firms and toward small enterprises is unequivocal: overall economic welfare is decreased since productivity and wages will be lower in small firms than in large firms. As Weiss (1979) argued in terms of efficiency and Brown, Hamilton, and Medoff (1990) in terms of employee compensation, *the implication for public policy*

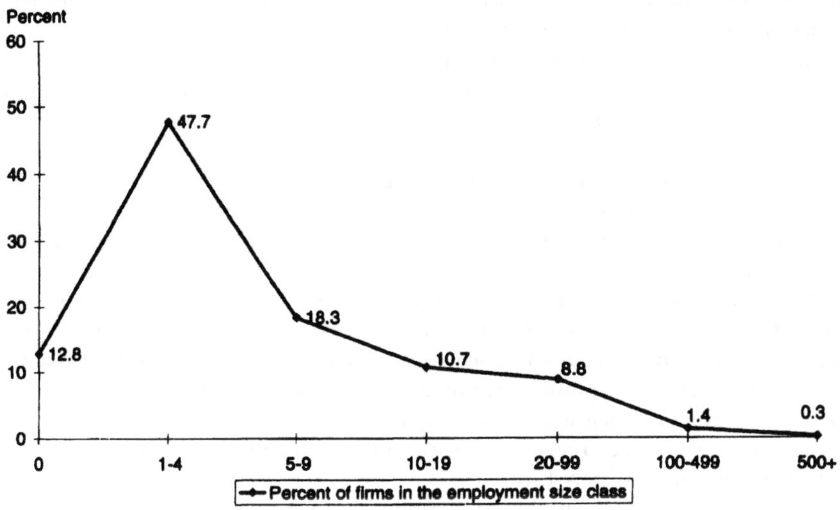

Figure 1.2. U.S. Distribution of Employer Firms, 1995.

is to implement polices to shift economic activity away from small firms and toward large enterprises.

Dynamic Theory

Why do firms exist? Ronald Coase (1937) was awarded a Nobel Prize for explaining why a firm should exist. His answer was, "To reduce transaction costs." But why should more than one firm exist in an industry? One answer is provided by the traditional economics literature focusing on industrial organization. An excess level of profitability induces entry into the industry. And this is why the entry of new firms is interesting and important—because the new firms provide an equilibrating function in the market, in that the levels of price and profit are restored to the competitive levels.

I provided an alternative explanation of the entry of new firms in my 1984 book on the changing structure of the U.S. economy. That book showed that the traditional model of entry was unable to explain the startup of firms in an industry where the incumbent firms were experiencing negative profits and a loss in market share to foreign companies. This is because what we notice is both entry and exit at the same time. Traditional static theory would support either entry or exit but not both at the same time. The alternative explanation is that *new firms entering the industry were to increase output not simply by being smaller replicas of large incumbent enterprises but also by serving as agents of change.*

In Chapter 2, David B. Audretsch suggests that there is nothing unique about firms. The firm is in no sense a natural unit of analysis. Only individuals can claim that distinction. All of us are potential entrepreneurs. It seems, then, that an economic theory of efficiency needs to build up from men and women rather than from firms. When the lens is shifted away from focusing on the firm as the relevant unit of observation to individuals, the relevant question becomes, "*How can entrepreneurs with a given endowment of new knowledge best appropriate the returns from that knowledge?*"

Given this new knowledge, each economic agent must choose how to best appropriate the value of his endowment of economic knowledge by comparing the wages he would earn if he remains employed by an incumbent enterprise, to the expected net present value of the profits accruing from a new firm. The model analyzing the decision confronting each individual economic agent—how best to appropriate the value of new economic knowledge—is useful to an understanding of entrepreneurs' actual decision to start new firms.

An additional layer of uncertainty pervades a new enterprise. Incumbent enterprises know something about their underlying competencies from past experiences. It is not known how competent a new firm really is, in terms of management, organization, and workforce—which is to say that a new enterprise is burdened with uncertainty as to whether it can produce and market the intended product as well as sell it. The degree of uncertainty will typically exceed that confronting incumbent enterprises.

Dynamic theory favors small firms because it shines the light on change. In the new information economy, continued innovation and change are the rule. Over half the sales of high-technology firms come from products that are less than eighteen months old. *What emerges from the new evolutionary theories of new and small firms is that markets are in motion*, with lots of new small firms entering the industry and a lot of firms exiting out of the industry. About 10 percent of firms are new each year, and about 9 percent exit each year.[10]

The persistence of an asystemic firm-size distribution biased toward small-scale enterprise reflects the continuing process of the entry of new firms into industries and not necessarily the permanence of such small and suboptimal enterprises over the long run. Although the skewed distribution of firms (a few large firms and lots of small firms) persists with remarkable stability over long periods of time, a constant set of small- and suboptimal-scale firms does not appear to be responsible for this skewed distribution. Rather, new small firms provide an essential source of new ideas and experimentation that otherwise would remain untapped in the economy. A constant supply of new firms seems to replace existing ones.

What are the welfare implications of dynamic theory? With dynamic theory the existence of small suboptimal firms does not represent a loss in economic efficiency. Seen through the dynamic lens of evolutionary theory, the economic welfare implications of the recent shift in economic activity away from large firms and toward small enterprises are welfare enhancing because new startups introduce change into the economy. As Schumpeter (1934) argued in terms of economic development and Kirchhoff (1994) argued in terms of dynamics, the implication for public policy is to implement policies that encourage the entry of new firms, support their survival, and promote their growth.[11]

Community

Before we continue, we need to understand "how an unrelated collection of small businesses can prosper in the face of competition from large firms" (Lazerson, 1988). There are two mechanisms by which small firms can succeed. First, they can become part of the value chain of an industry. For example, small firms can write software for a larger project. Second, small firms can become part of a larger social community like the Third Italy or Silicon Valley. In the latter case, what holds a disparate collection of small firms together is social capital. Social capital is a powerful force that only recently has been recognized by economists. Economists are assessing how the social fabric affects individual choice and economic growth. The essential qualities of social capital, as opposed to physical capital or human capital, are that it reflects a community or group and that it impinges on individuals regardless of their independent choice. What is important is the interplay between social dynamics in the community and economic performance over time. Strong community ties lead to strong commercial ties ("The Ties That Lead," 1997, p. 153).

Community comes in many flavors, from the high-tech communities of Silicon Valley to the Cuban immigrant communities of Miami. The essence of community is a shared set of values and customs concerning behavior and family. (Frishkoff and Kostecka, 1991).

INNOVATION, NEW-FIRM STARTUPS, AND JOB CREATION

Underneath the smooth path of macroeconomic aggregates there is a very active microeconomic world. Massive reshuffling of the factors of production is constantly taking place. Market economies seem to handle this overwhelming churn with remarkable success (Caballero and Hammond, 1996). Small and new firms are an integral part of the renewal process that pervades and defines market economies. New and small firms play a crucial role in experimentation and innovation that leads to technological change and employment growth.

In Chapter 3, Paul Almeida uses the semiconductor industry to explore the role of small firms and community in radical innovation. His chapter supports the view that small firms play an important role in innovation and in the evolution of markets. He argues that the importance of small firms lies not only in the productivity of their research relative to large firms but in the unique role that they play in the innovative process. Small firms play a critical role in technological (and economic) development by exploring and innovating in new technological fields.

He uses patent data to identify the patterns of innovation in large and small firms. Startups produce innovations in less crowded technological fields, while larger firms appear to succeed in more established fields. These discoveries for new small firms usually come just a few years after their founding. Therefore, small firms act as agents of change by providing an essential source of new ideas that otherwise would remain untapped, as suggested by Audretsch in Chapter 2.

The innovativeness of small firms and their ability to explore new technologies is, perhaps, surprising since often they are resource poor and have small R&D budgets and limited personnel. Small firms overcome their limited resources by turning to community networks. Small firms often rely on regional knowledge networks for important inputs into the innovation process. Through this process of accessing and sharing knowledge with geographically proximate firms, small firms help the circulation and building of regional networks (Saxennian, 1991).

Almeida found that both large and small firms cited local patents significantly more than would be expected, indicating localization effects. However, the results showed that these localization effects were much more significant for the startup sample. Startup firms were more closely tied to other firms within the same regional network.

In Chapter 4, John R. Baldwin and Joanne Johnson examine the role of new-firm entry and innovation. Entry is impressive in most economies. Over a five-year period, entry in manufacturing industries accounted for almost half of the net new employment increase in both the United States and Canada. However, while the size of the entry population is impressive, the importance of entry is due to its dynamic impact on innovation, as pointed out by Audretsch in Chapter 2. Entrants play a key role in the entrepreneurial process that constantly offer consumers new products in terms of both basic goods and services. Entrants are often seen as providing the dynamic new force in an industry that leads to change. This process is costly. Many entrants fail soon after they enter, but others grow.

Baldwin and Johnson surveys a large number of startups to better understand the innovation process. They examine firms' innovative competencies, their technological competencies, and their human capital development. The survey focused on new entrants that emerged from their early years and survived to their teen years. The sampling frame consists of all entrants to the commercial sector (both goods and services) in the period 1983 to 1986 that survived to 1993.

The Baldwin and Johnson results help generalize the importance of innovation to firms in all industries. While there is no doubt that firms in the semiconductor and electronics industries are innovative (as pointed out by Almeida in Chapter 3), it is also the case that firms elsewhere have developed the capacities that are needed for innovation in their particular industries. Innovations thus enhance firm survival. These capabilities often involve development of new technology, nurturing of worker skills, or devising of new products that are highly novel. The range and diversity of the innovative skills of new firms across all industries are remarkable.

The importance of the relationship between innovation and firm growth is also clear. The successful entrants that grow the most are those that develop some type of innovative activity, either with new products, new technology, or human resources. Therefore, the diffusion of new technologies throughout the economy plays a crucial role in keeping an economy vibrant and the small-firm sector dynamic and productive.

In Chapter 5, John Haltiwanger and C.J. Krizan examine the contribution of startups and small firms to job creation in the United States. The public discourse about the role of employer size has focused primarily on the contribution of small businesses to job creation. However, there is less agreement about this aspect of the role of employer size than, for example, innovation, compensation, or productivity. The widely cited claim that small businesses are the primary creators of jobs in the United States derives primarily from studies by David Birch and the U.S. Small Business Administration using the only data publicly available in the 1980s.

But what is the relationship between employer size and age? Strong arguments can be made for why employer age might be relevant. First and foremost, new and young businesses are inherently a part of the ongoing process of renewal that pervades market economies. The introduction of new ideas, products, and techniques involves a process of trial and error in which many new businesses fail while others are dramatic successes. Just a few years ago, computers did not talk to each other either within or between offices.[12]

Their research findings raise two sources of caution regarding the role of employer size. For manufacturing employment growth, it looks as if the more important factor is age and not size. That is, in manufacturing, most small establishments are new and young establishments. Thus, the role of small business in job creation may simply reflect the role of births and, in turn, young establishments.

These remarks do not deny that small (and young) businesses play important roles in the economy. The evidence here, as in the previous chapters, suggests that small businesses are undoubtedly an important part of the continuous renewal process of the U.S. economy.[13]

In Chapter 6, Bo Carlsson summarizes the contribution of small firms to the economy in terms of efficiency and dynamics. The essence of the *efficiency* argument is small firms do certain things better than large firms. As a result, through the division of labor between small and large firms, the efficiency of the economy is increased. This is especially important in production (Pratten, 1991) and innovation (Acs and Audretsch, 1988).

The argument with respect to *dynamics* is that small firms are needed to provide the entrepreneurship and variety required for macroeconomic growth and stability. In fact, the connection between entrepreneurship and small business is interesting from an economic growth perspective. While the static effects of the division of labor between large and small firms may be tied to the vast majority of small firms, the *dynamic* aspects are tied to a subset of firms that are entrepreneurial.

Small firms provide the lion's share of entrepreneurship in the economy, and a high rate of new firm entry is associated with *dynamics*. This is because highly structured organizations are inefficient when dealing with changes in the environment.

New small firms, therefore, are needed for the production of variety in the economy and the elimination of stagnation.

ENTREPRENEURSHIP, WOMEN, MINORITIES, AND IMMIGRANTS

Although change is important for the economy—since it directly affects productivity and growth—the broader social and political issues are just as important. Small firms are the essential mechanism by which millions enter the economic and social mainstream of American society. Small business is the vehicle by which millions access the American dream by creating opportunities. The American economy is a democratic system, as well as an economic system, that invites change and participation.

In Chapter 7 we begin by examining why women-owned businesses are important. According to Candida Brush and Robert D. Hisrich, the role of women-owned businesses has changed dramatically over the past decade. Since the 1970s, women's share of small business has increased from 5 percent to 38 percent. Therefore, *one reason that the U.S. economy has created so many new businesses in recent decades is that many women have chosen self-employment over wage employment.* Despite this dramatic increase little research has been conducted on women-owned businesses. The extent to which they are different needs to be researched, according to Brush and Hisrich.

They argue that the role of women-owned businesses can be better understood by taking a broader perspective about their role in society over time and examining the social context influencing women business owners. Of particular importance is the role of community, and paramount is the relationship between family and work. According to the authors, one of the key variables that has facilitated women in starting businesses has been the change in technology. As the economy continues to shift toward an information economy, innovations in telecommunications and computers have made it much easier to start home-based businesses, about a quarter of which are operated full time. The socioeconomic context of women-owned businesses is different from men, but technology is creating greater diversity in the reasons for business startups, as well as their costs.

Judged from the efficiency perspective of Audretsch, many of these small women-owned business are in most instances suboptimal from a static perspective. However, when we take an evolutionary perspective, as well as a contextual social perspective, many of these small businesses may in fact turn out to be socially efficient in the long run. This is because being a woman entrepreneur fulfills a large number of social and economic needs in society. For example, raising children and self-employment seem to go together, and home-based firms allow both to occur.

In Chapter 8, John Sibley Butler and Patricia Gene Greene continue to examine the role of entrepreneurship in the U.S. economy and the concept of community. However, instead of focusing on the role of women-owned or high-technology businesses, they shift the lens to the role of ethnic enterprises. Again, we see that there has been a significant increase in minority-owned businesses between 1987 and 1992, increasing from 8.8 percent to 12.5 percent of total firms.

Butler and Greene make a clear distinction between immigrant-owned businesses, minority-owned businesses, and ethnic entrepreneurship. Ethnic entrepreneurship has a special meaning in this context. Ethnic entrepreneurship consists of "*a set of connections and regular patterns of interaction among people sharing common national background or migration experiences.*"

The issue here is the role of entrepreneurship in shaping a community. This debate, according to Butler and Green, has a long history.[14] They present three case studies describing three immigrant- or minority-owned business communities. The case studies are drawn from different historical periods to clearly illustrate the dynamics of community entrepreneurship. Because community entrepreneurship has not always been driven by ethnicity or immigration, they take a case study from the history of black America also. For these groups, business enterprise is an important tool that contributes to the incorporation of ethnic immigrants into American society (see also Lusganten, 1994).

Two important lessons in these case studies are consistent with our concept of small firms. First, just as there are two views of efficiency in industrial organization, there are also two views of efficiency in ethnic entrepreneurship. The static view would suggest that most of these businesses are suboptimal, *while a dynamic view suggests that these businesses are building a community and networks and therefore will grow and prosper in the future.* Ethnic entrepreneurs probably have inside information about business opportunities and community that they are able to exploit. This information could be transferred to other organizations; however, as Audretsch suggests, there could be disagreement about the value of this information.

Second, just as community is important for small high-technology firms, it is just as important for ethnic entrepreneurship. In other words, small businesses—whether high tech or Main Street—need a community in which to survive and grow. These communities are characterized by Butler and Greene as instrumental networks, entrepreneurial apprenticeships, and funding networks. The crucial barometer for economic and social well-being is the continued high level of creation of new and small firms *in all sectors of the economy by all segments of society.*

EVOLUTION, COMMUNITY, AND THE GLOBAL ECONOMY

We have argued above that small firms make two indispensable contributions to the U.S. economy: first, they are an integral part of the renewal process that pervades market economies; second, small firms are the essential mechanism by which millions enter the economic and social mainstream of American society. However, small firms also make an important contribution to our role in the international community.

In this section, we develop the linkages among evolution, community, and the global economy. In Chapter 9, Zoltan J. Acs, Randall Morck, and Bernard Yeung examine the role that the innovations of small and medium-size firms play in the globalization process. Why are small firms radical innovators? Innovations arise only when property rights are properly aligned, and property rights may be less perfectly aligned in large firms than in small firms. It is difficult, if not impossible, for companies to differentially reward employees, even if one of them has a brilliant idea. Innovators in small firms can hold clear property rights.

However, small firms perform only limited amounts of R&D. Since small firms have fewer resources than large firms, they rely more on community and localized knowledge networks for important inputs into the innovation process. Comparing the innovative activity of startup firms and large firms reveals that small firms do explore new technological areas by innovating in less crowded areas and are tied into regional knowledge networks to a greater extent than large firms. In other words, community building is more important for small-firm innovations than for large firms.

Smaller firms can conduct international expansion on their own or by collaborating with a multinational firm. The intermediated form of international expansion has certain advantages. From the small-firm perspective, it benefits from having access to the multinational firm's global market reach. From the large firm's perspective, the arrangement enhances the value of its existing contributions to internationalization (see also Opperheimer, 1985; Vozikis, 1979).

Finally, they argue that the world is rapidly changing and that firm boundaries are blurred by competitive network connections. Firms can now be thought of as coordinating transaction units rather than merely integrating production units. In this way regions and multinational global networks are interconnected, with small firms playing an important dynamic role as radical innovators.

There are many public-policy issues, but in Chapter 10 Joshua Lerner examines one set of policy issues related to small firms, innovation, and industry dynamics—the role of the patent system. This is important since many small firms, as well as large firms, file for patents. Lerner argues that reforms in the patent system since 1982 have created a substantial innovation tax that afflicts some of America's most important and creative small firms (see also Acs and Yeung, 1999).

SUMMARY AND POLICY IMPLICATIONS

The impressive performance of the U.S. economy over the past six years can be contrasted with the rather lackluster performance in both Europe and Japan. We have argued that this divergent macroeconomic performance can be explained in part by differences in competition, entrepreneurship, and new firm startups. There are at least three entrepreneurial stories to the U.S. success: first, large firms have restructured themselves; second, new firm startups have been blossoming; and third, thousands of businesses have been founded by women, minorities, and immigrants. The last two entrepreneurial success stories overlap with small and new firms.

Small firms make two indispensable contributions to the American economy. First, they are an integral part of the renewal process that pervades and defines market economies. New and small firms play a crucial role in experimentation and innovation, which lead to technological change and productivity growth. *In short, small firms are about change and competition because they change market structure.* The U.S. economy is a dynamic organization always in the process of becoming, not an established one that has arrived.

Second, small firms are the essential mechanism by which millions enter the economic and social mainstream of American society. Small business is the vehicle by which millions access the American dream by creating opportunities for women, minorities, and immigrants. In this evolutionary process, community plays the crucial and indispensable role of providing the social glue and networking that bind small firms together in both high-tech and Main Street activities. The American economy is a democratic system, as well as an economic system, that invites change and participation.

A successful entrepreneurial environment features continual creative destruction, to use Joseph Schumpeter's apt term. New companies prosper and help the economy in part by destroying the markets of established competition. Nations that protect the markets and incomes of existing larger companies prevent the creative destruction so essential to progress.

The policy implications are clear. The crucial barometer for economic and social well-being is the continued high level of creation of new and small firms in all sectors of the economy by all segments of society. It should be the role of government policy to facilitate that process by eliminating barriers to entry and exit, lowering transaction costs, and minimizing anticompetitive behavior by large firms.

NOTES

1. This trend may be changing ("Startups to the Rescue," 1998, p. 50).

2. In this volume we do not deal with the question of entrepreneurial finance. It is, according to many, a barrier to entry. For a discussion of the issues, see Blanchflower and Oswald (1998); Lerner (1996), and Freear, Sohl, and Wetzel (1996).

3. This section draws heavily on Acs, Carlsson, and Karlsson (1999).

4. A notable early exception was the work of Steindl (1945).

5. For a review of the literature see Acs (1996), Admiraal (1996), OECD (1996), and Storey (1994).

6. For a discussion of scale economies in small firms, see Pratten (1991).

7. Research and data for this project were provided by the Office of Advocacy of the U.S. Small Business Administration.

8. The small business share of value added is the best measure of the relative importance of small business in the economy. Sales tend to understate the importance of small business, and employment tends to overstate the importance of small businesses because they are more labor intensive than large businesses.

9. Many of the issues raised in that book were examined by David B. Audretsch and Zoltan J. Acs at the Wissenschaftszentrum (WZB) in Berlin in the late 1980s. These findings are to be found in the inaugural issue of *Small Business Economics*, 1(1) (1989) and in Acs and Audretsch (1990a). Subsequent issues of *Small Business Economics* (6(2) 1994; 8(3) and 8(5) 1996) have reported more recent research findings from the second and third Global Workshops on Small Business Economics.

10. Office of Advocacy Statistics of U.S. Business (SUSB), Table 9S.

11. Perhaps the most important determinant of the survival and growth of new firms is the availability of human and financial capital (Cressey, 1996).

12. While the Longitudinal Research Datafile (LRD) may be inadequate to characterize the role of employer size in job creation for the U.S. economy, it can be used effectively to characterize the role of employer size for U.S. manufacturing, which is useful in its own right, and in so doing can serve as a testing ground for methodological and conceptual issues.

13. Although the LRD is limited to manufacturing data, a new longitudinal establishment and enterprise microdata (LEEM) set is being developed jointly by the U.S. Small Business Administration and

the U.S. Bureau of the Census. This file has the advantage of being longitudinal and has coverage of all private-sector establishments with employment. For documentation of the LEEM file, see Acs and Armington (1998), and for a discussion of job creation and destruction using the LEEM, see Acs, Armington, and Robb (1998).

14. For another perspective see Bates (1997). For a review of Bates, see Butler (forthcoming).

REFERENCES

Acs, Z.J. (1984). *The Changing Structure of the U.S. Economy*. New York: Praeger.

Acs, Z.J., ed. (1996). *Small Firms and Economic Growth* (vols. 1–2). Cheltenam: Elgar.

Acs, Z.J., and C. Armington. (1998). "Longitudinal Establishment and Enterprise Microdata (LEEM) Documentation." Working Paper 1998–10. Center for Economic Studies, U.S. Bureau of the Census, Washington, DC.

Acs, Z.J., C. Armington, and A. Robb. (1998). "Job Creation and Destruction in the U.S. Economy." Working Paper 1998, Center for Economic Studies, U.S. Bureau of the Census, Washington, DC.

Acs, Z.J., and D.B. Audretsch. (1988). "Innovation in Large and Small Firms." *American Economic Review*, 78, 678–690.

Acs, Z.J., and D.B. Audretsch. (1993). *Small Firms and Entrepreneurship: An East-West Perspective*. Cambridge: Cambridge University Press.

Acs, Z.J., B. Carlsson, and C. Karlsson. (1999). *Entrepreneurship, Small and Medium-Sized Enterprises, and the Macroeconomy*. Cambridge: Cambridge University Press.

Acs, Z.J., and D.S. Evans. (1995). "The Determinants of Variation in Self-Employment Rates Across Countries and Over Time." Working Paper, University of Maryland, College Park.

Acs, Z.J., and B. Yeung. (1999). *Small and Medium-Sized Enterprises in the Global Economy*. Ann Arbor: University of Michigan Press.

Acs, Zoltan J., and David, B. Audretsch. (1990). The Economics of Small Firms, Boston: Kluwer.

Admiraal, P.H., ed. (1996). *Small Business in the Modern Economy*. Oxford: Basil Blackwell.

Almeida P., and B. Kogut. (1997). "The Exploration of Technological Diversity and Geographic Localization in Innovation: Start-up Firms in the Semiconductor Industry." *Small Business Economics*, 9(1), 21–31.

Bates, T. (1997). *Race, Self-Employment, and Upward Mobility: An Elusive American Dream*. Baltimore: Johns Hopkins University Press.

Becker, Gary S. (1998). "Make the World Safe for Creative Destruction." *Business Week*. February 23, 20.

Birch, D. (1981). "Who Creates Jobs?" *The Public Interest*, 65, 3–14.

Blanchflower, D., and A. Oswald. (1998). "What Makes a Young Entrepreneur?" *Journal of Labor Economics*, 16(1), 26–60.

Brock, W.A., and D.S. Evans. (1986). *The Economics of Small Firms*. New York: Holmes and Meier.

Brock, W.A., and D.S. Evans. (1989). "Small Business Economics." *Small Business Economics*, 1(1), 7–20.

Brown, C., J. Hamilton, and J. Medoff. (1990). *Employers: Large and Small*. Cambridge: Harvard University Press.

Butler, J.S., (Forthcoming). "Review Essay," *Small Business Economics*.

Caballero, R.J., and L. Hammour. (1996). "On the Timing and Efficiency of Creative Destruction." *Quarterly Journal of Economics*, 111(3) (August), 805–852.

Carlsson, B. (1992). "The Rise of Small Business: Causes and Consequences." In W.J. Adams (ed.), *Singular Europe: Economy and Polity of the European Community After 1992*. Ann Arbor: Michigan University Press.

Committee of Inquiry on Small Firms. (1971). *Bolton Report*. Cmnd 4811. London: HMSO.

Coase, R. (1937). "The Nature of the Firm." *Economica*, 4, 386–405.

Cressey, R.C. (1996). "Are Business Startups Debt-Rationed?" *Economic Journal*, 106, 1253–1270.

Davis, S. (1990). "The Distribution of Employees by Establishment Size: Patterns of Change and Co-Movement in the United States, 1962–1985." Working Paper, University of Chicago.

Davis, S., and J. Haltiwanger. (1992). "Gross Job Creation, Gross Job Destruction and Employment Reallocation." *Quarterly Journal of Economics*, 107(3), 819–863.

Davis, S., J. Haltiwanger, and S. Schuh. (1996). *Job Creation and Destruction*. Cambridge: MIT Press.

De Jong, H.W. (1989). "Free Versus Controlled Competition." In B. Carlsson (ed.), *Industrial Dynamics: Technological, Organizational, and Structural Changes in Industries and Firms*. Boston: Kluwer.

Freear, J., J.E. Sohl, and W.E. Wetzel. (1996). "Creating New Capital Markets for Emerging Ventures." Prepared for the U.S. Small Business Administration, Office of Advocacy, Contract SBAHQ-95-m-1062, Washington, DC.

Frishkoff, Patricia A., and Alicja, M. Kostecka. (1991). "Business Contributions of Community Service," Office of advocacy, U.S. Small Business Administration, Washington DC.

Galbraith, J.K. (1956). *American Capitalism: The Concept of Countervailing Power*, 2nd ed. Boston: Houghton Mifflin.

Garten, Jeffery E. (1992). *A Cold Peace: America, Japan, Germany, and the Struggle for Supremacy*. New York: Times Books.

Harrison, Bennett (1994). Lean and Mean, New York: Basic Books.

Hebert, R.F., and A.N. Link. (1989). "In Search of the Meaning of Entrepreneurship." *Small Business Economics*, 1(1), 39–50.

Joel Popkin and Company. (1997). "Small Business Share of Private, Nonfarm Gross Domestic Product." Prepared for the U.S. Small Business Administration, Office of Advocacy, Contract SBAHQ-95-C-0021, February, Washington, DC.

Kirchhoff, B. (1994). *Entrepreneurship and Dynamic Capitalism*. London: Praeger.

Lazerson, M. (1988). "Organizational Growth of Small Firms: An Outcome of Markets and Hierarchies?" *American Sociological Review*, 53(3), 330–342.

Lerner, J. (1996). "The Government as Venture Capitalist." Working Paper 96-038, Harvard Business School, Boston, MA.

Loveman, G., and W. Sengenberger. (1991). "The Re-emergence of Small-Scale Production: An International Comparison." *Small Business Economics*, 3(1), 1–39.

Lusgarten, Steve. (1994). "The Role of Small Firms in the Uward Mobility of New Immigrants." Office of Advocacy, U.S. Small Business Administration, Contract SBA-8139-OA-94, Washington, DC.

Lynch, P., and John Rothchild. (1996). *Learn to Earn*. New York: Simon and Schuster.

OECD. (1996). *SMEs: Employment, Innovation and Growth*. Washington Workshop. Paris: OECD.

Oppenheimer, Michael, E. (1985). The Effect of Non-tariff Trade Barriers on Corporate strategy in High-Technology Sectors," Office of Advocacy, U.S. Small Business Administration, Washington DC.

Piore, M.J., and C.F. Sabel. (1984). "Possibilities for Prosperity: International Keynesianism and Flexible Specialization." In *The Second Industrial Divide* (pp. 251–280). New York: Basic Books.

Pratten, C. (1991). *The Competitiveness of Small Firms*. Cambridge: Cambridge University Press.

Robb, Alicia and Bruce D. Phillips, *New Data for Analysis of Small Business Job Creation*. Washington, DC: U.S. Small Business Administration, forthcoming.

Saxenian, A. (1991). "The Origins and Dynamics of Production Networks in Silicon Valley." *Research Policy*, 20, 423–437.

Schumacher, E.F. (1973). *Small Is Beautiful*. New York: Harper and Row.

Schumpeter, J.A. (1934). *The Theory of Economic Development*. Cambridge: Harvard University Press.

Schumpeter, J.A. (1942). *Capitalism, Socialism, and Democracy*. New York: Harper and Row.

Smith, A. (1776). *The Wealth of Nations*. Oxford: Clarendon Press.

"Startups to the Rescue." (1998). *Business Week*. March 23, p. 50.

Steindl, J. (1945). *Small and Big Business*. Oxford: Basil Blackwell.

Storey, D.J. (1994). *Understanding the Small Business Sector*. London: Routledge.

Thurow, Lester. (1992). *Head to Head: The Coming Battle Among Japan, Europe, and America*. New York: Morrow.

"Ties That Lead to Prosperity, The." (1997). *Business Week*. December 15, 153.

Trueheart, Charles. (1997). "French Proudly Hold Fast to Benevolent Central Rule." *Washington Post*. July 14, p. A1.

Tyson, Laura D" Andrea. (1992). *Who's Bashing Whom? Trade Conflict in High Technology Industries*. Washington, DC: Institute for International Economics.

"U.S. Sails on Tranquil Economic Seas." (1996). *Washington Post*. December 2, 1.

U.S. Small Business Administration. (1994). "Health Insurance Coverage: A Profile of the Uninsured by Firm Size and Employment Size" in *The State of Small Business: A Report of the President*, 65–108. Washington, DC: US Government Printing Office.

U.S. Small Business Administration, Office of Advocacy Statistics of U.S. Business (SUSB), prepared under contract by the U.S. Bureau of the Census, table 9S.

Vozikis, George. (1979). A Strategic Disadvantage Profile of the Stages of Development and the Stages

of the Exporting Process: the Experiences of the Small Business Exporters in Georgia," Washington DC, Office of Advocacy, U.S. Small Business Administration.
Weiss, Leonard W. (1979). "The Structure-Performance Paradigm and Antitrust." *University of Pennsylvania Law Review*, 127 (April), 1104–1140.
You, J. (1995). "Small Firms in Economic Theory." *Cambridge Journal of Economics*, 19, 441–462.

2. SMALL FIRMS AND EFFICIENCY

DAVID B. AUDRETSCH

THE TWO VIEWS ABOUT SMALL FIRMS

Two disparate views about the impact of small firms on economic efficiency have emerged in the economics literature. On the one hand is the traditional view in the field of industrial organization that views small firms as imposing excess costs on the economy as a result of a scale of production that is too small to be efficient. According to this traditional view, the inefficient scale of operations results in lower levels of productivity for small firms and lower wages for their workers. The shift in economic activity that has taken place over the previous two decades away from large corporations and toward new and small firms is interpreted as causing a decrease in the standard of living of Americans. Shifting employment out of high-productivity and high-wage firms and into lower-productivity and lower-wage (small) firms reduces the well-being of the American population. According to this traditional view of small firms, any policies that shift economic activity out of small firms and back into large corporations should be encouraged, since they will increase the American standard of living.

With the publication of *The Changing Structure of the U.S. Economy: Lessons from the Steel Industry*, Zoltan J. Acs (1984) shattered the prevalent conventional wisdom. While the industrial organization literature portrayed small firms as less efficient clones of the large corporations, Acs introduced a radically different view of the small firm. By arguing that entrepreneurs started new firms not simply to duplicate the incumbent firms but rather to deviate in an innovative manner, Acs challenged the conventional wisdom in industrial organization by proposing a second view of small firms—as agents of change. Under this alternative view, the dynamic contributions made by small firms far offset any static efficiency losses.

The purpose of this chapter is to ask which of these two competing views about the efficiency of small firms is correct—the traditional view of industrial organization or that proposed by Acs some fifteen years ago. The answer is found by sifting through what has now become a large and compelling literature about the economic role of small firms—viewed through the static lens provided by the traditional industrial organization literature and through the dynamic lens of evolutionary economics.

With the hindsight of some fifteen years, it is clear that the dynamic view of small-firm efficiency introduced by Acs (1984) is more consistent with not just the recent wave of theories about the evolutionary role of small and new firms but also with the compelling empirical evidence that analyzes firms and industries through a dynamic lens.

THE STATIC VIEW OF SMALL FIRMS

In thinking about the economic role of small firms, the obvious starting point is the theory of the firm. The field of economics that focuses the most on links between the organization of firms in industries and the resulting economic performance has been industrial organization. The ascendancy of industrial organization in the postwar period as an important and valued field economics came from the recognition not only by scholars but also by policymarkers that industrial organization matters. The widespread fear of the Soviet Union that was pervasive throughout the United States in the late 1950s and early 1960s was not just that the Soviets might bury the Americans because they were the first into space with the launching of the *Sputnik* but that the superior organization of industry facilitated by centralized planning was generating greater rates of growth in the Soviet Union.[1] After all, the nations of Eastern Europe, and the Soviet Union in particular, had a "luxury" inherent in their systems of centralized planning—a concentration of economic assets on a scale beyond anything imaginable in the West, where the commitment to democracy seemingly imposed a concomitant commitment to economic decentralization.

Although there may have been considerable debate about what to do about the perceived Soviet threat some three decades ago, there was little doubt at that time that the manner in which enterprises and entire industries were organized mattered. And even more striking, when one reviews the literature of the day, there seemed to be near unanimity about the way in which industrial organization mattered. It is no doubt an irony of history that a remarkably similar version of the giantism embedded in Soviet doctrine, fueled by the writings of Marx and ultimately implemented by the iron fist of Stalin, was also prevalent throughout the West. This was the era of mass production when economies of scale seemed to be the decisive factor in dictating efficiency. This was the world so colorfully described by John Kenneth Galbraith (1956) in his theory of counterveiling power, in which the power of big business was held in check by big labor and by big government.

It became the task of the industrial organization scholars to sort out the issues involving this perceived tradeoff between economic efficiency on the one hand and political and economic decentralization on the other. The scholars of industrial organization responded by producing a massive literature focusing on essentially three issues:

1. What are the economic gains to size and large-scale production?
2. What are the economic welfare implications of having an oligopolistic market structure (is economic performance promoted or reduced in an industry with just a handful of large-scale firms)? and
3. Given the overwhelming evidence from 2 that large-scale production resulting in economic concentration is associated with increased efficiency, what are the public-policy implications?

A fundamental characteristic of the industrial organization literature was not only that it was obsessed with the oligopoly question but that it was essentially static in nature. There was considerable concern about what to do with the existing firms and industrial structure, but little attention was paid to where they came from and where they were going. Oliver Williamson's classic 1968 article in the *American Economic Review*, "Economies as an Antitrust Defense: The Welfare Tradeoffs," became something of a final statement demonstrating this seemingly inevitable tradeoff between the gains in productive efficiency that could be obtained through increased concentration and gains in terms of competition that could be achieved through decentralizing economic policies, such as antitrust. But it did not seem possible to have both, certainly not in Williamson's completely static model.

One of the most striking findings emerging in this static view of industrial organization is that small firms generally operate at a level of output that is too small to sufficiently exhaust scale economies, even when the standard definition of a small firm employing fewer than 500 employees is applied. A large number of studies found that because of the minimum efficient scale (MES) of output, or the lowest level of output where the minimum average cost is attained, large-scale production is typically required to exhaust scale economies in manufacturing. Any enterprise or establishment that was smaller than required by the MES was branded as being *suboptimal* or inefficient, in that it produced at average costs in excess of more efficient larger firms. Weiss (Audretsch and Yamawaki, 1991, p. 403) assumed that "the term 'suboptimal' capacity describes a condition in which some plants are too small to be efficient."

The importance of scale economies in the typical manufacturing industry relegated most small firms to being classified as suboptimal.[2] For example, Weiss (1964) found that suboptimal plants accounted for about 52.8 percent of industry value off shipments, Scherer (1973) found that 58.2 percent of value of shipments emanated from the suboptimal plants in twelve industries, and Pratten (1971) identified the suboptimal scale establishments accounting for 47.9 percent of industry shipments. After reviewing the literature on the extent of suboptimal firms, Weiss

(Audretsch and Yamawaki, 1991, p. xiv) concluded, "In most industries the great majority of firms is suboptimal. In a typical industry there are, let's say, one hundred firms. Typically only about five to ten of them will be operating at the MES level of output, or anything like it."

What are the economic welfare implications? Weiss (1979, p. 1137) argued that the existence of small firms that are suboptimal represented a loss in economic efficiency and therefore advocated any public policy that "creates social gains in the form of less suboptimal capacity." This actually translated into an ingenuious argument against market power, since empirical evidence suggested that the price umbrella provided by monopoly power encouraged the existence of suboptimal capacity firms. Weiss (1979) went so far as to argue that the largest inefficiency associated with market power was not that higher prices were charged to consumers but rather that it facilitated the existence of suboptimal scale-small firms.

Wages and productivity would be expected to reflect the degree to which small firms are less efficient than their larger counterparts. There is a large body of empirical evidence spanning a broad range of samples, time periods, and even countries that has consistently found wages (and nonwage compensation as well) to be positively related to firm size. Probably the most cited study is that of Brown, Hamilton, and Medoff (1990, pp. 88–89), who conclude that

> Workers in large firms earn higher wages, and this fact cannot be explained completely by differences in labor quality industry, working conditions, or union status. Workers in large firms enjoy better benefits and greater security than their counterparts in small firms. When these factors are added together, it appears that workers in large firms do have a superior employment package.

Seen through the static lens provided through traditional industrial organization and labor economics, the economic welfare implications of the recent shift in economic activity away from large firms and toward small enterprises is unequivocal: overall economic welfare is decreased since productivity any wages will be lower in small than in large firms. As Weiss (1979) argued in terms of efficiency and Brown, Hamilton, and Medoff (1990) in terms of employee compensation, the implication for public policy is to implement policies to shift economic activity away from small firms and toward larger enterprises.

THE EVOLUTIONARY VIEW

Coase (1937) was awarded a Nobel Prize for explaining why a firm should exist. But why should more than one firm exist in an industry?[3] One answer is provided by the traditional economics literature focusing on industrial organization. An excess level of profitability induces entry into the industry. And this is why the entry of new firms is interesting and important—because the new firms provide an equilibrating function in the market, in that the levels of price and profit are restored to the competitive levels. The new firms are about business as usual: they simply equilibrate the market by providing more of it.

An alternative explanation for the entry of new firms was provided for by Zoltan Acs (1984) in his seminal work on the emergence of the minimills in the United States steel industry. Acs showed how the traditional model of entry was unable to explain the startup of the minimills in an industry where the incumbent firms were experiencing negative profits and a loss in market share to foreign companies. Rather, Acs argued that the new firms entered the industry not simply to increase output by being a smaller replica of the large incumbent enterprises but by serving as *agents of change.* The minimills produced a different product using different inputs and different production processes. This suggested that small firms, at least in some situations, were not about being smaller clones of the larger incumbents but rather about serving as *agents of change* through innovative activity.

The starting point for most theories of innovation is the firm.[4] In such theories the firms are exogenous, and their performance in generating technological change is endogenous.[6] For example, in the most prevalent model found in the literature of technological change, the model of the *knowledge-production function*, formalized by Zvi Griliches (1979), firms exist exogenously and then engage in the pursuit of new economic knowledge as an input into the process of generating innovative activity.

The most decisive input in the knowledge production function is new economic knowledge. And as Cohen and Klepper (1991, 1992) conclude, the greatest source generating new economic knowledge is generally considered to be R&D. Certainly a large body of empirical work has found a strong and positive relationship between knowledge inputs, such as R&D, on the one hand, and innovative output, on the other hand.

The knowledge production function has been found to hold most strongly at broader levels of aggregation. The most innovative countries are those with the greatest investments to R&D. Little innovative output is associated with less developed countries, which are characterized by a paucity of production of new economic knowledge. Similarly, the most innovative industries also tend to be characterized by considerable investments in R&D and new economic knowledge. Industries such as computers, pharmaceuticals, and instruments are high not only in R&D inputs that generate new economic knowledge but also in innovative outputs (Audretsch, 1995). By contrast, industries with little R&D—such as wood products, textiles, and paper—also tend to produce only a negligible amount of innovative output. Thus, the knowledge-production model linking knowledge-generating inputs to outputs certainly holds at the more aggregated levels of economic activity.

Where the relationship becomes less compelling is at the disaggregated microeconomic level of the enterprise, establishment, or even line of business. For example, while Acs and Audretsch (1990) found that the simple correlation between R&D inputs and innovative output was 0.84 for four-digit standard industrial classification (SIC) manufacturing industries in the United States, it was only about half, 0.40, among the largest U.S. corporations.

The model of the knowledge production function becomes even less compelling in view of the recent wave of studies revealing that small enterprises serve as the engine of innovative activity in certain industries. These results are startling because, as Scherer (1991) observes, the bulk of industrial R&D is undertaken in the largest corporations; small enterprises account only for a minor share of R&D inputs. Thus the knowledge production function seemingly implies that, as the Schumpeterian hypothesis predicts, innovative activity favors those organizations with access to knowledge-producing inputs—the large incumbent organization. The more recent evidence identifying the strong innovative activity raises this question: "Where do new and small firms get the innovation-producing inputs—that is, the knowledge?"

One answer, proposed by Audretsch (1995), is that, although the model of the knowledge production function may still be valid, the implicitly assumed unit of observation—at the level of the firm—may be less valid. The reason that the knowledge-production function holds more closely for more aggregated degrees of observation may be that investment in R&D and other sources of new knowledge spills over for economic exploitation by third-party firms.

A large literature has emerged focusing on what has become known as the *appropriability problem* (see Cohen and Levin, 1989; Baldwin and Scott, 1987). The underlying issue revolves around how firms that invest in the creation of new economic knowledge can best appropriate the economic returns from that knowledge (Arrow, 1962). Audretsch (1995) proposes shifting the unit of observation away from exogenously assumed firms to individuals—agents with endowments of new economic knowledge. As J. de V. Graaf (1957) observed nearly four decades ago,

> When we try to construct a transformation function for society as a whole from those facing the individual firms comprising it, a fundamental difficulty confronts us. There is, from a welfare point of view, nothing special about the firms actually existing in an economy at a given moment of time. The firm is in no sense a "natural unit." Only the individual members of the economy can lay claim to that distinction. All are potential entrepreneurs. It seems, therefore, that the natural thing to do is to build up from the transformation function of men, rather than the firms, constituting an economy. If we are interested in eventual empirical determination, this is extremely inconvenient. But it has conceptual advantages. The ultimate repositories of technological knowledge in any society are the men comprising it, and it is just this knowledge which is effectively summarized in the form of a transformation function. In itself a firm possesses no knowledge. That which is available to it belongs to the men associated with it. Its production function is really built up in exactly the same way, and from the same basic ingredients, as society's.

But when the lens is shifted away from focusing on the firm as the relevant unit of observation to individuals, the relevant question becomes this: How can economic agents with a given endowment of new knowledge best appropriate the returns from that knowledge?

The appropriability problem confronting the individual may converge with that confronting the firm. Economic agents can and do work for firms, and even if they do not, they can potentially be employed by an incumbent firm. In fact, in a model of perfect information with no agency costs, any positive economies of scale or scope will ensure that the appropriability problems of the firm and individual converge. If an agent has an idea for doing something different than is currently being practiced by the incumbent enterprises—both in terms of a new product or process and in terms of organization—the idea, which can be termed an innovation, will be presented to the incumbent enterprise. Because of the assumption of perfect knowledge, both the firm and the agent would agree on the expected value of the innovation. But to the degree that any economies of scale or scope exist, the expected value of implementing the innovation within the incumbent enterprise will exceed that of taking the innovation outside the incumbent firm to start a new enterprise. Thus, the incumbent firm and the inventor of the idea would be expected to reach a bargain splitting the value added to the firm contributed by the innovation. The payment to the inventor—either in terms of a higher wage or some other means of remuneration—would be bounded by (1) the expected value of the innovation if it was implemented by the incumbent enterprise on the upper end and (2) the return that the agent could expect to earn if he used it to launch a new enterprise on the lower end. Or, as Frank Knight (1921, p. 273) observed more than seventy years ago,

> The laborer asks what he thinks the entrepreneur will be able to pay, and in any case will not accept less than he can get from some other entrepreneur, or by turning entrepreneur himself. In the same way the entrepreneur offers to any laborer what he thinks he must in order to secure his services, and in any case not more than he thinks the laborer will actually be worth to him, keeping in mind what he can get by turning laborer himself.

Thus, each economic agent would choose how to best appropriate the value of his endowment of economic knowledge by comparing the wage he would earn if he remains employed by an incumbent enterprise, w, to the expected net present discounted value of the profits accruing from starting a new firm, π. If these two values are relatively close, the probability that he would choose to appropriate the value of his knowledge through an external mechanism such as starting a new firm, $Pr(e)$, would be relatively low. On the other hand, as the gap between w and π becomes larger, the likelihood of an agent choosing to appropriate the value of his knowledge externally through starting a new enterprise becomes greater, or

$$Pr(e) = f(\pi - w). \tag{2.1}$$

This model analyzing the decision of how best to appropriate the value of new economic knowledge confronting an individual economic agent seems useful when considering an entrepreneur's actual decision to create a new firm. For example, Chester Carlsson started Xerox after his proposal to produce a (new) copy machine was rejected by Kodak. Kodak based its decision on the premise that the new copy machine would not earn very much money and, in any case, that Kodak was in a different line of business—photography. It is perhaps no small irony that this same entrepreneurial startup, Xerox, decades later turned down a proposal from Steven Jobs to produce and market a personal computer because it did not think that a personal computer would sell and, in any case, Xerox was in a different line of business—copy machines (Carrol, 1993a). After seventeen other companies turned down Jobs for virtually identical reasons, including IBM and Hewlett Packard, Jobs resorted to starting his own company, Apple Computer.

Similarly, IBM turned down an offer from Bill Gates—"the chance to buy ten percent of Microsoft for a song in 1986, a missed opportunity that would cost $3 billion today" ("System Error," 1993, p. 99). IBM reached its decision on the grounds that "neither Gates nor any of his band of thirty some employees had anything approaching the credentials or personal characteristics required to work at IBM" (Carrol, 1993a, p. 18).

Divergences in beliefs with respect to the value of a new idea need not be restricted to what is formally known as a product or even a process innovation. Rather, the fact that economic agents choose to start a new firm due to divergences in the expected value of an idea applies to the sphere of managerial style and organization as well. One of the most vivid examples involves Bob Noyce, who founded Intel. Noyce had been employed by Fairchild Semiconductor, which is credited with being the pioneering semiconductor firm. In 1957 Noyce and seven other engineers left Schockley Semiconductor to form Fairchild Semiconductor, an enterprise that in turn is considered the start of what is today known as Silicon Valley. Although Fairchild Semiconductor had "possibly the most potent management and technical team ever assembled" (Gilder, 1989, p. 89),

> Noyce couldn't get Fairchild's eastern owners to accept the idea that stock options should be part of compensation for all employees, not just for management. He wanted to tie everyone, from janitors to bosses, into the overall success of the company. . . . This management style still sets the standard for every computer, software, and semiconductor company in the Valley today. . . . Every CEO still wants to think that the place is run the way Bob Noyce would have run it. (Cringley, 1993, p. 39)

That is, Noyce's vision of a firm excluded the dress codes, reserved parking places, closed offices, executive dining rooms, and other trappings of status that were standard in virtually every hierarchical and bureaucratic U.S. corporation. But when he tried to impress this vision on the owners of Fairchild Semiconductor, he was flatly rejected. The formation of Intel in 1968 was the ultimate result of the divergence in beliefs about how to organize and manage the firm.

The key development at Intel was the microprocessor. When longtime IBM employee Ted Hoff approached IBM and later DEC with his new microprocessor in the late 1960s, "IBM and DEC decided there was no market. They could not imagine why anyone would need or want a small computer; if people wanted to use a computer, they could hook into time-sharing systems" (Palfreman and Swade, 1991, p. 108).

The model proposed by Audretsch (1995) refocuses the unit of observation away from firms deciding whether to increase their output from a level of zero to some positive amount in a new industry and to individual agents in possession of new knowledge that, due to uncertainty, may or may not have some positive economic value. It is the uncertainty inherent in new economic knowledge, combined with asymmetries between the agent possessing that knowledge and the decision-making vertical hierarchy of the incumbent organization with respect to its expected value that potentially leads to a gap between the valuation of that knowledge.

How the economic agent chooses to appropriate the value of his knowledge—that is, either within an incumbent firm or by starting or joining a new enterprise—will be shaped by the knowledge conditions underlying the industry. Under the routinized technological regime the agent will tend to appropriate the value of his new ideas within the boundaries of incumbent firms. Thus, the propensity for new firms to be started should be relatively low in industries characterized by the routinized technological regime.

By contrast, under the entrepreneurial regime the agent will tend to appropriate the value of his new ideas outside of the boundaries of incumbent firms by starting a new enterprise. Thus, the propensity for new firms to enter should be relatively high in industries characterized by the entrepreneurial regime.

Audretsch (1995) suggests that divergences in the expected value regarding new knowledge will, under certain conditions, lead an agent to exercise what Albert O. Hirschman (1970) has termed as *exit* rather than *voice* and to depart from an incumbent enterprise to launch a new firm. But who is right—the departing agents or those agents remaining in the organizational decision-making hierarchy who, by assigning the new idea a relatively low value, have effectively driven the agent with the potential innovation away? In hindsight, the answer may not be too difficult, but given the uncertainty inherent in new knowledge, the answer is anything but trivial *a priori*.

Thus, when a new firm is launched, its prospects are shrouded in uncertainty. If the new firm is built around a new idea—a potential innovation—it is uncertain whether there is sufficient demand for the new idea or if some competitor will have the same or even a superior idea. Even if the new firm is formed to be an exact replica of a successful incumbent enterprise, it is uncertain whether sufficient demand for a new clone, or even for the existing incumbent, will prevail in the future. Tastes can change, and new ideas emerging from other firms will certaintly influence those tastes.

Finally, an additional layer of uncertainty pervades a new enterprise. It is not known how competent the new firm really is, in terms of management, organization, and workforce. At least incumbent enterprises know something about their underlying competencies from past experience. A new enterprise is burdened with uncertainty as to whether it can produce and market the intended product as well as sell it. In both cases the degree of uncertainty will typically exceed that confronting incumbent enterprises.

This initial condition—of not just uncertainty but a greater degree of uncertainty about incumbent enterprises in the industry—is captured in the theory of firm selection and industry evolution proposed by Boyan Jovanovic (1982). Jovanovic presents a model in which the new firms, which he terms *entrepreneurs*, face costs that are random and that differ across firms. A central feature of the model is that a new firm does not know what its cost function (its relative efficiency) is but rather discovers this through the process of learning from its actual postentry performance. In particular, Jovanovic (1982) assumes that entrepreneurs are unsure about their ability to manage a new-firm startup and therefore their prospects for success. Although entrepreneurs may launch a new firm based on a vague sense of expected postentry performance, they discover their true ability—in terms of managerial competence and of having based the firm on an idea that is viable on the market—only once their business is established. Those entrepreneurs who discover that their ability exceeds their expectations expand the scale of their business, whereas those who discover that their postentry performance is less than commensurate with their expectations will contact the scale of output and possibly exit from the industry. Thus, Jovanovic's model is a theory of *noisy selection*, where efficient firms grow and survive and inefficient firms decline and fail.

The role of learning in the selection process has been the subject of considerable debate. On the one hand is what has been referred to as the *Larackian* assumption that learning refers to adaptations made by the new enterprise. In this sense, those new firms that are the most flexible and adaptable will be the most successful in adjusting to whatever the demands of the market are. As Nelson and Winter (1982, p. 11) point out, "Many kinds of organizations commit resources to learning; organizations seek to copy the forms of their most successful competitors."

On the other hand is the interpretation that the role of learning is restricted to discovering if the firm has the *right stuff* in terms of the goods it is producing as well as the way they are being produced. Under this interpretation the new enterprise is not necessarily able to adapt or adjust to market conditions but receives information based on its market performance with respect to its *fitness* in terms of meeting demand more efficiently than rivals. The theory of organizational ecology proposed by Michael T. Hannan and John Freeman (1989) most pointedly adheres to the notion that "we assume that individual organizations are characterized by relative inertia in structure." That is, firms learn not in the sense that they adjust their actions as reflected by their fundamental identity and purpose but in the sense of their perception. What is then learned is whether the firm has the right stuff but not whether it knows how to change that stuff.

The theory of firm selection is particularly appealing in view of the rather startling size of most new firms. For example, the mean size of more than 11,000 new-firm startups in the manufacturing sector in the United States was found to be fewer than eight workers per firm (Audretsch, 1995).[6] While the minimum efficient scale (MES) varies substantially across industries and even to some degree across various product classes within any given industry, the observed size of most new firms is sufficiently small to ensure that the bulk of new firms will be operating at a suboptimal scale of output. Why would an entrepreneur start a new firm that would immediately be confronted by scale disadvantages?

An implication of the theory of firm selection is that new firms may begin at a small, even suboptimal, scale of output and then, if merited by subsequent performance, expand. Those new firms that are successful will grow, whereas those that are not successful will remain small and may ultimately be forced to exit from the industry if they are operating at a suboptimal scale of output.

Subsequent to entering an industry, an entrepreneur must decide whether to maintain its output expand, contract, or exit. Two different strands of literature have identified several major influences shaping the decision to exit an industry. The first and most obvious strand of literature suggests that the probability of a business exiting will tend to increase as the gap between its level of output and the minimum efficient scale (MES) level of output increases.[7] The second strand of literature points to the role that the technological environment plays in shaping the decision to exit. As Dosi (1988) and Arrow (1962) argue, an environment characterized by more frequent innovation may also be associated with a greater amount of uncertainty regarding not only the technical nature of the product but also the demand for that product. As technological uncertainty increases, particularly under the entrepreneurial regime, the likelihood that the business will be able to produce a viable product and ultimately be able to survive decreases.

An important implication of the dynamic process of firm selection and industry evolution is that new firms are more likely to be operating at a suboptimal scale of output if the underlying technological conditions are such that there is a greater chance of making an innovation—that is, under the entrepreneurial regime. If new firms successfully learn and adapt or are just plain lucky, they grow into viably sized enterprises. If not, they stagnate and many ultimately exit from the industry. This suggests that entry and startup of new firms may not be greatly deterred in the presence of scale economies. As long as entrepreneurs perceive that there is some prospect for growth and ultimate survival, such entry will occur. Thus, in industries where the MES is high, it follows from the observed general small size of new-firm startups that the growth rate of the surviving firms would presumably be relatively high.

At the same time, those new firms not able to grow and attain the MES level of output would presumably be forced to exit from the industry, resulting in a relatively low likelihood of survival. In industries characterized by a low MES, neither the need for growth nor the consequences of its absence are as severe, so that relatively lower growth rates but higher survival rates would be expected. Similarly, in industries where the probability of innovating is greater, more entrepreneurs may actually take a chance that they will succeed by growing into a viably sized enterprise. In such industries, one would expect that the growth of successful enterprises would be greater but that the likelihood of survival would be correspondingly lower.

THE CONTRIBUTION OF SMALL FIRMS TO EFFICIENCY IN THE EVOLUTIONARY ECONOMY

What emerges from the new evolutionary theories and empirical evidence on the economic role of new and small firms is that markets are in motion, with a lot of new firms entering the industry and a lot of firms exiting out of the industry. But is this motion horizontal (are the bulk of firms exiting comprised of firms that entered relatively recently?) or vertical (are most exiting firms established incumbents that were displaced by younger firms?)? In trying to shed some light on this question, Audretsch (1995) proposes two different models of the evolutionary process of industries over time. Some industries can be best characterized by the model of the conical revolving door, where new businesses enter but where there is a high propensity to subsequently exit from the market. Other industries may be better characterized by the metaphor of the forest, where incumbent establishments are displaced by new entrants. Which view is more applicable apparently depends on three major factors—the underlying technological conditions, scale economies, and demand. Where scale economies play an important role, the model of the revolving door seems to be more applicable. While the rather startling result discussed above (that the startup and entry of new businesses is apparently not deterred by the presence of high scale economies), a process of firm selection analogous to a revolving door ensures that only those establishments successful enough to grow will be able to survive beyond more than a few years. Thus the bulk of new entrants that are not so successful ultimately exit within a few years subsequent to entry.

There is at least some evidence also suggesting that the underlying technological regime influences the process of firm selection and therefore the type of firm with a higher propensity to exit. Under the entrepreneurial regime new entrants have a greater likelihood of making an innovation. Thus, they are less likely to decide to exit from the industry, even in the face of negative profits. By contrast, under the routinized regime the incumbent businesses tend to have the innovative advantage, so that a higher portion of exiting businesses tend to be new entrants. Thus, the model of the revolving door is more applicable under technological conditions consistent with the routinized regime, and the metaphor of the forest (where the new entrants displace the incumbents) is more applicable to the entrepreneurial regime.

Why is the general shape of the firm-size distribution strikingly similar across virtually every industry—that is, skewed with only a few large enterprises and numerous small ones—and why has it persisted with tenacity across developed countries and over a long period of time? The evolutionary view of the process of industry evolution is that new firms typically start at a very small scale of output. They are motivated by the desire to appropriate the expected value of new economic knowledge. But depending on the extent of scale economies in the industry, the firm may not be able to remain viable indefinitely at its startup size. Rather, if scale economies are anything other than negligible, the new firm is likely to have to grow to survival. The temporary survival of new firms is presumably supported through the deployment of a strategy of compensating factor differentials that enables the firm to discover whether it has a viable product.

The empirical evidence supports such an evolutionary view of the role of new firms in manufacturing because the postentry growth of firms that survive tends to be spurred by the extent to which there is a gap between the MES level of output and the size of the firm. However, the likelihood of any particular new firm surviving tends to decrease as this gap increases. Such new suboptimal-scale firms are apparently engaged in the selection process. Only those firms offering a viable product that can be produced efficiently will grow and ultimately approach or attain the MES level of output. The remainder will stagnate and, depending on the severity of the other selection mechanism (the extent of scale economies), may ultimately be forced to exit the industry. Thus, the persistence of an asymmetric firm-size distribution biased toward small-scale enterprise reflects the continuing process of the entry of new firms into industries and not necessarily the permanence of such small and suboptimal enterprises over the long run. Although the skewed size distribution of firms persists with remarkable stability over long periods of time, a constant set of small- and suboptimal-scale firms does not appear to be responsible for this skewed distribution. Rather, by serving as agents of change, new firms provide an essential source of new ideas and experimentation that otherwise would remain untapped in the economy.

CONCLUSIONS

When viewed through the static lens provided by industrial organization, small firms place an efficiency burden on the economy. Their small scale of production inflicts a substantial loss in terms of higher production costs. However, when viewed through a more evolutionary lens, such static losses in production efficiency are more than offset in gains in dynamic efficiency. The greatest contribution to economic efficiency by small firms is dynamic and evolutionary in nature: small firms serve as agents of change.

In the current debate on the relationship between employment and wages, it is typically argued that the existence of small firms that are suboptimal within the organization of an industry represents a loss in economic efficiency. This argument is based on a static analysis, however. When viewed through a dynamics lens, a different conclusion emerges. One of the most striking results in the new literature is the finding of a positive impact of firm age on productivity and employee compensation, even after controlling for the size of the firm. Given the strongly confirmed stylized fact linking both firm size and age to a negative rate of growth (that is, the smaller and younger a firm, the faster it will grow, but the lower is its likelihood of survival), this new finding that links firm age to employee compensation and productivity suggests that not only will some of the small and suboptimal firms of today become the large and optimal firms of tomorrow, but there is at least a tendency for the low productivity and wage of today to become the high productivity and wage of tomorrow.

The public policies emerging in the postwar period dealing with business have been shaped by the static view of industrial organization and therefore are essentially constraining in nature. There were three general types of public policies toward business—antitrust (competition policy), regulation, and public ownership. All three of these policy approaches toward the firm in the market restricted the firm's freedom to contract. While specific policy approaches tended to be associated more with one country than with others, such as antitrust in the United States or public ownership in France and Sweden, all developed countries shared a common policy approach of intervening to restrain what otherwise was perceived as too much market power held by firms. Public policies constraining the freedom of the firm to contract were certainly consistent with the *Weltanschauung* emerging from the theories and empirical evidence regarding the firm in the market during the postwar period. Left unchecked, the large corporation in possession of market power would allocate resources in such a way as to reduce economic welfare. Through state intervention, the Williamsonian tradeoff between efficiency and fairness would be solved in a manner that presumably would be more socially satisfying.

But more recently the relevant policy question has shifted away from "How can the government constrain firms from abusing their market power?" to "How can governments create an environment fostering the success and viability of firms?" The major issues of the day have shifted away from concerns about excess profits and abuses of market dominance to the creation of jobs, growth, and international competitiveness. the concern about corporations is now more typically not that they are too successful and powerful but that they are not successful and powerful enough. Thus, the government policies of the 1990s have increasingly shifted away from *constraining* to *enabling*. Governments are increasingly fostering efforts to create new firms in order to promote job creation and economic growth within their jurisdictions. While this policy emphasis on small and new firms as engines of dynamic efficiency may seem startling after decades of looking to the corporate giants to bestow efficiency, it is anything but new. Before the country was even half a century old, Alexis de Tocqueville, in 1835, reported, "What astonishes me in the United States is not so much the marvellous grandeur of some undertakings as the innumerable multitude of small ones" (*Business Week*, 1993, p. 12).

ACKNOWLEDGMENTS

An earlier version of this chapter was presented at the U.S. Small Business Administration conference on the role of small firms. I am grateful to the participants of the conference, and in particular Zoltan J. Acs, for valuable suggestions. Any omissions or errors remain my responsibility.

NOTES

1. See Moore (1992, p. 72) for a recent documentation of the "view held widely at the time that Soviet central planning would produce persistently higher growth rates into the foreseeable future."

2. Although it was acknowledged that small firms were able to avoid direct competition by occupying strategic niches, Weiss (Audretsch and Yamawaki, 1991, p. 404) observed that "the survival of smaller plants within any given industry may be due to their specialization in items with short production runs or to their service of small geographic markets within which their relatively small national market share is irrelevant. To the extent that such explanations hold, small plants are not necessarily suboptimal. However, such explanations seem unlikely to hold for a number of the industries where the percentage of suboptimal capacity is larger."

3. Coase (1937, p. 23) himself asked, "A pertinent question to ask would appear to be (quite apart from the monopoly considerations raised by Professor Knight), why, if by organizing one can eliminate

certain costs and in fact reduce the cost of production, are there any market transactions at all? Why is not all production carried on by one big firm?"

4. For reviews of this literature, see Baldwin and Scott (1987), Cohen and Levin (1989), Scherer (1984, 1992), and Dosi (1988).

5. See, for example, Scherer (1984 and 1991), Cohen and Klepper (1991 and 1992), and Arrow (1962 and 1983).

6. A similar startup size for new manufacturing firms has been found by Dunne, Roberts, and Samuelson (1989) for the United States, Mata (1994) and Mata and Portugal (1994) for Portugal, and Wagner (1994) for Germany.

7. For example, Weiss (1976, p. 126) argues that "In purely competitive long-run equilibrium, no suboptimal capacity should exist at all."

REFERENCES

Acs, Zoltan J. (1984). *The Changing Structure of the U.S. Economy: Lessons from the Steel Industry*. New York: Praeger.

Acs, Zoltan J. (ed.). (1995). *Small Firms and Economic Development*. (vol. 1 and 2) Cheltenham, UK: Elgar.

Acs, Zoltan J., and David B. Audretsch. (1988). "Innovation in Large and Small Firms: An Empirical Analysis." *American Economic Review*, 78(4) (September), 678–690.

Acs, Zoltan J., and David B. Audretsch. (1990). *Innovation and Small Firms*. Cambridge: MIT Press.

Arrow, Kenneth J. (1962). "Economic Welfare and the Allocation of Resources for Invention." In R.R. Nelson (ed.), *The Rate and Direction of Inventive Activity*. Princeton: Princeton University Press.

Audretsch, David B. (1991). "New Firm Survival and the Technological Regime." *Review of Economics and Statistics*, 73(3) (August), 441–450.

Audretsch, David B. (1995). *Innovation and Industry Evolution*. Cambridge: MIT Press.

Audretsch, David B., and Maryann P. Feldman. (1996). "R&D Spillovers and the Geography of Innovation and Production." *American Economic Review*, 86(3) (June), 630–640.

Audretsch, David B., and Talat Mahmood. (1995). "New-Firm Survival: New Results Using a Hazard Function." *Review of Economics and Statistics*, 77(1) (February), 97–103.

Audretsch, David B., and Paula E. Stephan. (1996). "Company-Scientist Locational Links: The Case of Biotechnology." *American Economic Review*, 86(3) (June), 641–652.

Audretsch, David B., and Hideki Yamawaki (eds.). (1991). *Structure, Conduct and Performance: Leonard Weiss*. New York: New York University Press.

Baldwin, John R. (1995). *The Dynamics of Industrial Competition*. Cambridge: Cambridge University Press.

Baldwin, John R., and Paul K. Gorecki. (1991). "Entry, Exit, and Production Growth." In P. Geroski and J. Schwalbach (eds.), *Entry and Market Contestability: An International Comparison*. Oxford: Basil Blackwell.

Baldwin, John R., and M. Rafiquzzaman. (1995). "Selection Versus Evolutionary Adaptation: Learning and Post-Entry Performance." *International Journal of Industrial Organization*, 13(4) (December), 501–523.

Baldwin, William L., and John T. Scott. (1987). *Market Structure and Technological Change*. London and New York: Harwood Academic Publishers.

Brown, Chalres, James Hamilton, and James Medoff. (1990). *Employers Large and Small*. Cambridge: Cambridge University Press.

Business Week. (1993). Bonus Issue, p. 12.

Carrol, Paul. (1993a). *Big Blues: The Unmaking of IBM*. New York: Grown.

Carrol, Paul. (1993b). "Die Offene Schlacht." *Die Zeit*, no. 39 (September 24), 18.

Coase, R.H. (1937). "The Nature of the Firm." *Economica*, 4(4), 386–405.

Chandler, Alfred D., Jr. (1977). *The Visible Hand: The Managerial Revolution in American Business*. Cambridge: Harvard University Press.

Cohen, Wesley M., and Richard C. Levin. (1989). "Empirical Studies of Innovation and Market Structure." In R. Schmalensee and R. Willig, eds. *Handbook of Industrial Organization*, Vol. 2, Amsterdam: North-Holland, 1059–1107.

Cringley, Robert X. (1993). *Accidental Empires*. New York: Harper Busienss.

Dosi, Giovanni. (1988). "Sources, Procedures, and Microeconomic Effects of Innovation." *Journal of Economic Literature* 26(3): 1120–1171.

Dunne, T., M.J. Roberts, and L. Samuelson. (1989). "The Growth and Failure of U.S. Manufacturing Plants." *Quarterly Journal of Economics*, 104, 671–698.
Galbraith, John Kenneth. (1956). *American Capitalism*. Boston: Houghton Mifflin.
Geroski, Paul A. (1991). "Some Data-Driven Reflections on the Entry Process." In Paul Georski and Joachin Schwalbach (eds.), *Entry and Market Contestability: An International Comparison*. Oxford: Basil Blackwell.
Geroski, Paul A. (1995). "What Do We Know About Entry?" *International Journal of Industrial Organization*, 13(4) (December) (Special Issue on The Post-Entry Performance of Firms edited by D.B. Audretsch and J. Mata).
Geroski, Paul A., and Joachim Schwalbach (eds.). (1991). *Entry and Market Contestability: An International Comparison*. Oxford: Basil Blackwell.
Gilder, George. (1989). *Microcosm*. New York: Touchstone.
Graf, J. de V. (1957). *Theoretical Welfare Economics*. Cambridge: Cambridge University Press.
Griliches, Zvi. (1979). "Issues in Assessing the Contribution of R&D to Productivity Growth." *Bell Journal of Economics*, 10 (Spring), 92–116.
Hall, Bronwyn H. (1987). "The Relationship Between Firm Size and Firm Growth in the U.S. Manufacturing Sector." *Journal of Industrial Economics*, 35 (June), 583–605.
Hannan, Michael T., and John Freeman. (1989). *Organizational Ecology*. Cambridge: Harvard University Press.
Hirschman, Albert O. (1970). *Exit, Voice, and Loyalty*. Cambridge: Harvard University Press.
Ijiri, Yuji, and Herbert A. Simon. (1977). *Skew Distributions and Sizes of Business Firms*. Amsterdam: North Holland.
Jovanovic, Boyan. (1982). "Selection and Evolution of Industry." *Econometrica*, 50(2), 649–670.
Knight, Frank H. (1921). *Risk, Uncertainty and Profit*. New York: Houghton Mifflin.
Mansfield, Edwin. (1962). "Entry, Gibrat's Law, Innovation, and the Growth of Firms." *American Economic Review*, 52(5), 1023–1051.
Mata, Jose. (1994). "Firm Growth During Infancy." *Small Business Economics*, 6(1), 27–40.
Mata, Jose, and Pedro Portugal. (1994). "Life Duration of New Firms." *Journal of Industrial Economics*, 27(3), 227–246.
Mata, Jose, Pedro Portugal, and Paulo Guimaraes. (1995). "The Survival of New Plants: Start-Up Conditions and Post-Entry Evolution." *International Journal of Industrial Organization*, 13(4) (December), 459–482.
Moore, John H. (1992). "Measuring Soviet Economic Growth: Old Problems and New Complications." *Journal of Institutional and Theoretical Economics*, 148(1), 72–92.
Nelson, Richard R., and Sidney G. Winter. (1982). *An Evolutionary Theory of Economic Change*. Cambridge: Harvard University Press.
Neumann, Manfred. (1993). "Review of Entry and Market Contestability: An International Comparison." *International Journal of Industrial Organization*, 11(4), 593–594.
Palfreman, Jon, and Doron Swade. (1991). *The Dream Machine: Exploring the Computer Age*. London: BBC Books.
Pratten, C.F. (1971). *Economies of Scale in Manufacturing Industry*. Cambridge: Cambridge University Press.
Scherer, F.M. (1976). "Industrial Structure, Scale Economies, and Worker Alienation." In Robert T. Masson and P. David Qualls (eds.), *Essays on Industrial Organization in Honor of Joe S. Bain* (pp. 105–122). Cambridge, MA: Ballinger.
Scherer, F.M. (1991). "Changing Perspectives on the Firm Size Problem." In Z.J. Acs and D.B. Audretsch (eds.), *Innovation and Technological Change: An International Comparison*. Ann Arbor: University of Michigan Press.
Scherer, F.M. (1973). "The Determinants of Industry Plant Sizes in Six Nations" *Review of Economics and Statistics* 55(2): 135–175.
Schumpeter, Joseph A. (1911). *Theorie der wirtschaftlichen Entwicklung. Eine Untersuchung hber Unternehmergewinn, Kapital, Kredit, Zins und den Konjunkturzyklus*. Berlin: Duncker und Humblot.
Schumpeter, Joseph A. (1942). *Capitalism, Socialism and Democracy*. New York: Harper and Row.
Simon, Herbert A., and Charles P. Bonini. (1958). "The Size Distribution of Business Firms." *American Economic Review*, 48(4), 607–617.
"System Erron." (1993). *The Economist*. September 18, p. 99.
Wagner, Joachim. (1992). "Firm Size, Firm Growth, and Persistence of Chance: Testing Gibrat's Law with Establishment Data from Lower Saxony, 1978–1989." *Small Business Economics*, 4(2), 125–131.
Wagner, Joachim. (1994). "Small Firm Entry in Manufacturing Industries: Lower Saxony, 1979–1989." *Small Business Economics*, 6(3), 211–224.

Weiss, Leonard W. (1979). "The Structure-Performance Paradigm and Antitrust." *University of Pennsylvania Law Review*, 127 (April), 1104–1140.
Weiss, Leonard W. (1964). "The Survival Technique and the Extent of Suboptimal Capacity." *Journal of Political Economy* 72(3): 246–261.
Williamson, Oliver E., (1968). "Economies as an Antitrust Defense: The Welfare Tradeoffs." *American Economic Review*, 58(1), 18–36.
Williamson, Oliver E. (1975). *Markets and Hierarchies: Antitrust Analysis and Implications*. New York: Free Press.
Winter, Sidney G. (1984). "Schumpeterian Competition in Alternative Technological Regimes." *Journal of Economic Behavior and Organization*, 5 (September–December), 287–320.

3. SEMICONDUCTOR STARTUPS AND THE EXPLORATION OF NEW TECHNOLOGICAL TERRITORY

PAUL ALMEIDA

Georgetown University, Washington, DC

INTRODUCTION

Why are small firms important? The answer to this question often points to the critical role played by small firms in innovation. Research conducted by small firms has, after all, been shown to be more productive than that conducted by larger firms (Bound, Cummins, Griliches, Hall, and Jaffe, 1984). For instance, Acs and Audretsch (1990) find that small firms produce innovations with twice the productivity of larger firms. However, this superiority of small firms in research productivity has not been supported universally. The higher productivity of small-firm research is evident only in some industries and is more conclusive for the United States than for other countries (Scherer, 1984).

This chapter supports the view that small firms play an important role in innovation. We argue that the importance of small firms lies not only in the productivity of their research relative to larger firms but in the unique role that small firms play in the innovative process. By analyzing the role of startup firms in the semiconductor industry, we suggest that these small firms play a critical role in technological (and thus economic) development by exploring and innovating in new technological fields. In addition, by using and diffusing knowledge within geographic regions, small semiconductor firms help sustain and build regional knowledge networks.

SMALL FIRMS AND THE EXPLORATION OF NEW TECHNOLOGICAL TERRITORY

Anecdotal evidence of innovation in today's technology-intensive industries such as semiconductors, biotechnology, and software suggests an important role for small firms. The role of small firms in innovation is, however, neither new nor confined to recent high-technology industries. Substantial qualitative evidence supports the role of small firms and individuals in introducing important, or in Schumpeterian terminology *radical*, innovations even in the first half of this century. While examining fifty important and successful innovations, Jewkes, Sawers, and Stillerman (1958) find that a critical role was played by the individual inventor: more than half of these innovations were introduced outside established research organizations. Scherer and Ross (1990) highlight several revolutionary inventions by startup firms that departed significantly from the technologies in use at the time of the invention. Among the inventions mentioned are the incandescent lamp (Edison), the FM radio (Armstrong), the microwave oven (Raytheon), the microcomputer (Altair and Apple), and the microprocessor (Intel). They point out that invitations to collaborate with the inventors of these technological breakthroughs were often turned down by larger firms.

The conventional explanation for the lead role played by small firms in innovation appeals to the deficiency of internal incentives in larger firms to pursue radical innovation and the lack of flexibility of these larger companies to permit internal change. (Monopolistic motivations are pertinent in industries less characterized by the potential for the introduction of radical innovations.) The drawback to large-firm research is that innovation in large firms becomes routinized and this results in a reluctance to explore new technological fields. A wide variety of organizational studies support the idea that inertia within an organization increases with the firm's age and size (Hannan and Freeman, 1984). This inertia perpetuates innovation along established directions but prevents these firms from exploring new opportunities and hence developing radical innovations. Even Schumpeter's (1934) early work emphasized the dynamic role played by new-firm innovations. It was his pessimism over the supply of entrepreneurs (Schumpeter, 1943, p. 152) that led him to characterize the process of a creative destruction that is increasingly driven by large firms that are capable of innovating within a routinized regime.

Small firms do not have the resources to compete with larger firms in innovating in routinized regimes. They also are more likely to possess the organizational characteristics that permit the adjustments necessary to take advantage of and explore new opportunities. Further, factors including financing, government regulations, and the motives and goals of entrepreneurs provide condition for small firms that are more amenable to the exploration of diversity (Nooteboom, 1994). Hence small firms are better equipped to exploit new technological opportunities through the exploration of diversity. Some support for the link between new firms and radical innovation is provided by Henderson (1993). In a study of the photolithographic alignment equipment industry, Henderson shows that larger incumbent firms were less productive than startup firms in exploiting radical innovations.

SEMICONDUCTOR STARTUPS AND TECHNOLOGICAL EXPLORATION

An examination of innovation in the semiconductor industry reveals a clearer picture of the relationship between small firms and radical innovation. The semiconductor industry is, after all, the apotheosis of a innovative industry and originated from the invention of the first solid-state transistor at the laboratories of AT&T (Bell Laboratories) in New Jersey in 1947. The industry has been characterized by waves of startup activity that each results in the exploration of new fields and the discovery of major innovations. Ever since William Shockley left Bell Labs to start Shockley Semiconductors in Palo Alto, California, entrepreneurship and hence startups have played an important role in the diffusion of knowledge in and the evolution of the industry (Moore, 1986). Several of Shockley's assistants left his firm to form Fairchild Semiconductors in 1957. The newly formed Fairchild was the source of one of the most important innovations in the semiconductor industry. In 1959, Robert Noyce of Fairchild developed the planar process, which permitted large-scale production of integrated circuits. This important advance helped launch the era of the integrated circuit, and Fairchild itself spawned a host of new spinoffs. In fact, the origins of almost every firm in Silicon Valley can be traced back to Fairchild. Several of these startups, via successful innovation, grew into large firms that often dominated sections of the industry.

Though larger firms came to dominate more established fields (the memory segment is dominated by large Japanese and, more recently, Korean firms), new waves of startups continued to bring about technological changes. In the 1980s, small firms dominated innovation in the areas of application-specific integrated circuits (ASICs)—high-performance CMOS memory and logic chips. As ASICs have become more popular, many of the startups of the 1980s have grown rapidly. A new wave of startups in the middle 1990s is investigating new and emerging fields such as three-dimensional integrated circuits, voice recognition and synthesis, bioelectronics, and optoelectronics. While semiconductor startups continue to drive new design technologies, larger firms dominate in the manufacture of integrated circuits and the development of more mature segments of the industry. Thus, though innovation is driven by firms of all sizes, the entry of new firms continues to play an important role in new technology development.

Though most of the evidence supporting the role of small firms in innovation is descriptive in nature, empirical evidence too supports this view. Almeida and Kogut (1997) provide some empirical support for the role of small firms in innovation by analyzing patent data for semiconductor firms from 1980 to 1995. Their research identified patents corresponding to major innovations produced by large and small firms in the semiconductor industry and then identified the technology classes[1] in which these innovations were classified. They then plotted the total number of patents granted by the U.S. patent office in (1) the technology classes in which the larger firms had their major patents and (2) the technology classes in which the startup firms had their major patents. The results are shown in Figure 3.1.

The figure reveals interesting differences regarding the technologies in which small and large firms produce major innovations. While startups produce major innovations in less crowded technological fields, larger firms appear to succeed in more established fields, which have a larger concentration of innovative activity.

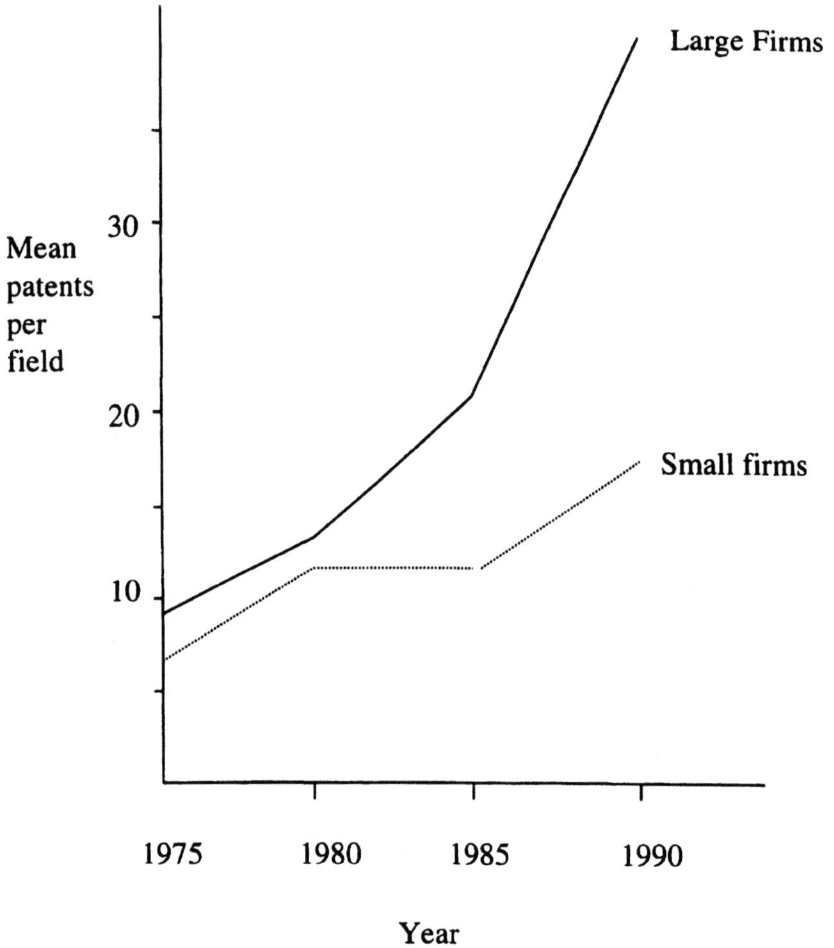

Figure 3.1.

Almeida and Kogut (1997) also applied the student's t-test to test for significance in the differences between sample means and found significant results. This analysis provides some support for the proposition that small firms are more likely to explore technologically diverse and uncrowded territories, leaving the domination of more mature technologies to larger firms. An examination of the market niches of semiconductor firms lends further support for this proposition. For instance, established firms like Intel, Motorola, Toshiba, and Siemens dominate patenting and sales in microprocessor and dynamic random-access memory (DRAM) technologies. Smaller firms are more active in patenting and sales in the areas of application-specific integrated circuits, gallium arsenide, and analog-integrated circuits.

Other studies of the technological activities of semiconductor firms further clarify the patterns of technological investigation of semiconductor firms. Stuart and Podolny (1996) studied large Japanese semiconductor firms and showed that these firms exhibited technologically local search tendencies: their exploration of technology tended to be in the neighborhood of their current technological expertise. This finding was not surprising: large firms have an acknowledged tendency to innovate along standard and well-explored fields. However, Kogut and Kim (1996) also found similar local search tendencies among semiconductor startups. This finding of local technological search for small semiconductor firms appears to be odds with the role of these firms in exploring new technological territory. An explanation for this apparent contradiction can be found in Almeida and Rosenkopf (1997), who further investigate the patterns of technological exploration of semiconductor startups by tracking interfirm learning using patent citation data. They confirmed the notion that small firms tend to conduct technologically local search. Small firms formed alliances with and hired engineers away from technologically similar firms to facilitate learning. However, this research showed that small firms also conducted technologically more distant searches and that successful innovations often resulted from this distant search. Thus, though small firms (like large firms) tend to search locally, success is often tied to their more distant exploration in fields not already dominated by larger firms.

An additional explanation for the success of small firms in new technological areas lies in the timing of the production of innovations. Major innovations in the semiconductor industry are often produced in the years immediately after a firm's founding (before the firm has an established area of expertise). The motivation of entrepreneurs is often to exploit new ideas that would not have been possible in established firms. Intel, for instance, produced its two most important inventions, the microprocessor and memory-integrated circuits, in the years immediately following its formation. As these two technologies grew more established, the technological fields came to be dominated by a now larger Intel and by other large Japanese, American, and Korean semiconductor firms. Thus, the descriptive and empirical evidence in the semiconductor industry points to an important role of small semiconductor firms in innovating in new technological territories and thus extending the opportunities for further technological exploration for firms in the industry.

KNOWLEDGE LOCALIZATION AND REGIONAL NETWORKS

The innovativeness of small firms and their ability to explore new technologies is perhaps surprising since they are often resource poor and have small R&D budgets and limited manpower (Rothwell, 1989). As early Schumpeter (1934) noted, startup companies are hampered by limits to financial and human resources to support their activities. However, the evidence from several empirical studies is that though small firms often spend less on R&D, they are at least as innovative as large firms (Nooteboom, 1994). Feldman (1994) suggests that small firms overcome their internal limitations by turning to outside sources of knowledge to build their innovative abilities. We suggest here that, given their resource limitations, small firms often rely on regional knowledge networks for important inputs to the innovative process. While accessing knowledge they also share knowledge with other firms locally. Through this process of accessing and sharing knowledge with geographically proximate firms, small firms help the circulation and building of regional knowledge. Thus, small firms play the important role of linking firms in regional knowledge networks.

Case studies of various small-firm clusters point to the use of informal mechanisms for local knowledge building. The presence of spatially concentrated mutually supportive networks has been well documented in many regions of the world. Localized information sharing was common among geographically clustered firms in the steel industry in nineteenth-century England (Allen, 1983). Case studies of regional clusters of small and medium-size firms in Italy (Piore and Sabel, 1984) and Baden-Wuerttemberg in Germany (Herrigel, 1993) indicate extensive interdependencies between the usually small firms located in these regions.

More recent statistical studies have conclusively found that innovations have a strong regional character. In a recent study, Jaffe, Trajtenberg, and Henderson (1993) analyzed patent citation data pertaining to domestic university and corporate patents to test the extent of localization of knowledge spillovers. They found evidence that patents tend to be cited in the same area where the originating patents are located, even after controlling for the existing concentration of patenting activity. Similarly, Almeida (1996a) studied the spatial diffusion of technological knowledge of larger firms through the analysis of important semiconductor innovations and through field interviews with engineers and scientists in the industry. His findings indicate that knowledge remains localized in the United States and particularly in some regions like Silicon Valley.

But why should this phenomenon of localized knowledge flows benefit smaller firms rather than larger ones? We suggest that large firms are more self-reliant than smaller firms and do not perceive the need to build relationships with other local organizations. Further, larger firms can be seen to have the resources permitting global scanning and reach and hence do not need to concentrate on local networking activities. An important reason for the reliance of small firms on local knowledge sources is that the paucity of resources in the firm creates an incentive to rely on outside sources of knowledge. These sources of knowledge are best obtained through building relationships with other institutions within the region. Small firms may have not only a greater motivation but also a greater opportunity to absorb local knowledge. By definition, the personnel in a startup company will have, on average, a short tenure in the company and, hence, recent employment and learning experiences in other firms or research institutions.

The presence of a local or regional social network holds several advantages in resource acquisition for small firms. One of the advantages of regional networks for small firms is that locational proximity reduces the cost and increases the frequency of personal contacts and serves to build social relations. Professional relationships are often embedded in these social networks. These professional and social networks are especially important in the process of innovation. An idea for a new product or process may originate from individuals or small groups within or outside a firm. The development of ideas into a usable product or process requires the combination of knowledge from several perspectives. This development of ideas is facilitated by face-to-face discussion and knowledge sharing either within a firm or across it. The commercial exploitation of a new product (or process) also requires interaction between and the involvement of employees of a firm and members of the community at large—buyers, suppliers, and even engineers and scientists from rival firms. Thus the participation of small firms in regional social networks provides an important opportunity for knowledge acquisition and sharing. Regional networks also aid the transmission of job-related information and thereby facilitate the movement of people across firms. Besides rich communication across firms, interfirm mobility of engineers aids the exploitation of new innovations and the sharing of knowledge between firms. Mobility within a region is also enhanced by personal costs for job switching within a region that are lower than those for interregional mobility. Almeida and Rosenkopf (1997) show that the mobility of engineers to small firms in the semiconductor industry is primarily intraregional and that engineers transfer useful knowledge across firms when they change jobs.

Much of this interfirm mobility, of course, may be directed to the exploitation of new knowledge through entrepreneurial activity. Local social and professional networks decrease the uncertainty and costs associated with startup activity, which encourages the provision of venture capital. The flow of information that serves as a common stock of knowledge in the region for innovations also sets the foundations for the exploration and exploitation of new knowledge by startups. Evidence to support the proposition that local networks are more important to small firms than to large firms is offered by Feldman (1994). Using U.S. Small Business Administration innovation data to ascertain the importance of inputs to innovation for firms of different sizes, she finds that although large firms benefit from local innovation, for small firms the benefit are more significant: small firms are two times more sensitive to local university research.

SEMICONDUCTOR STARTUPS AND REGIONAL NETWORKS

The semiconductor industry is remarkable for the role played by regional networks in knowledge development. Technology diffusion within regions has been facilitated by the culture of networking and information exchange between engineers. Managers within the industry are known to actively seek outside information useful in various stages of innovation, and this practice is particularly strong among entrepreneurial firms (Saxenian, 1991). Engineers at different companies share problem-solving information by discussing failed avenues of exploration; solutions are less likely to be communicated (Rogers, 1982). Many of these conversations take place at social occasions. In their history of the semiconductor industry, Braun and Mac-

Donald (1982) provide the example of a bar located close to Intel, Fairchild, Raytheon, and other semiconductor companies that served as a place where engineers "drank, exchanged information, and hired employees."

Much of the lore of the semiconductor industry is associated with one region—Silicon Valley. This region has been characterized by several waves of entrepreneurial activity. Much of the startup activity in Silicon Valley has been directed toward the exploitation of new ideas by an individual or a group of entrepreneurs (Rogers and Larsen, 1984). Entrepreneurs use their knowledge of local suppliers, venture capitalists, and other firms to further the success of their new firms. Eisenhardt and Schoonhoven (1990) showed that entrepreneurs in Silicon Valley are closely networked with venture capitalists and also with other firms in the region. Since the founders of new firms play an important role in the networking activities of these firms, one would expect that previous experience in the region where the startup is located would be an important prerequisite to successful networking activity. Almeida and Kogut (1997) show that over 88 percent of the founders of semiconductor firms were employed in the same region prior to the formation of the startup. As can be seen, previous local experience of entrepreneurs influences the location of startup activity and therefore the new firm's networking potential.

Statistical studies in the semiconductor industry have confirmed the importance of local sourcing of resources by small firms. Almeida and Kogut (1997), while contrasting the knowledge acquiring practices of small and large firms, compared the citation patterns to major patents of two matched samples of semiconductor firms. Their results showed that both small and large firms cited local patents significantly more than would be expected, indicating localization effects. However, the results showed that these localization effects were much more significant for the startup sample. Startup firms were more closely tied to other firms within the same regional network.

Interestingly, in the above study, the greatest localization of knowledge was found in Silicon Valley, where a large majority of new firms are located. Of the 176 startups founded around the world between 1977 and 1989, 55 percent were located in Silicon Valley (Dataquest, 1990). Almeida (1996b) has shown that Silicon Valley is unique in terms of its sociology, with extensive interfirm mobility of engineers, resulting in significant localization of design knowledge. Could the significant localization of knowledge of startup firms be due only to the characteristics of the region (Silicon Valley) rather than to the characteristics of small firms themselves?

To investigate this question, Almeida and Kogut (1997) identified the major patents from both samples that belonged to Silicon Valley and conducted localization tests on those samples. Knowledge emanating from startup firms was more localized than for larger firms even within Silicon Valley, indicating greater integration into knowledge networks for smaller firms. Apparently, regions with a higher proportion of small firms (like Silicon Valley) exhibit greater regional networking of activities. Even within highly networked regions, small firms are more linked with other regional organizations than are large firms.

This local networking of small firms may be important not just to themselves but also to larger firms in the region. In a rich ethnography of regions in the semiconductor industry, Saxenian (1994) contrasted the industrial systems of the Route 128 region (around Boston) and the Silicon Valley area (near San Francisco) to explain the comparative success of the Bay Area. She noted that the Silicon Valley region with its greater share of startup firms is characterized by local collective learning and experimentation resulting in extensive interfirm knowledge exchange. The Route 128 region is dominated by larger firms that are more insulated from the surrounding institutions. These firms did not build relationships with other firms in that region, and Saxenian concludes that this isolation of larger firms contributed, in part, to the decline of that region in recent years. Thus small firms, through their local knowledge-building activities, can be seen to be important links in a regional knowledge network, acquiring and sharing knowledge and thus contributing to the dynamism of both small and large firms in a region.

THE COMPLIMENTARY ROLES OF LARGE AND SMALL FIRMS

Our description of the role of small firms in innovation offers some insights to the perennial question of the relationship between firm size and innovation ability. Based on varying interpretations of Schumpeter's reflections on the routinization of research in the large laboratory, most studies have sought a cross-sectional relationship between firm size and innovation. But the cross-sectional evidence, as Cohen and Levin (1989) conclude in their review, is very mixed. There appears to be no hard and fast statement regarding optimal firm size or scale economies in reference to innovative activities.

The lack of robustness of the relationship between firm size and innovation is not surprising: size is a moving target driven, partly, by a firm's research success. The evidence—of the startup firm as an important driver of radical innovation and its role in linking regional knowledge networks—points to a more complex relationship between firm size and innovative ability. We should view firm size and innovative ability as linked in a dynamic process in which firms of various sizes are codependent. Not only do successful small firms grow to be large firms, but the success of large firms in regional networks may depend on the innovative ability of (and the new technological opportunities provided by) smaller firms. The most striking example of the process of growth through innovation is the case of Intel. Intel, one of the "Fairchildren," was started by a group of entrepreneurs in the late 1960s. Within a few years of its formation, Intel introduced both the memory chip and the microprocessor—the two types of integrated circuits that came to dominate the semiconductor industry. With the growing popularity of the personal computer in the 1980s and 1990s, the demand for memory and microprocessor chips exploded. Though Intel dropped out of the memory market, the firm continued to dominate the microprocessor segment. Today, Intel produces 70 percent of the world's microprocessors and is the largest semiconductor manufacturer in the world. This view of the relationship between firms was best summed up by Jewkes, Sawers, and Stillerman (1958, p. 168, cited in Cohen and Levin, 1989, pp. 1073–1074): "It may well be," they note, "that there is no optimum size of firm but merely an optimal pattern for any industry, such a distribution of firms by size, character, and outlook as to guarantee the most effective gathering together and commercially perfecting of the flow of new ideas."

After all, small and large firms both have advantages (Cohen and Klepper, 1996). Small firms may be superior in the generation of new knowledge in industries characterized by technological opportunities. Larger firms are superior in their ability to appropriate returns from these innovations, either by buying and selling property rights (sometimes through cooperative ventures), acquiring the firms, or benefiting through spillovers. Thus small and large firms play complementary roles in innovation, and small firms should be viewed, along with large firms, as partners in the continuous process of technological and regional development.

CONCLUSIONS

In many industries, startups receive funding because they explore new technological spaces and opportunities that are ignored by larger firms. Since their technological exploration is facilitated through close ties to other innovating institutions and startup firms, their activities also generate a geographic space in which technology diffuses more rapidly within a local network of firms. As long as this technological space is sufficiently rich, the interaction of diffusion and innovation creates a positive feedback that reinforces further innovative efforts. Small firms thus play a crucial role in innovation and technological development.

There is an interesting policy issue embedded in this discussion. Small firms, with their geographically local activities, are important to the building of research intensive regions within a country. Yet financial constraints on small firms often make them vulnerable to acquisition. The twin conditions of being small and holding knowledge that is local and not internationally diffused would seem to make these startup firms vulnerable to foreign acquisition. Small firms in regions such as Silicon Valley have been attractive acquisition targets of larger firms seeking technological knowledge inputs. Over the last decade, several firms—including Philips, Thomson-CSF, Toshiba, Sony, Samsung, and a number of other electronic firms—have bought into local knowledge networks by acquiring semiconductor startups. These foreign firms in U.S. regions then use local regional knowledge extensively in their innovation activities (Almeida, 1996b).

This discussion, besides its relevance to policy debates over foreign technological acquisition, is important in underlying the problem in focusing solely on the individual firm. Innovation is an activity that shifts the size distribution of firms. It is closely linked to the general progress of science and technology in society. For small firms, innovation is more often than not the product of a firm's efforts to benefit from its own research and from a local network of entrepreneurs and innovators. The difficulty of recreating such networks, as evident in Silicon Valley, is certainly one of the leading candidates for explaining why the distribution of innovations varies among regions and countries.

ACKNOWLEDGMENTS

I am grateful to Jerome Romano for his research assistance. An earlier version of this chapter was presented at the seminar on "Why Small Firms Are Important" at the U.S. Small Business Administration Washington, DC, May 1997.

NOTE

1. Approximately 400 technology classes and 100,000 technology subclasses are identified by the U.S. Patent Office. Every U.S. patent is assigned to one or more subclass.

REFERENCES

Acs, Zoltan, and David Audretsch. (1990). *Innovation and Small Firms.* Cambridge, MA: MIT Press.

Allen, Robert. (1983). "Collective Invention." *Journal of Economic Behavior and Organization*, 4, 1–24.

Almeida, Paul. (1996a). "The Geographic Localization of Technological Knowledge in the International Semiconductor Industry." Ph.D. dissertation, Wharton School, University of Pennsylvania, Philadelphia, PA.

Almeida, Paul. (1996b). "Knowledge Sourcing by Foreign Multinationals: Patent Citation Analysis in the U.S. Semiconductor Industry." *Strategic Management Journal*, 17, 155–165.

Almeida, Paul, and Bruce Kogut. (1997). "The Exploration of Technological Diversity and the Geographic Localization of Innovation." *Small Business Economics*, 9(1), 21–31.

Almeida, Paul, and Lori Rosenkopf. (1997). "Interfirm Knowledge Building by Semiconductor Startups: The Role of Alliances and Mobility." Working Paper, Huntsman Center for Global Competition and Innovation, Wharton School, Philadelphia, PA.

Bound, J.C., C. Cummins, Z. Griliches, B.H. Hall, and A. Jaffe. (1984). "Who Does R&D and Who Patents." In Z. Griliches (ed.), *R&D: Patents and Productivity*. Chicago: Chicago University Press.

Braun, Ernest, and Stuart MacDonald. (1982). *Revolution in Miniature* (2nd ed.), New York: Cambridge University Press.

Cohen, W., and S. Klepper. (1996). "The Trade-off Between Firm Size and Diversity in the Pursuit of Technological Progress." *Small Business Economics*, 4(1), 1–14.

Cohen, Wes, and Richard Levin. (1989). "Innovation and Market Structure." In Richard Schmalensee and Robert Willig (eds.), *Handbook of Industrial Organization*. Amsterdam: North Holland.

Dataquest. (1990). *A Decade of Semiconductor Start-ups*. San Jose, CA: Dataquest.

Eisenhardt, K.M., and C.B. Schoonhoven. (1990). "Organizational Growth: Founding Teams Strategy and Environment and Growth Among U.S. Semiconductor Ventures 1978–1988." *Administrative Science Quarterly*, 35(3), 504–529.

Feldman, Maryann. (1994). "Knowledge Complimentarity and Innovation." *Small Business Economics*, 6(5), 363–372.

Hannan, Michael, and John Freeman. (1984). "Structural Inertia and Organizational Change." *American Sociological Review*, 49, 149–164.

Henderson, R. (1993). "Underinvestment and Incompetence as Responses to Radical Innovation: Evidence from the Photolithographic Alignment Equipment Industry." *RAND Journal of Economics*, 24(2), 248–270.

Herrigel Gary. (1993). "Large Firms, Small Firms, and the Governance of Flexible Specialization: The Case of Baden Wuttemberg and Socialized Risk." In Bruce Kogut (ed.), *Country Competitiveness*. New York: Oxford University Press.

Jaffe, A., M. Trajtenberg, and R. Henderson. (1993). "Geographic Localization of Knowledge Spillovers as Evidenced by Patent Citations." *Quarterly Journal of Economics*, 108(3), 577–598.

Jewkes, J., D. Sawers, and R. Stillerman. (1958). *The Sources of Invention*. London: St. Martin's Press.

Kogut, Bruce, and Dong-Jae Kim. (1996). "Diversification and Platform Technologies." *Organization Science*, 7(3), 283–301.

Moore, Gordon E. (1986). "Entrepreneurship and Innovation: The Electronics Industry." *The Positive Sum Strategy*. Washington, DC: National Academy Press.

Nooteboom, Bart. (1994). "Innovation and Diffusion in Small Firms: Theory and Evidence." *Small Business Economics*, 6(5), 327–348.

Piore, M., and C. Sabel. (1984). *The Second Industrial Divide: Possibilities for Prosperity*. New York: Basic Books.

Rogers, Everett. (1982). "Information Exchange and Technological Innovation." In D. Sahal (ed.), *The Transfer and Utilization of Technical Knowledge* (pp. 105–123). Lexington, MA: Lexington Books.
Rogers, Everett, and Judith Larson. (1984). *Silicon Valley Fever.* New York: Basic Books.
Rothwell, R. (1989). "Small Firms, Innovation and Industrial Change." *Small Business Economics,* 1, 51–64.
Saxenian, Anna Lee. (1991). "The Origins and Dynamics of Production Networks in Silicon Valley." *Research Policy,* 20, 423–437.
Saxenian, Anna Lee. (1994). *Regional Advantage.* Cambridge, MA: Harvard University Press.
Scherer, F.M. (1984). *Innovation and Growth: Schumpeterian Perspectives.* Cambridge, MA: MIT Press.
Scherer, F.M., and D. Ross. (1990). *Industrial Market Structure and Economic Performance.* Boston: Houghton Mifflin.
Schumpeter, J.A. (1934). *Theory of Economic Development.* Boston: Harvard University Press.
Schumpeter, J.A. (1943). *Capitalism, Socialism and Democracy.* London: Unwin.
Stuart, T., and J. Podolny. (1996). "Local Search and the Evolution of Technological Capabilities." *Strategic Management Journal,* 17, 21–38.

4. ENTRY, INNOVATION AND FIRM GROWTH

JOHN R. BALDWIN

Statistics Canada, Ottawa, Ontario, Canada

JOANNE JOHNSON

Statistics Canada, Ottawa, Ontario, Canada

INTRODUCTION

Recent studies have demonstrated the quantitative importance of entry, exit, growth, and decline in the industrial population (see Baldwin, 1995). This turnover rewards innovative activity and contributes to productivity growth. Entry is not the only process that causes turnover in the firm population. Growth and decline also occur in the incumbent population. But entry and exit make a significant contribution to the total amount of turnover that takes place.

The importance of entry can be gauged in the first instance by the percentage of firms that is new each year or the percentage of employment that can be found in these firms. The annual entry rates for the manufacturing sector (defined as the employment in entrants divided by total employment) from 1972 to 1986 averaged about 1.9 percent for the United States and 2.4 percent for Canada (Baldwin, Dunne, and Haltiwanger, 1995, p. 127). When calculated over five-year periods (1972 to 1977 and 1977 to 1982), the U.S. average across two-digit industries was 11.3 percent, while the Canadian was 10.9 percent (Baldwin, Dunne, and Haltiwanger, 1995, p. 137).

The importance of entry and exit can also be calculated as the share of job growth that is accounted for by entry or the share of job decline that is accounted for by exit. The share of job change accounted for by entry and exit is quite similar for the two countries when comparable manufacturing databases for Canada and the United States are used. For year-to-year changes from 1970 to 1985, job creation due to entry in the United States averaged 21 percent of the total increase in jobs;

in Canada, it averaged 27 percent (Baldwin, Dunne, and Haltiwanger, 1995, p. 126). Calculated over two comparable five-year periods (1972 to 1977 and 1977 to 1982), entry accounted for 44 percent in the United States and 45 percent in Canada. As we increase the length of period over which the importance of entry is calculated, entry becomes relatively more important.

While new firms are important, they are more prone to failure. Young firms are also more at risk; data drawn from a longitudinal file of Canadian entrants in both the goods and service sectors show that over half the new firms that fail do so in the first two years of life (see Baldwin, 1998b). Life is short for the majority of entrants. Only one in five new firms survive to their tenth birthday.

These failures involve a cost—both in human and financial terms. But these resources should not be regarded as wasted, anymore than the resources that are expended on obtaining information in a world of imperfect information are wasted. Failures are an investment that society makes in the dynamic competitive process. New firms provide an important stimulus to the industrial population. A few small entrants grow to become the new dynamos of the industrial system. Others remain relatively small but provide an important source of innovation in the small-firm sector—especially when it comes to quality differentiation. Smaller firms excel in their ability to provide quality and flexibility of service (Baldwin et al., 1994). Small firms are constantly changing their product offerings—with respect to both types of products and services offered. Small firms are adept at ascertaining changing consumer tastes with regards to the amount of services that are bundled with a product or being flexible with regards to other aspects of the product offering. New small firms that are better able to sense consumer requirements are constantly replacing other small firms that are less able to do so (Baldwin, 1995). One manifestation of the success of small entrants is their tendency to pay higher wages and to be more productive than those firms that they force out of the market (Baldwin, 1995, 1996). The process of entry and exit generates information about which combinations of products and services best satisfy consumer tastes.

Therefore, while the size of entry and exit is large, its importance must be found in its impact on innovation in the economy. Experimentation is key to a dynamic, market-based economy. A key part of the experimentation comes from entrants. New entrepreneurs constantly offer consumers new products—both in terms of the basic good and the level of service that accompanies it.

While the benefits from entry are perceived to be extensive, there are few studies that fully describe the types of entrants that survive or the rich nature of the innovative process that can be found in small firms. The development of longitudinal databases on exit and entry has allowed us to better estimate the amount of entry taking place and to determine that this aspect of turnover shifts significant amounts of market share and changes the identity of market participants. But the longitudinal databases derived from administrative records do not contain very rich descriptions of the participants. Therefore, survey data are presented here that are meant to allow us to better understand the underlying characteristics of entrants—their competencies not only with regard to innovation but also in such areas as human resource development, marketing, management, and training and how these activities relate to innovation. These survey data are linked to longitudinal data on firm performance, such as growth in sales, so that differences in competencies can be related to performance differences.

The first objective of this chapter is to delineate the environment and the strategies that are emphasized by new firms that survive beyond infancy. Since so many entrants fall by the wayside, it is of inherent interest to understand the conditions that are associated with survival—the conditions that allow the potential in new entrepreneurs to come to fruition. The second is to demonstrate the variety of innovation that takes place in new firms. The third is to outline the competencies are associated with growth in new firms. Success in the industrial population is associated with different capabilities. To understand how these capabilities contribute to growth, it is necessary to study how the performance of entrants relates to differences in strategies and pursued activities.

DATA

We make use of firm-level data on entrants to examine the nature of their innovative capabilities. The firm-level data are taken from *The Survey of Operating and Financial Practices of Entrants* performed by Statistics Canada (1996). The focus on new firms permits us to examine in general terms the strategic emphasis of entrants and the innovative capabilities of new firms in particular. The richness of the survey database allows both output- and input-based measures of innovation and technological and skill-based competencies of smaller firms to be developed.

The survey focused on entrants that emerged from their early childhood and survived to their early teen years. In light of the high death rate of new firms, these are the more successful entrants. The frame consisted of all entrants to the commercial sector (both goods and services) in the period 1983 to 1986 that survived to 1993; the survey was conducted in 1996. The sample included 3,991 firms from both the goods and services sector. The response rate to the survey was 80 percent.

The survey provides a broad overview of the financing and operating practices of entrants. The questionnaire contains information on (1) management (the extent of managerial and industry experience and the degree of ownership in the firm), (2) the nature of the competitive environment (whether products quickly become obsolete, whether production technology changes rapidly, whether the threat of new entry is high), (3) the firm's competencies in the area of management, technology, human resources, financing, marketing, and production, with special attention paid to various facets of competencies in each area, (4) the extent and nature of financial planning, (5) the importance of investment in R&D, technology, and training, (6) whether the firm engaged in formal training, and (7) the manner by which various activities were financed.

A PROFILE OF ENTRANTS

The survey on entrants outlines the type of environment that entrants face, the emphasis that they place on different strategies, the types of innovations pursued, and the connection between growth, innovation, and associated competencies that these firms develop.

The Competitive Environment

The competitive environment that new entrants face affects the skills required for survival and growth. Competition has many dimensions: it depends on the type of rivals an entrant faces, the pressures placed on it by buyers and suppliers, and the rapidity of changes in products and technology.

The type of competition in an industry is partially determined by the maturity of the market. Industries vary by the stage of development of the market for their primary product:

- The introductory stage consists of those markets where the product demand is just starting to grow but the product is unknown to many potential users;
- The growth stage occurs when product demand is growing and the product is becoming familiar to many potential users;
- The maturity stage is when product demand growth is slowing and the product is familiar to most potential users;
- Finally, postmaturity occurs when no growth in product demand occurs and there are few potential new users.

The stage of the product is expected to influence the firm because previous work (Gort and Klepper, 1982) suggests that early stages in the product life cycle involve a high degree of uncertainty since product and technological innovations follow one another in quick succession. In later phases, the type of problems changes. Reducing production costs via technological change becomes more important. The problems faced by firms vary according to the stage of product life cycle in which they are located. In the early phases of the life cycle, product innovations are dominant. In later phases, the type of problems changes. Reducing production costs via technological change becomes more important.

Despite the fact that successful entrants are new, they generally serve mature markets. While 29 percent of successful entrants are in a growing product market, 50 percent are in mature markets. Moreover, a greater percentage is in the postmaturity phase (18 percent) than in the introductory phase (3 percent). As the life-cycle model would have predicted, successful entrants as a whole reported more rapid technological than product obsolescence. When asked to indicate if they felt that products quickly become obsolete and production technology changes rapidly in their industry, only 24 percent of entrants felt that product obsolescence was rapid in their industry[1] (Figure 4.1). Yet 45 percent said production technology changed rapidly.

The number of competitors also serves as a measure of the amount of competition that entrants face. About 40 percent face between five and nineteen competitors. Another 38 percent compete with over twenty firms. However, the number of competitors is only a rough proxy for competitiveness; firms face competition from potential as well as existing competitors. Even when the number of competitors is

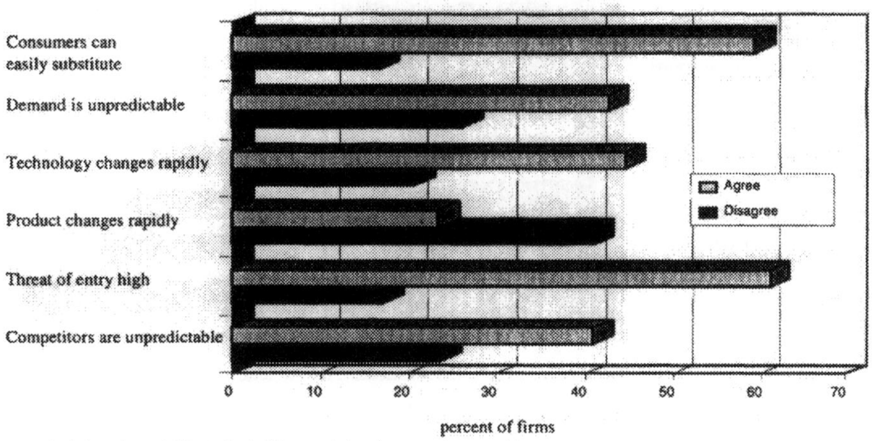

Figure 4.1. Entrants' Perceptions About Their Industry Environment.

small, rivalry can be intense.[2] In order to gauge the intensity of competition, entrants were asked if they disagreed or agreed with two propositions—that the threat of entry was high and that their competitors' actions were predictable. Most entrants (41 percent felt their competitors' actions were difficult to predict. However, some 61 percent of entrants felt that threats from entry were high (Figure 4.1).

Customer relations also affect the nature of the competitive environment. Firms with only one customer face uncertainty due to bilateral bargaining and the loss of the customer. Firms with few repeat customers cannot build customer loyalty. Neither factor is very important for successful entrants. Over half obtain less than 10 percent of their revenue from one customer, and over two-thirds of their customers are repeat customers.

To examine the uncertainty associated with demand, successful entrants were asked if they agreed or disagreed with these statements: (1) consumer demand is difficult to predict, and (2) consumers can easily substitute among competing products. The ease of substitutability represents the largest source of uncertainty, as almost 60 percent of entrants felt consumers could easily substitute competing products (Figure 4.1). Unpredictability of consumer demand was less of a problem; just 40 percent of successful entrants rated this hard to predict.

The final element that can be used to describe the competitive environment that successful entrants face is the nature of product competition. Entrants ranked competition in their industry on a scale of 1 (low) to 5 (high) in seven areas—price, customer service, quality, flexibility in responding to customers, product range, product customization, and frequency of introducing new or improved products. The percentage of successful entrants that ranked each area as highly competitive (4 or 5) is plotted in Figure 4.2. In keeping with their functioning mainly in mature

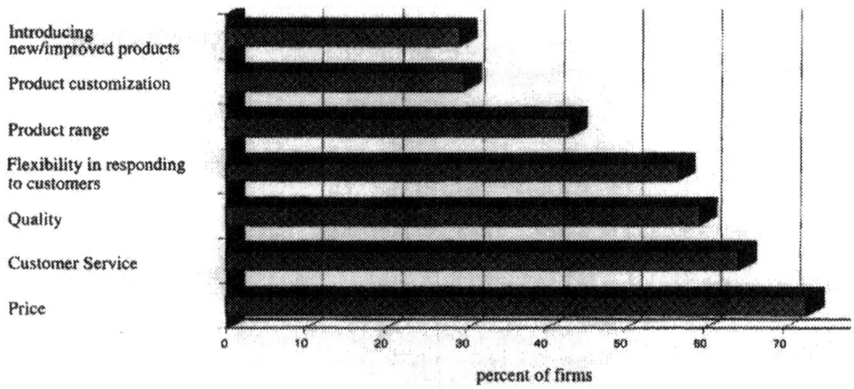

Figure 4.2. Percentage of Entrants Reporting Intense Industry Competition.

markets, successful entrants report that competition in their industry is greatest with respect to price, customer service, and quality. In contrast, factors that mark growth industries—customization or introducing new products—are less important.

The Focus of Entrants

What, then, are the product and production strategies adopted by new firms in the face of the environment that they face? A firm's product-based strategies are directed at making their existing products as attractive as possible to consumers. There are several ways in which firms can do this: they can offer an attractive price, focus on quality, provide superior customer service, or offer flexibility in meeting their customers' needs. Alternatively, firms can try to alter their product line. In doing so, they might choose to customize their products, develop a product line that carries a wide range of related products, or continually expand and update their product line by frequently introducing new or improved products.

Of these strategies, successful entrants give the highest priority (scored on a scale of 1 to 5) to strategies related to quality and service. Each of the strategies here—quality, customer service, and flexibility in responding to customers and price—is deemed to be important (Figure 4.3). Alternate strategies that involve updating, expanding, or enhancing their product line are perceived to be less important by successful entrants.

The quality-oriented niche strategies are concentrated at maintaining existing customers. This broad strategy includes specific strategies such as "satisfying existing customers" or slightly more aggressive strategies directed at "promoting company and products reputation and "improving position in existing markets" (Figure 4.4).

The third component examined here is the production strategy of entrants. They may seek to improve their production by doing it better, doing it faster, doing it

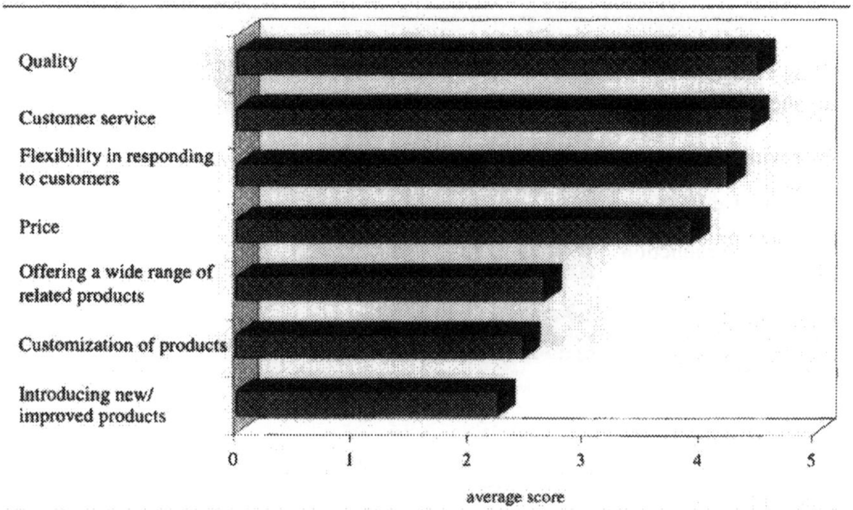

Figure 4.3. Importance of Product-Based Strategies.

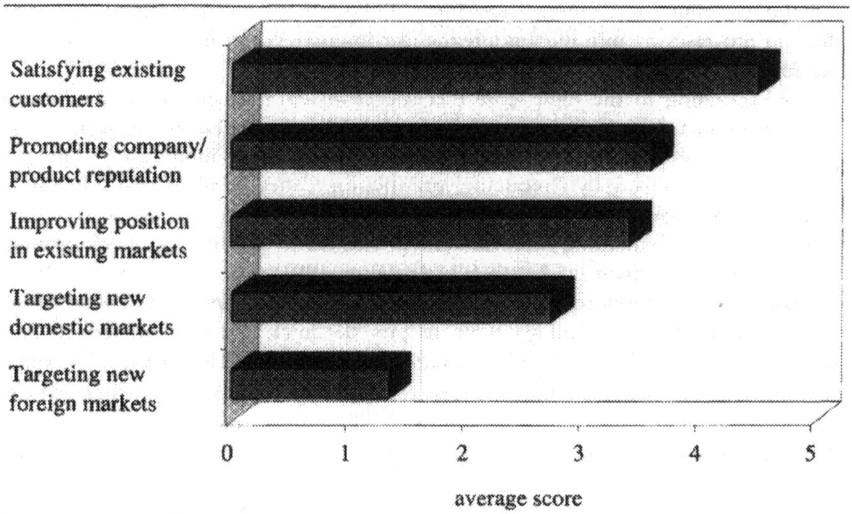

Figure 4.4. Importance of Market-Based Strategies.

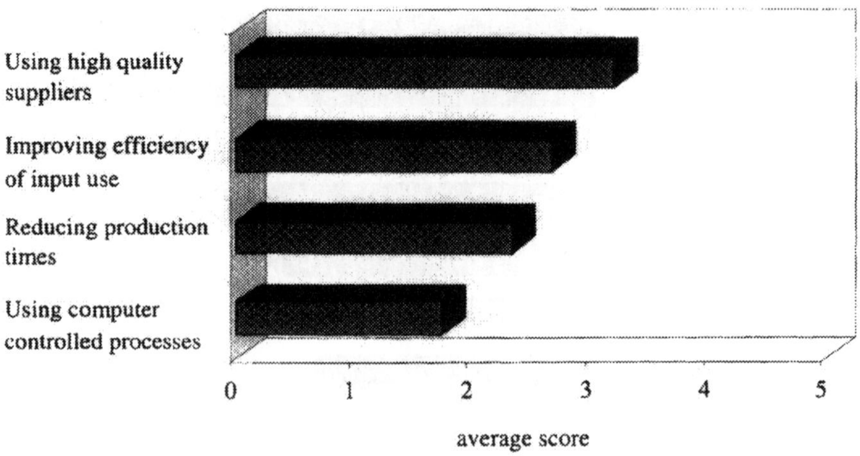

Figure 4.5. Importance of Production Strategies.

more efficiently, or using better inputs. To do so, they may reduce their use of material inputs, reduce their production times, focus on the functioning of their production processes by introducing integrated computer-controlled processes, or stress the importance of using high-quality suppliers.

Corresponding to the high score that successful entrants give to quality as part of their product strategy, "using high-quality suppliers" is rated the most important production strategy (Figure 4.5). "Improving efficiency of input use" is next in importance, followed by "reducing production times" and "using computer-controlled processes."

This picture of emerging successful entrants confirms the finding of other studies on small firms (Baldwin et al., 1994; D'Amboise, 1991). The success of small firms depends on their ability to produce a high-quality output; their comparative advantage is the flexibility that allows them to provide quick and efficient service. Successful entrants develop a customer-oriented business focus. Their product strategies are aimed at enhancing the attractiveness of their current products in their existing market: they focus on quality and responsiveness to customer needs, and their process strategies are concentrated on improving the efficiency and quality of the production process.

Innovation Among Entrants

Entrants are often seen as providing the dynamic new force in an industry that leads to change. Productivity growth is one way in which this is manifested. Geroski (1991) relates technical progress, efficiency, and productivity growth at the industry level in the United Kingdom to entry rates and finds that roughly 30 percent of productivity growth is related to entry. Entry is seen to have a significant impact on productivity growth in the Canadian manufacturing sector when micro plant-level data are used (Baldwin, 1995, p. 234). Somewhere between 20 and 25 percent of productivity growth in a manufacturing industry in the 1970s came from entry and exit. Haltiwanger (1998) reports the U.S. share as 18 percent, using a similar microeconomic database.

Changes in productivity are the result of either product or process innovation. While there are few studies of the effect of new firms on productivity growth, much more attention has been paid to the role of small firms on innovation. Audretsch (1995), for example, uses data from the SBA innovation database to argue that the U.S. small-firm sector is more innovative than the large-firm sector.

The empirical work on small-firm innovation capability has had to wrestle with a paucity of usable data on innovations. Exercises to measure innovations using experts or trade journals have provided data on innovative tendencies; however, in doing so, they have tended to reduce the world of innovation to a single dimension.

Innovations are not easily pigeonholed in one compartment. Some innovations involve new products; others consist of new processes. Some firms will focus on the use of advanced technologies. Others will incorporate new ideas by embodying skills in their employees who will, in turn, devise and design new products. Technology and skills will be combined in different proportions across firms.

The variety of innovations that are being continuously introduced means that there is no single measure of innovativeness that any study of innovations, whether arising from innovation surveys or trade-journal searches, should be expected to yield. It is not sufficient to argue that this could be resolved by specifying that it is only major innovations that should be included in the definition of an innovation since it is only major breakthroughs that should interest us. First, this still leaves the problem of defining *major*. Second, this position ignores the important contribution that marginal innovations make. Hollander (1965), for example, studied the course of productivity growth in Dupont's rayon division and found that much of its productivity growth arose from marginal innovations. Freeman (1982) notes that substantial progress is made in the way of incremental process innovation and these types of improvements tend not to be captured in major event studies that focus on innovations. Incremental innovations are not measured by patent statistics, since they are not patented, or by historical studies that focus on major breakthroughs.

If we are to understand the importance of new firms in the innovation process, it is essential to move beyond the very simple, partial analysis based on a single definition of innovation and develop a classification scheme based on a number of innovative competencies. Only by doing so can we fully appreciate the complexity of an innovation process that is multidimensional rather than unidimensional.

This section therefore explores the types of innovation that are occurring in new firms. When variants and combinations of strategies are examined, two themes stand out. First, innovativeness is not a dichotomous factor: it occurs along a continuum. Second, innovativeness is a multidimensional concept.

In order to study the innovative capability of successful entrants, we make use of questions taken from four areas—on the innovative capabilities of firms, on their human-resource competencies, on their technological capacities, and on their competitive strategies. Each of these will be used to define the extent to which new firms followed an innovation, a technovation (an advanced high-tech input strategy), or a knowledge (a skill-based) strategy.

Two types of questions are used to provide information on the competencies of entrants. First, there are questions that characterize an entrant as following certain strategies—producing a product innovation, having formal training, or the percentage of investment in R&D or in training. These take on 0–1 values or are expressed as percentages. Second, there are answers to questions about the emphasis that entrants placed on factors such as R&D capabilities or training activities that contributed to the ongoing success of the firm. These questions were scored on a five-point Likehart scale of 1 (low importance) to 5 (high importance). These are used here to gauge the entrant's competencies.[3] In what follows, entrants are deemed to possess a particular competency or to be stressing a particular strategy if they score that strategy as 4 or 5 on the five-point Likehart scale.

In order to catch the diversity of the innovative activity in entrants, the stress that new, small firms place on innovation is measured with ten different variables. Each captures a different though related concept of innovation.

Several of the measures make use of a question that asked whether an entrant had introduced an innovation. An innovation was defined as the introduction of a new or improved product or process but not the introduction of aesthetic changes that did not affect the technical construction or performance of the product. These innovations were, in turn, characterized as being either entirely new products, modifications of existing products, entirely new processes, or modifications of existing processes. Finally, entrants indicated whether these innovations were protected with intellectual property rights. Combinations of these measures are then used to define whether the entrants were introducing innovations of varying degrees of novelty and importance.

These variables are as follows:

INGEN Whether an entrant reports any innovation.

INIMP1 Whether an entrant reports an innovation that is protected by an intellectual property right such as a patent or whether the firm reports that a strategy of protecting its innovations with intellectual property is important or very important (a score of 4 or 5). Baldwin (1997) finds that the most novel innovations are those availing themselves of intellectual property protection.

INIMP2 Whether an entrant reports an innovation that is either a completely new product or a completely new process.

INPROD Whether an entrant is a product innovator.

INPROC Whether an entrant is a process innovator.

INCOMP Whether an entrant is both a product and a process innovator.

Innovation is also measured by the emphasis that is given to a prime (though not the only) input to innovation—research and development. The variables are as follows:

INRD Whether an entrant scored 4 or 5 on the importance given to R&D capabilities.

INIMP Whether an entrant's percent of investment devoted to R&D was above the median of all other entrants who devoted a portion of their investment to R&D.

Finally, the innovative tendencies are measured by the scores that are given to the importance that an entrant attributes to different competitive strategies that involve a broader concept of innovation. The first of these variables complements the other innovation measures by focusing on the frequency of new-product introduction. Since a new product (as opposed to an innovation) can involve product differentiation changes, the coverage of this variables is broader than the variable that captures whether a firm has had a product or process innovation. The first variable used is

INFREO Whether an entrant scores 4 or 5 on the extent to which it frequently introduces new or improved products.

The second broader variable captures the extent to which entrants focus on providing a different type of innovation—customization and quality variation. The majority of small firms cannot compete directly on prices with larger firms because of the cost disadvantages associated with size. Instead they stress a niche strategy by varying the quality of product, offering slightly better levels of customer service, showing flexibility to customer needs, or customizing their product for individual customer requirements. The value of a product to consumers is a function of its quality. All firms, but small firms in particular, are constantly experimenting with variations in quality to attract customers. These experiments all involve innovations—though, in most cases, they are incremental in nature. While incremental, their importance should not be discounted. The cumulative effect of the sum of many changes at the margin can be large. The variable used to catch this aspect of innovation is

INTRAD Whether an entrant scores at least eighteen out of a possible twenty points on the importance attributed to quality, customer service, flexibility in responding to customer needs, and customization.

Technological Competencies

The second advanced competency focuses specifically on whether technological innovation (technovation) in an entrant is important. Technological innovation involves a different though related dimension of innovation—the extent to which an entrant focuses on advanced technology, increases its efficiency of input use, and introduces new production processes. The variables used here are as follows:

INTECH1 Whether an entrant scores 4 or 5 on the importance attached to developing new and refining existing technology.

INTECH2 Whether an entrant scores 4 or 5 on the importance attached to purchasing technology from others.

TEDEV Whether an entrant both develops or refines new technology and purchases it.

TECOMP Whether an entrant scores 4 or 5 on the importance given to using computer-controlled processes in production.

TEINFO Whether an entrant scores 4 or 5 on using information technology for management purposes.

TEINP Whether an entrant's percentage of investment devoted to technology acquisition and licensing was above the median of all other entrants who devoted a portion of their investment to technology acquisition and licensing.

PROD1 Whether an entrant scores 4 or 5 on improving efficiency of input use in the production process or reducing production times.

Human-Capital Development

The final set of competencies considered here is worker skills. Entrants incorporate these skills either by focusing their human-resource strategies on hiring skilled workers or by implementing training programs. In both cases, a firm's innovative competencies depend critically on the amount of human capital that it possesses. Baldwin and Johnson (1996a) report that a human-capital strategy is pursued more intensely by innovators in both the goods and the services sectors.[4] In the goods sector, it is often combined with an emphasis on R&D or the development of new machinery and equipment. In the services sector, the innovation strategy often *is* the human-resource strategy.

The skill emphasis of entrants is measured here by the value that an entrant attaches to recruiting skilled labor, on the emphasis it gives to training, and finally on the extent to which it implements a formal training program and invests in training. The variables are as follows:

LABSKLL Whether an entrant scores 4 or 5 on the importance given to recruiting skilled employees.

LABSCOR Whether an entrant scores 4 or 5 on the importance attached to training.

LABFOR Whether an entrant does *formal* training.

LABTRAIN Whether an entrant's share of investment devoted to training is positive.

LABINT Whether the percentage of investment that is devoted to training is above the median percentage for all other entrants that invest in training.

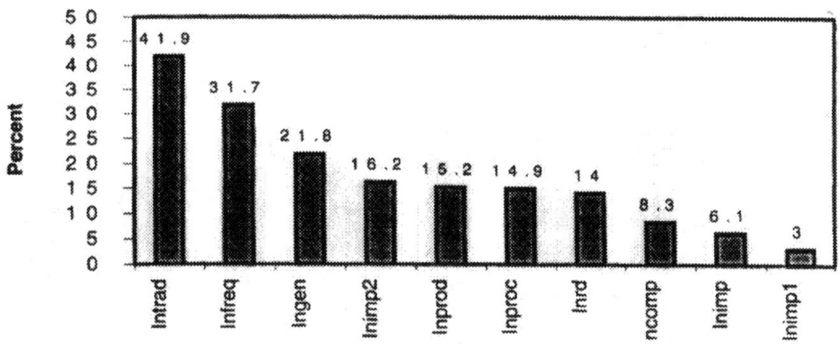

Figure 4.6. Innovation Types.

Comprehensiveness of Innovation in the Entrant Population

The percentage of the population of entrants that is innovative differs considerably depending on which of the summary measures is used (Figure 4.6). Judged by the traditional measure (Intrad), entrants are quite innovative. Many firms are experimenting with the type of innovation that requires bundling service or quality with a good. About 42 percent place a heavy emphasis on varying quality to provide a unique product to the consumer (Intrad). Somewhat fewer are introducing new products. Some 32 percent place more than average importance on frequently introducing new products (Infreq). When *new product* is interpreted to mean an *innovation*, fewer firms fall into this category. Some 22 percent have introduced an innovation over the 1992–1994 period (Ingen). Some 14 percent emphasized an R&D strategy (Inrd), but some 29 percent either report an innovation or that they place above average importance on R&D—about the same percentage that emphasize the frequent introduction of new products. When the constraint of novelty is imposed on the innovation, the percentage declines-by amounts that vary depending on the definition of novelty that is imposed. Only 16 percent introduced what they consider to be an entirely new product or process (Inimp2). Even fewer (3 percent) introduced an innovation that was protected by formal intellectual property rights (Inimp1).

The various measures of the firm's technological capabilities also indicate both a diversity and universality of technological competencies (Figure 4.7). In accord with the finding of Baldwin and Sabourin (1996) that communications technologies have been expanding fastest, the largest group of firms (47 percent) emphasize the importance of computer-based information technologies (Teinfo). The next largest percentage of entrants (34 percent) focus on methods to reduce the cost of inputs and to reduce production times (Prod1). About 25 percent place heavy emphasis on

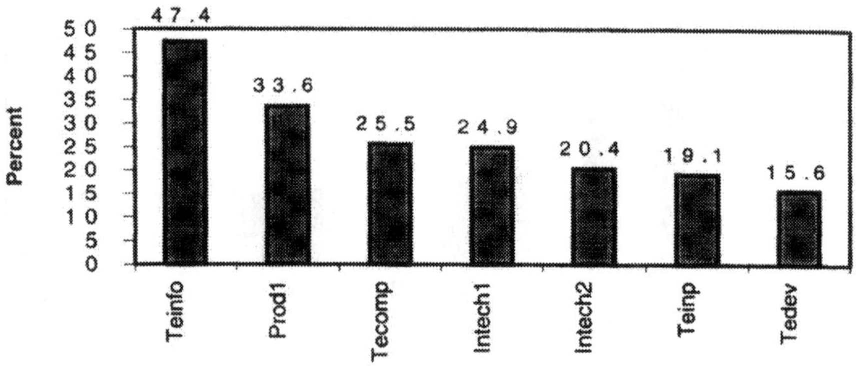

Figure 4.7. Technology Types.

developing new technologies (Intech1) or use computer-controlled processes in production (Tecomp). There are about 20 percent who stress the purchase of new technologies (Intech2). About 16 percent of firms both develop new technologies and purchase new technologies from others (Tedev).

When the entrants' responses to the importance of skills and training are used to estimate the extent to which human capital is important, a large percentage of the population is seen to emphasize human capital (Figure 4.8). Some 56 percent indicate that training is important (Labscor) and devote considerable importance to recruiting skilled labor (Labsk1). Some 52 percent have implemented a formal training program (Labfor). Even if we judge whether firms are performing substantial activity in this area—on the basis of whether they report that they devote part of their investment to training (Labtrain)—some 30 percent still are seen to be serious participants in upgrading human capital.

These data show that a substantial proportion of new entrants consider themselves to be either innovative or technologically advanced or to depend on skilled workers. Moreover, when we consider the characteristics jointly, the percentage of entrants that fall into at least one category increases. For example, some 22 percent report an innovation, some 14 percent place a very high importance on R&D, and 29 percent do at least one of these two. Similarly, 25 percent of entrants report that they develop new or refine existing technology, while 20 percent bring in outside technology; but some 30 percent do at least one of these two. Some 47 percent use information technology in management, and 25 percent use computers for process control, but 53 percent of entrants do at least one of the two. When we expand our definitions of innovation to encompass a characteristic from more than just the innovative group, the percentage of entrants that can be said to be innovative is

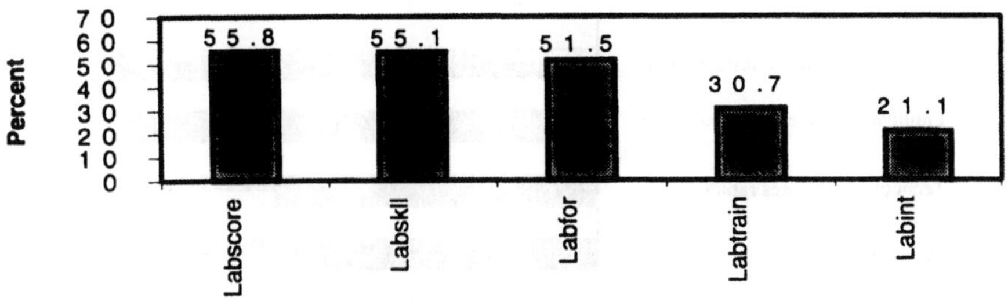

Figure 4.8. Incidence of Skill Emphasis.

quite large. Some 39 percent report an innovation, or perform R&D, or emphasize either the development or purchase of technology. Some 65 percent do one of the above or emphasize computer-controlled processes or stress the use of information technologies. Finally, some 83 percent do the above or stress advanced labor skills or do formal training.

Innovation and the Competitive Environment

Do innovators face a quieter environment than noninnovators? Is innovation in the small-firm segment encouraged by concentrated market structures? The life-cycle model of entry offered by Abernathy and Utterback (1978) or by Gort and Klepper (1982) would suggest that innovative entrants generally should be found in highly fluid, highly competitive situations.

In order to examine this issue, entrants are defined to be innovative if they are introducing new products or processes. Then differences between entrants who are introducing new products and processes and those who are not doing so are examined.

How does the competitive environment of innovators differ from noninnovators? First, innovating successful entrants face more competitors; only three-quarters of noninnovative entrants face more than four competitors, compared to 87 percent of innovators.

Second, innovators are generally found in segments of industries where certain key aspects of competition focus on innovation. When the perceptions of innovators and noninnovators about the nature of competition that they face are compared (Figure 4.9), it is clear that changes that are related to innovation are far more intense in the innovators' industries. Technology is more likely to be changing rapidly. Products are more likely to face rapid obsolescence. Demand is unpredictable, probably because competitor actions are also more difficult to forecast.

It should be pointed out that, in other environmental areas, competition is just

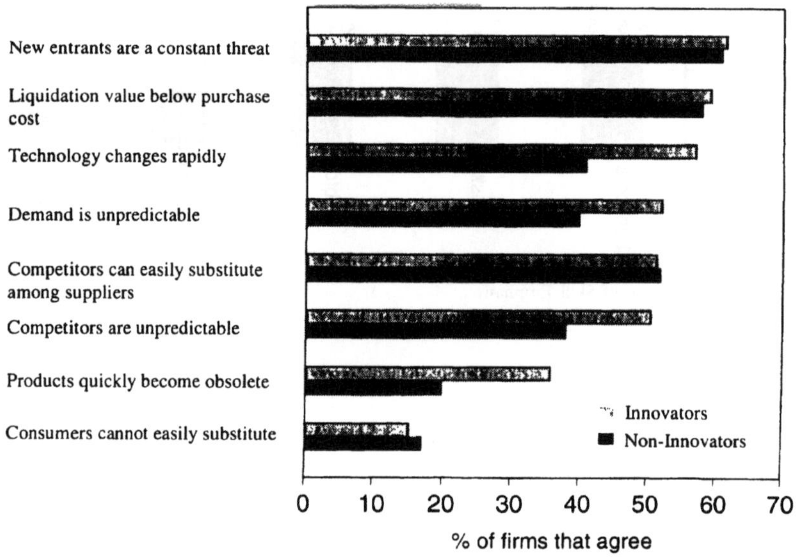

Figure 4.9. Innovators and Noninnovators' Perceptions of Industry Risk.

as intense for both innovators and noninnovators alike. The threat of entry is high everywhere. Firms are just as capable of switching suppliers. Both groups face the same threat that consumers can easily substitute products if they should so choose.

While small firms may have to find a niche strategy in order to survive, the innovators among them do not lead a protected existence. In general, all entrants continuously face the threat of entry. Innovators are also faced with continuous changes as a result of new product introduction and technological change that are related to the innovative nature of their industry.

Growth of Entrants and the Importance of Innovation

Growth Differences Across All Markets

We have already demonstrated that despite the emphasis that the economics literature has placed on the connection between innovation and firm size, small firms and entrants in particular demonstrate many different types of innovative behavior. Nevertheless, small firms do face a highly competitive environment as demonstrated above, and there are those who argue that competition does not encourage innovation. We can investigate whether this is so by asking whether innovation is rewarded by faster growth. In order to investigate the differences between faster- and slower-growing firms, we separate firms into two groups based on the annual average growth in real revenue from their first full year to 1993.

Faster-growing entrants are found to be more innovative than slower-growing

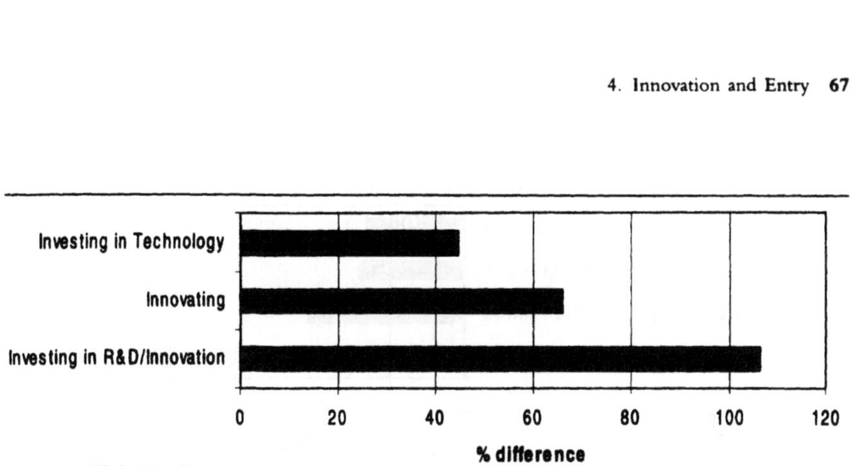

Figure 4.10. Differences in the Percentage of Entrants Investing and Innovating Between Faster- and Slower-Growing Entrants.

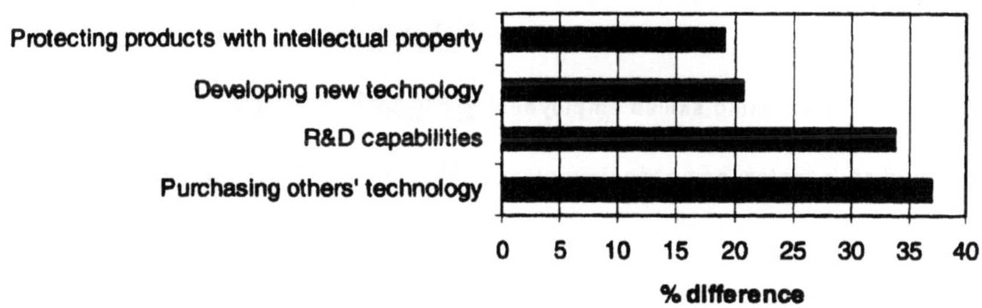

Figure 4.11. Differences in the Importance of Technological Strategies Between Faster- and Slower-Growing Entrants.

entrants in several different ways. They are twice as likely to invest in technology and R&D (Figure 4.10). These investments in inputs to the innovation process are rewarded: faster-growing entrants are more than 50 percent more likely to innovate than are slower-growing entrants. All of these differences are significantly different from zero at the 5 percent level using a one-tailed t-test.

Faster-growing entrants are more innovative in a number of other associated ways. They are more likely to introduce new or improved products, seek out new markets, and strive for efficiency gains through process innovation.

Accompanying these differences in investment activities associated with innovation and innovation itself comes a considerable difference in the emphasis that is given to technological competencies and R&D capabilities (Figure 4.11). The largest difference (over 35 percent) can be found in the extent to which the firm introduces new technologies by purchasing them from others. But differences in R&D capabilities are a close second though they are less statistically significant. Differences between faster- and slower-growing firms are somewhat smaller for developing new technologies and protecting products using intellectual property rights.[5]

The greater emphasis on innovative inputs, whether R&D or technology, is also

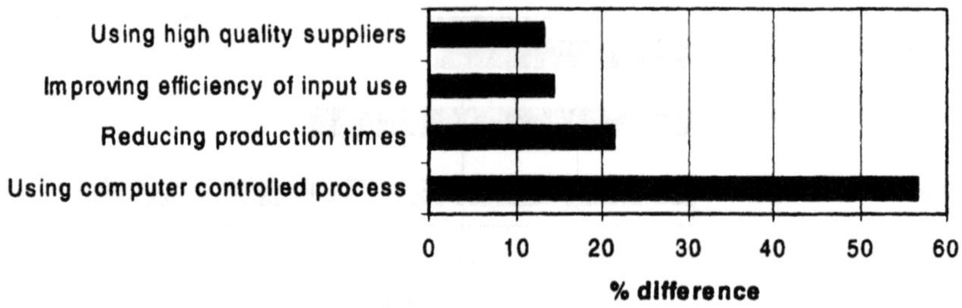

Figure 4.12. Differences in the Importance of Production Strategies Between Faster- and Slower-Growing Entrants.

Figure 4.13. Differences in the Importance of Human-Resource Strategies Between Faster- and Slower-Growing Entrants.

accompanied by a greater emphasis on other aspects of the production process that are associated with improving production efficiencies. Faster-growing entrants also rate each of the production-related strategies more highly than slower-growing entrants, with the largest differential being associated with the use of computer-controlled processes (Figure 4.12).[6]

The purchase of advanced technologies enhances the physical capital that is critical to innovation. The development of R&D contributes to one type of intangible knowledge capital. The other type of intangible knowledge capital is embedded in the human capital of the firm. Since both of the former receive greater emphasis from faster-growing entrants, it is not surprising to find that faster-growing entrants also give greater emphasis to each of the strategies associated with creating and maintaining high levels of human capital (Figure 4.13). Faster-growing entrants give a greater emphasis to incentive compensation plans. Plans such as these provide the incentive to be inventive where risk and rewards need to be shared if innovative projects are to be brought to market. But faster-growing entrants also place more emphasis on recruiting skilled employees and on training.[7]

Faster-growing entrants rate almost all of the product-specific strategies higher

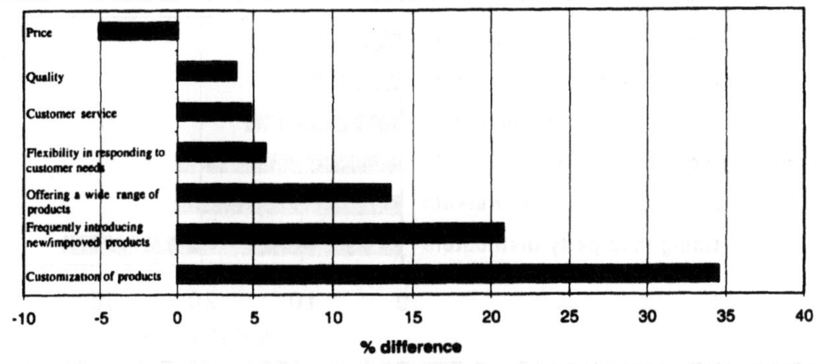

Figure 4.14. Differences in the Importance of Competitive Strategies Between Faster- and Slower-Growing Entrants.

than slower-growing entrants. They are most distinguished from slower-growing firms in the value they place on product innovation-related strategies such as customizing their products, frequently introducing new or improved products, and offering a wide range of products (Figure 4.14).

Innovative strategies in faster-growing firms do not replace the attention that these firms give to enhancing existing products. Growing entrants also place more value on flexibility in responding to customer needs, customer service, and quality; moreover, the former two differences are statistically significant. Growing entrants do not maintain unchanged product lines; rather they focus on introducing new products that are of a higher quality and on improving the delivery of the product.[8]

The innovative stance of growing entrants is evident in their marketing strategy as well. Growing entrants place significantly greater emphasis on expanding their market reach (Figure 4.15). The greatest differential occurs in the emphasis that is placed on using third-party distributors. The next most important differentials exist in the emphasis that is placed on targeting new foreign markets and improving their position in existing markets.[9]

Growth Differences in New and Mature Markets

Examining differences between faster- and slower-growing firms for the entire population of entrants establishes which competencies are associated with growth, irrespective of the specific environmental factors affecting the entrants. Yet there is reason to believe that the importance of these factors may vary across industries. In particular, the stage of the industry is likely to affect the type of innovative activity and the complementary strategies that are adopted by faster growing entrants.

In new-product markets that are in their early growth phase, the characteristics

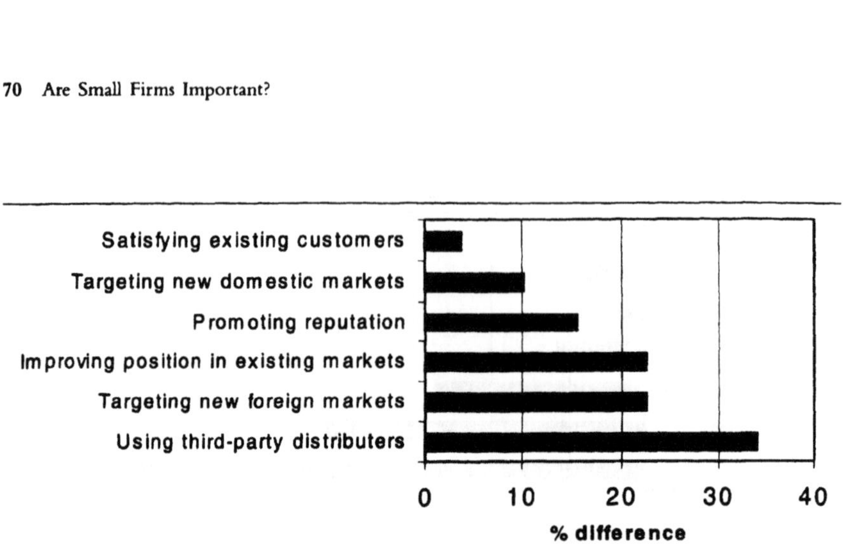

Figure 4.15. Differences in the Importance of Marketing Strategies Between Faster- and Slower-Growing Entrants.

of the product are continually changing. In these volatile markets, the entrants that grow should be those that keep pace with or lead product changes. Entrants that grow in these markets are those that anticipate and stimulate demand for new product features and focus on product development. At this stage of development, product change is so rapid that firms have little time to focus on process innovation, and there is relatively less to gain by focusing on improving the efficiency with which existing products are produced. The emphasis that firms give to improving the way existing products are produced or to extending their market reach is likely to become more important as markets mature.

In order to examine the extent to which there are differences in the innovation profile of entrants and differences in the types of competencies that are associated with growth, entrants are separated into two groups—those in markets that are in their introductory or growth stage (new markets) and those in markets that are in their mature or postmature stage (mature markets). Differences in the competencies of faster and slower growers are then examined in order to determine the extent to which the stage of the market changes the conclusions previously derived as to the nature of competencies associated with growth.

When this is done, innovation is still found to be strongly associated with growth, regardless of the market's maturity. Innovation is more prevalent in faster-growing firms than in slower-growing firms in both new and mature markets (Figure 4.16). In new markets, an emphasis on product innovation serves to distinguish faster from slower growers; this is not the case for process innovation. In mature markets, faster growers are more likely to be doing more of both process and product innovation. Our hypotheses about the differences in the importance of innovation across the product life-cycle are only partially confirmed. It is true that process innovation matters more in mature markets than it does in new markets. But product innovation is equally important in terms of growth in both markets.

In keeping with the importance of human capital to the growth process, growing

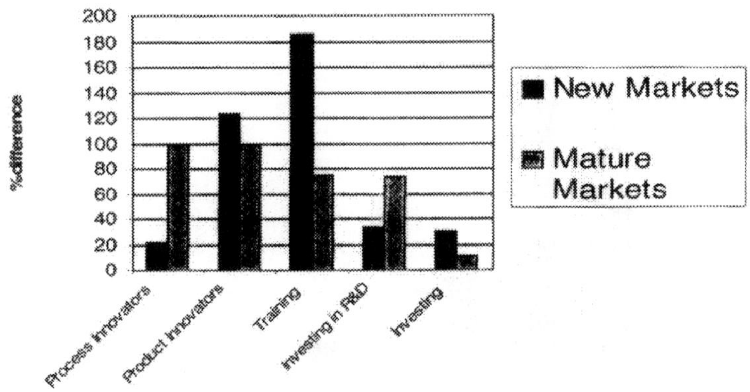

Figure 4.16. Differences in Innovative Activities Between Faster- and Slower-Growing Firms.

firms are more likely to train in both new and mature markets (Figure 16). We know that innovation brings about greater skill requirements (Baldwin and Johnson, 1996b), and firms that innovate tend to train more. Consequently, it is not surprising to find that faster-growing firms, in each of the groups, are more likely to train than are slower-growing firms.

The training differences between faster- and slower-growing firms are greater in new than in mature markets. Mature markets are more likely to require skills that can be obtained by hiring workers with existing skill sets. In new markets, new products are being introduced so rapidly that new skills are constantly required. The very novelty of the products often requires skills that are so new or firm-specific that companies have to train workers to match the desired skill level. Training then is important in both phases, but it is more critical to the growth process in markets where the product is in the earlier stages.

R&D also serves to distinguish faster- from slower-growing firms in both stages of product development (Figure 4.16). However, the difference is greater for mature markets. At first glance, this is counterintuitive since R&D is associated with new product development, which in turn is linked with new markets. But as we have seen, product development is equally important in both market stages, while process innovation is more important in mature markets. If R&D is a critical component required for both types of innovation, then R&D differences should be greater for mature markets—as they are.

While the connection between growth and the intensity of product innovation does not serve to distinguish new from mature markets, other aspects of the customer product strategy do so (Figure 4.17). There are positive differences between faster- and slower-growing firms with regards to both customization of new products and the frequency of introducing new or improved products for both mature and new markets. This is what one would expect since the emphasis on product

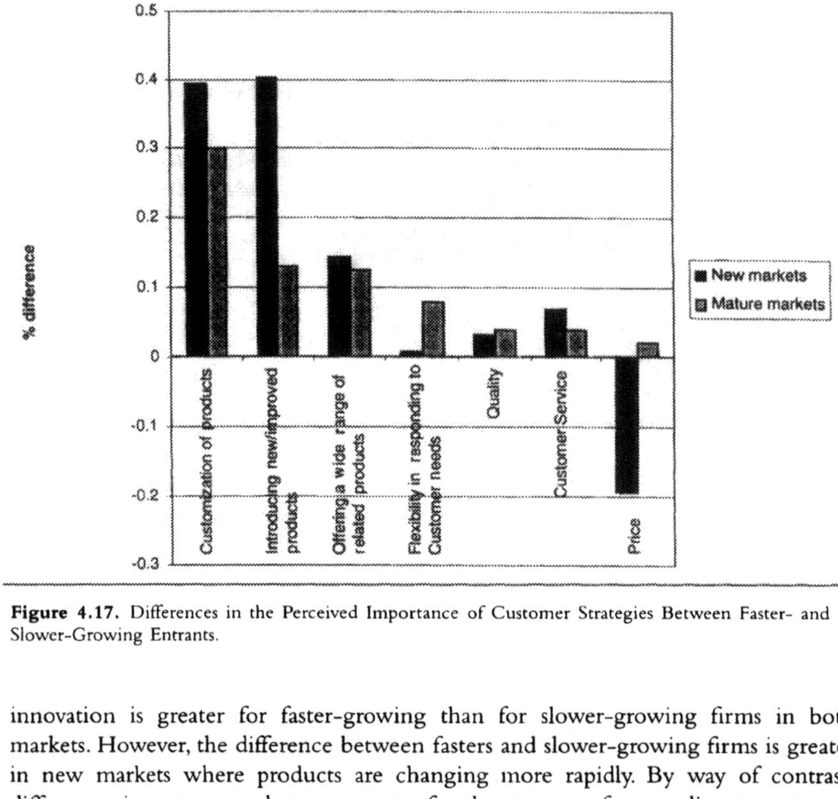

Figure 4.17. Differences in the Perceived Importance of Customer Strategies Between Faster- and Slower-Growing Entrants.

innovation is greater for faster-growing than for slower-growing firms in both markets. However, the difference between fasters and slower-growing firms is greater in new markets where products are changing more rapidly. By way of contrast, differences in mature markets are greater for the strategy of responding to customer needs in a flexible manner. There are smaller differences between faster- and slower-growing firms for the two conventional aspects of competition—quality and customer service—but the differences are nonetheless positive. The difference is statistically significant in new markets for a quality strategy; in mature markets, it is significant for a customer-service strategy.

Associated with a greater stress by growing firms on product innovation and other new-product strategies comes a greater emphasis on a number of different marketing strategies (Figure 4.18). Faster-growing firms in both markets are significantly more likely to stress product reputation. Faster-growing firms in both markets are more likely to stress market expansion—but the source of that expansion differs because the markets are not at the same point in the life-cycle. Faster-growing firms in mature markets are more likely to target new foreign markets and new domestic markets than are faster-growing firms in new markets (Figure 4.18). Despite the fact that mature markets offer less growth on average, faster-growing firms in the mature stage of a product life-cycle expand by targeting both new domestic and foreign markets.

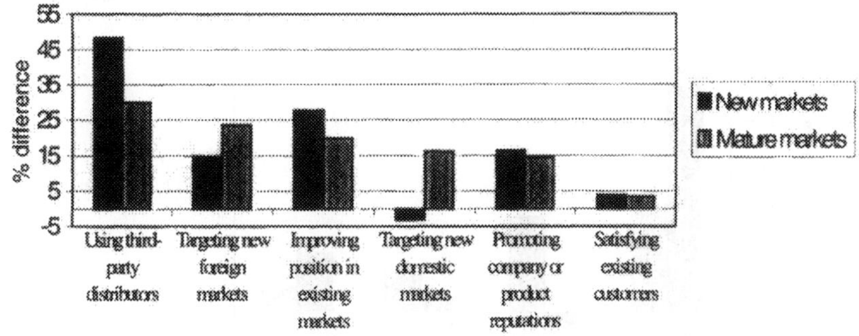

Figure 4.18. Differences in the Perceived Importance of Marketing Strategies Between Faster- and Slower-Growing Entrants.

All firms in the initial stage of the product life-cycle are producing new products for new markets. Therefore, the stress on new markets does not distinguish between faster and slower growers here. However, it is true that the percentage difference in the stress that is placed on improving existing market position, which for firms in new markets means expanding market share in their new product markets, is greater between faster and slower growers in new markets than in mature markets. Therefore, growing firms in this phase of the product life cycle do place a greater emphasis on the aspect of market expansion that was relevant to them.

More important, what serves to distinguish faster growers from slower growers in new markets is the extent to which third-party distributors are used. The demands being made on new firms in the early stages of the life-cycle are sufficiently large that relying on outside parties for distribution, where they are available, husbands scarce resources.

The previous section demonstrated the universal importance of product innovation in markets that differ in terms of their position in their life-cycle. While differences in emphasis exist, they involve detail only—with more new products and more customization in the early stages of the life-cycle. Where differences are more marked is in the degree of process innovation. Mature markets are those where growth is more closely related to process innovation.

This finding should not be interpreted to mean that an emphasis on production strategies is unimportant in new markets. While faster-growing firms in new markets place relatively less stress on process innovations (Figure 4.19), they are more likely to stress new computer-based production strategies. On the other hand, faster growers in mature markets are more likely to focus on reducing production times or using high-quality suppliers.

In summary, similarities in the importance of product innovation can be found across markets that are both young and old. The generalizations that originated in comparing faster- and slower-growing firms in the entire population are qualified but are not overturned when the analysis is extended to markets that differ by

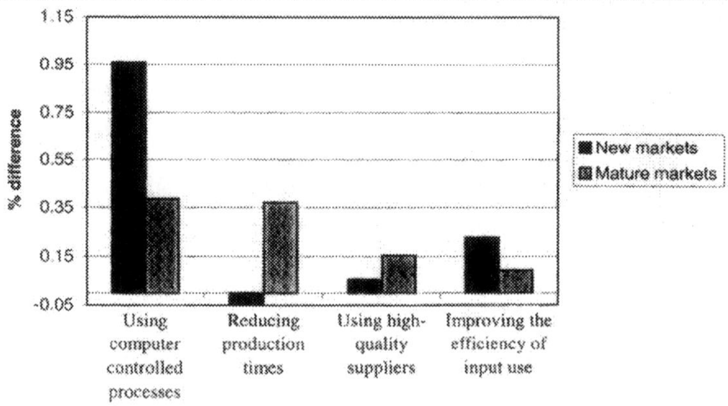

Figure 4.19. Differences in the Perceived Importance of Production Strategies Between Faster- and Slower-Growing Entrants.

degree of maturity. Adding detail by examining different markets provides insights that bolster the original conclusion that innovation is critical for growth. In particular, product innovation is important in both young and old product markets alike.

Successful entrants are those that reach beyond the bounds of their established product markets. They introduce new or improved products and seek out new customers. They look inside the firm and continually strive to improve, update, and modify their operations—but in different ways. Despite the primary focus of entrants on established markets that has been drawn in the previous section, innovation in new firms in most markets is rewarded with growth. These results corroborate those found in the GSME survey (Baldwin, Chandler, Le, and Papailiadis, 1994), where more-successful[10] firms outperform less successful firms in every area, but where innovation is the key factor that discriminates between more- and less successful firms.

CONCLUSION

Entry is important. At any point in time, a substantial amount of market share or employment is accounted for by firms that entered in the recent past—not a gargantuan amount but an amount that cannot be dismissed as marginal.

Entry is an inherent part of the dynamic competitive process that leads some firms to grow and others to decline. And it is within this context that it needs to be appreciated. It is not the only process at work—but it is an important part of it.

The entry process involves trial and error. Firms have to develop basic skills before they can survive—and large numbers appear not to have these skills at birth. Firms that fall by the wayside generally start off smaller, pay lower wages, and have lower labor productivity (Baldwin and Rafiquzzaman, 1995). Moreover, their management lacks knowledge of basic management skills in many cases (Baldwin et al., 1997). Nevertheless, a subset of new entrants survives and grows—and the growth of this group is substantial.

It is in the area of innovation that entrants make a widespread contribution. The contribution of entrants to some industries is well understood. New technology-based firms play an important role in the early stages of the life-cycle of many industries. They are the means by which the ideas of new entrepreneurs are initially commercialized. Whether in electronics, instruments, medical equipment, steel, or biotechnology, new firms have played an important role in the innovation process.

Despite the high profile of entrants in industries such as electronics and biotechnology, the role of small firms is still questioned. As important as these high-profile firms are, generalizing their impact to other sectors is difficult based just on case studies. And it is all too easy to infer that firms in sectors other than electronics and biotechnology are not innovative. This chapter argues that this is inappropriate.[11] While there is no doubt that firms in the electronics industries are innovative, it is also the case that firms elsewhere have developed the capacities that are needed for innovation in their particular industries. These capabilities often involve development of new technology, nurturing of worker skills, or devising of new products that are highly novel. The range and diversity of the innovative skills of new firms across all industries is remarkable.

The importance of the innovation process is attested to by the connection between growth and innovation. The successful entrants that grow the most are those that develop one or other type of innovative activity—either with respect to the introduction of new products, an emphasis on technology, or human resources.

This innovation process, to be successful, requires complementary skills. Firms that develop new products have to focus more intensely on human-resource capabilities. They develop competencies in a number of different areas. On the one hand, innovation activities are accompanied by a greater emphasis on accompanying skills; but they also require balance. An innovative firm focuses more intensely on a broad range of competencies.

ACKNOWLEDGMENTS

I am indebted to Daniel Stripinis and Bob Gibson, who assisted with the data preparation.

NOTES

1. That is, they scored 4 or 5 on a scale of 1 to 5.

2. See Baldwin (1995) for data that show that the intensity of competition, as measured by market share turnover, is not closely related to concentration.

3. Where possible the two sets of questions were cross-tabulated in order to validate the nature of the Likehart scale. For example, there is a high correlation between the importance given to R&D and the percentage of investment devoted to R&D—or the score given to training and whether a firm had implemented a formal training program (see Baldwin, 1998a). This has also been found in previous

surveys that ask firms to score their competencies and to indicate the intensity of their activities (Baldwin et al., 1994).

4. See also Baldwin, Gray, and Johnson (1996) for a study of the connection between the adoption of advanced manufacturing technologies and a firm's emphasis on training.

5. Only the difference "purchasing others' technology" is statistically significant at the 5 percent level using a one-tailed t-test. R&D capabilities is significant at the 10 percent level.

6. Differences for computer-controlled processes and high-quality suppliers are statistically significant at the 5 percent level using a one-tailed t-test; the others are statistically significant at the 10 percent level using a one-tailed t-test.

7. All these differences are statistically significant at the 5 percent level using a one-tailed t-test.

8. Except for customer service and range of products, all the positive differences are statistically significant at the 5 percent level for a one-tailed t-test. The former are significant at the 10 percent level.

9. Promoting reputation, improving position in existing markets, and using third-party distributors are statistically significant at the 2.5 percent level; the other differences are statistically significant at the 10 percent level using a one-tailed t-test.

10. In the 1994 study, success is defined by an index consisting of growth in market share, productivity, and profitability.

11. For a more detailed analysis of cross-industry differences, see Baldwin and Gellatly (1998).

REFERENCES

Abernathy, W.J., and J.M. Utterbach. (1978). "Patterns of Industrial Innovation." *Technology Review*, 80 (June–July), 41–47.

Audretsch, D.B. (1995). *Innovation and Industry Evolution*. Cambridge, MA: MIT Press.

Baldwin, J.R. (1995). *The Dynamics of Industrial Competition*. Cambridge: Cambridge University Press.

Baldwin, J.R. (1996). "Productivity Growth, Plant Turnover and Restructuring in the Canadian Manufacturing Sector." In D. Mayes (ed.), *Sources of Productivity Growth*. Cambridge: Cambridge University Press.

Baldwin, J.R. (1997). *Innovation and Intellectual Property*. Catalogue No. 88–515. Ottawa: Statistics Canada.

Baldwin, J.R. (1998a). *Are There High-Tech Industries or Only High-Tech Firms*? Research Paper No. 120 Analytical Studies Branch. Ottawa: Statistics Canada.

Baldwin, J.R. (1998b). *Entry and Exit*. Research Paper No. 121. Ottawa: Statistics Canada.

Baldwin, J.R., W. Chandler, C. Le, and T. Papailiadis. (1994). *Strategies for Success: A Profile of Small and Medium-Sized Enterprises in Canada*. Catalogue No. 61-523R. Ottawa: Statistics Canada.

Baldwin, J.R., T. Dunne, and J. Haltiwanger. (1995). "Plant Turnover in Canada and the United States." In J. Baldwin (ed.), *The Dynamic of Industrial Competition*. Cambridge: Cambridge University Press.

Baldwin, J.R., and G. Gellatly. (1998). "Developing High-Tech Classification Schemes: A Firm-Based Approach." Proceedings of the sixth Annual International Conference at the University of Twente, The Netherlands.

Baldwin, J.R., T. Gray, and J. Johnson. (1996). "Advanced Technology Use and Training in Canadian Manufacturing." *Canadian Business Economics*, 5(1), 51–70.

Baldwin, J.R., T. Gray, J. Johnson, J. Proctor, M. Rafiquzzaman, and D. Sabourin. (1997). *Failing Concerns: Business Bankruptcy in Canada*. Catalogue No. 61-525. Ottawa: Statistics Canada.

Baldwin, J.R., and J. Johnson. (1996a). "Business Strategies in More- and Less-Innovative Firms in Canada." *Research Policy*, 25, 785–804.

Baldwin, J.R., and J. Johnson. (1996b). "Human Capital Development and Innovation: A Sectoral Analysis." In Peter Howitt (ed.), *The Implications of Knowledge-Based Growth for Micro-Economic Policies*. Calgary: Calgary University Press.

Baldwin, J.R., and J. Johnson. (1998). "Innovator Typologies, Related Competencies and Performance." In G. Eliasson and C. Green (eds.), *Microfoundations of Economic Growth*. Ann Arbor: University of Michigan Press.

Baldwin, J.R., and M. Rafiquzzaman. (1995). "Selection Versus Evolutionary Adaption: Learning and Post-entry Performance." *International Journal of Industrial Organization*, 13, 501–522.

Baldwin, J.R., and D. Sabourin. (1996). Technology Adoption in Canadian Manufacturing, Catalogue number 88-514XPE, Ottawa: Statistics Canada.

D'Amboise, G. (1991). *The Canadian Small and Medium-Sized Enterprise: Situations and Challenges.* Halifax: Institute for Research on Public Policy.
Dunne, T., M. Roberts, and L. Samuelson. (1988). "Patterns of Firm Entry and Exit in U.S. Manufacturing Industries." *Rand Journal of Economics*, 19(4), 495–515.
Freeman, C. (1982). *The Economics of Industrial Innovation.* Cambridge, MA: MIT Press.
Geroski, P.A. (1991). *Market Dynamics and Entry.* Basil Blackwell.
Gort, M., and S. Klepper. (1982). "Time Paths in the Diffusion of Product Innovations." *Economic Journal*, 92, 630–653.
Haltiwanger. J. (1998). "Measuring and Analyzing Aggregate Fluctuations: The Importance of Building from Micro-Economic Evidence." *St. Louis Federal Reserve Bank Economic Review.* 79(3), 55–77.
Hollander, S. (1965). *The Sources of Increased Efficiency: A Study of Dupont Rayon Plants.* Cambridge, MA: MIT Press.
Picot, G., J.R. Baldwin, and R. Dupuy. (1994). "Employment Generation by Small Producers in the Job-Turnover Process." *Canadian Economic Observer* (pp. 3.1–3.18). Catalogue 11-010. Ottawa: Statistics Canada.
Statistics Canada. (1996). *The Survey of Operating and Financial Practices of Entrants.* Ottawa: Statistics Canada.

5. SMALL BUSINESS AND JOB CREATION IN THE UNITED STATES: THE ROLE OF NEW AND YOUNG BUSINESSES

JOHN HALTIWANGER

U.S. Bureau of the Census and University of Maryland, College Park, MD

C.J. KRIZAN

U.S. Bureau of the Census

INTRODUCTION

There is widespread agreement that employer size matters for a variety of economic outcomes. Previous academic research convincingly establishes strong connections between employer size and important economic outcomes like the level and inequality of wages, the incidence of fringe benefits, workforce quality, the pace of technological innovation and adoption, and the likelihood of unionization.[1] The public discourse about the role of employer size has focused primarily on the contribution of small businesses to job creation.[2] However, there is less agreement about this aspect of the role of employer size. The widely cited claim that small businesses are the primary creators of jobs in the United States derives primarily from a couple of studies by Birch (1979, 1987) and many reports from the U.S. Small Business Administration (SBA). Recently, Davis, Haltiwanger, and Schuh (1994, 1996) examined these studies on small businesses and job creation and raised a variety of conceptual, methodological, and measurement questions.[3]

In many respects, the problems with the existing studies are connected to the finding that there are high and pervasive rates of gross job creation and destruction in every sector and accompanying high rates of establishment births and deaths. The tremendous turbulence, while interesting in and of itself, yields conceptual, measurement, and methodological problems in considering the role of employer size in job creation. One of the interesting aspects of these problems is characterizing the role of new and young businesses. Their role is intimately linked to the role of employer size since new and young businesses tend to be small. In this chapter, we focus our attention on this aspect of the conceptual, measurement, and methodological issues.

Focusing on the role of new and young businesses helps to consider the deep underlying issue: Why should employer size be of any importance in accounting for differences in behavior across employers? There are arguably several reasons that employer size might be relevant, but its connection to employer age is obvious and compelling. New and young businesses are inherently part of the ongoing process of renewal that pervades market economies. The introduction of new ideas, products, and techniques involves a process of trial and error so that many new businesses fail while others are dramatic successes. The evidence we present in this chapter will highlight the volatile nature of new and young businesses and reveal their overall average success rate. Moreover, our results demonstrate the vital importance of distinguishing between employer age and size effects.

We first discuss the limitations that existing databases impose on the analysis of our questions of interest and then review some important methodological issues. Since these issues have already been discussed at length in prior studies (see Davis, Haltiwanger, and Schuh, 1994, 1996), we review these issues only briefly, and then we turn our attention to exploring the distinction between employer age and employer size.

WHAT DATABASE TO USE? WHAT DATABASE NOT TO USE?

Measuring gross job creation and gross job destruction and assessing the contribution of small businesses to net job creation requires longitudinal establishment-level data for a representative sample of establishments over an extended period of time, including a representative sample of establishment births and deaths.[4] Further, not only must the establishment-level longitudinal linkages be accurate, the establishment-level data must contain a firm identifier to permit analysis of the relationship between the gross job flows and firm size. These are formidable requirements, and the United States statistical agencies are only now developing fully operational database that will satisfy these requirements on an economywide basis.[5] Thus, at present, we cannot accurately assess the contribution of small business to job creation on a comprehensive basis in the United States. Even as economywide databases are developed and become available for use, it will take time to build a significantly long time series that can be employed to accurately analyze and assess the contribution of employer size in this context. In this section of the chapter, the relevant databases that have been used in the key studies are discussed.

Many early studies of job creation and job destruction are based on the Dun and Bradstreet Market Identifier (DMI) files (see, e.g., Birch, 1979, 1987; U.S. Small Business Administration, numerous years). In principle, the DMI file represents a longitudinal database on individual employers that can be used to measure job creation and destruction on an annual basis for virtually all sectors of the U.S. economy. Unfortunately, while the Dun and Bradstreet database has many impressive attributes and represents an unparalleled source of information for many commercial purposes, it is not designed or maintained to maximize its usefulness as a tool for statistical analysis of job creation and job destruction. Numerous studies have highlighted severe problems with the DMI files as a tool for measuring job creation and destruction or business births and deaths.[6] Identifying establishment births and deaths and tracking businesses over time is most difficult in the case of small employers. Given that these data are particularly ill suited for the study of small employers, it seems ironic that the DMI files have been the source of many of the claims of role of small businesses in job creation.

The Longitudinal Research Datafile (LRD) housed at the Center for Economic Studies at the U.S. Bureau of the Census has been the source of numerous recent studies of gross job flows by employer size (see, e.g., Dunne, Roberts, and Samuelson, 1989; Davis and Haltiwanger, 1990, 1992; Davis, Haltiwanger, and Schuh, 1994, 1996). Currently, the LRD links plant-level data for the Census of Manufactures (CM) and Annual Survey of Manufactures (ASM) for the period 1963 to 1993. The LRD contains a wealth of information that permits construction of annual and quarterly measures of job creation and destruction for the U.S. manufacturing sector cross-tabulated by a variety of sectoral and plant characteristics.

The LRD has several key advantages relative to other datasets that have been used to measure gross job flows, primarily the comprehensive scope of its sampling frame for a major sector of the U.S. economy, but also the large probability-based samples that minimize sampling error, the incorporation of births into ongoing panels, a careful distinction between firms and establishments, and a careful distinction between ownership transfers and the birth and death of establishments. Of fundamental importance here is that the Bureau of the Census, through its economic censuses and the Company Organization Survey (COS), assigns individual establishments unique, time-invariant identifiers that enable accurate tracking of the activity at individual establishments over an extended period of time.

Another key advantage of using the LRD to measure gross flows is that the ASM (and other Census surveys that can be linked to the ASM) contains a wealth of information about the characteristics of the plant and the firm (such as industry, location, size, age, capital intensity, energy intensity, productivity, wages) that can be cross-tabulated with the measures of gross job flows. Thus, the LRD provides a basis for providing a wide range of information about the characteristics of the plants that are creating and the plants that are destroying jobs.

The LRD also has limitations—primarily, in the present context, that the data are restricted to the manufacturing sector. Additionally, though, the sample frame for each ASM five-year panel, which is drawn from an Economic Census, is based on all establishments with more than five employees. This is likely not a significant limitation for manufacturing since the very small establishments account for only about 4 percent of manufacturing employment. Moreover, the ASM is replenished annually with a representative sample of establishment births and some ASM establishments experience periods where their employment is less than five. (Note that once an establishment is selected for an ASM panel, it stays in for the entire panel.) Accordingly, there are a large number establishments in the ASM with less than five employees, and thus the sample frame restriction to establishments in the Census with five or more employees is less binding than it may first appear.

These limitations (especially the restriction to manufacturing) are such that the LRD by itself is inadequate for the purpose of characterizing the role of employer size in job creation in the United States. However, the LRD can be used effectively to characterize the role of employer size for U.S. manufacturing, which is useful in its own right, and in so doing can serve as a testing ground for methodological and conceptual issues. In particular, one of the advantages of the LRD is the ability to measure other employer characteristics, including establishment age. For the purposes of this chapter, we exploit its ability to measure both establishment size and establishment age to further our understanding of the connection between these two variables.

METHODOLOGICAL ISSUES

Beyond the formidable database requirements, the analysis of the contribution of small businesses to job creation is fraught with difficult methodological and measurement issues, as explained briefly in the following subsections.[7]

Analysis of the Time Series of the Size Distribution of Employment Is Misleading

Some analyses of the role of small business in employment growth have attempted to make inferences based on changes over time in the employer-size distribution of employment. The problem with this approach is that firms can migrate between size categories from one year to the next. That is, it may be that the share of employment among small businesses increases because some large businesses shrank. How important is such migration across firm size categories in reality? The large magnitude of gross job flows discussed in the Evidence section below—and the concentration of job flows in plants that undergo big employment changes (see Davis, Haltiwanger, and Schuh, 1996)—indicates that migration across categories is frequent and important. Especially during periods of slow employment growth, firm migration from large to small is likely to occur quite often. This pattern creates the appearance of a booming small-firm sector. The implication is that analyzing the contribution of small businesses to employment growth requires tracking individual businesses over time—longitudinal business data.

Confusion Between Net and Gross Job Creation

Even with longitudinal business data, there are a host of methodological difficulties. One difficulty stems from the importance of distinguishing between net and gross job-creation statistics. A well-known finding is that gross job-creation rates (for all groups) dwarf net job-creation rates. The evidence for manufacturing discussed in the Evidence section below indicates that gross job-creation rates average approximately 10 percent per year while net job creation is typically one-tenth of this magnitude. Available evidence suggests this pattern of large gross rates relative to net rates is the norm in all sectors of the economy. The large disparity between gross and net job-creation rates implies that there are many possible groupings of expanding plants that can each separately account for all of the net job creation. In short, longitudinal studies that focus on the "share" of net job growth accounted for by small businesses present a misleading picture of the actual distribution of newly created jobs by size of employer. A more meaningful way to represent this distribution is to focus on the small-employer share of gross job creation.

Regression-to-the Mean Effects

Another potential for bias arises whenever employers experience transitory fluctuations in size or whenever measurement error introduces transitory fluctuations in observed size. Both phenomena are important features of longitudinal data on employers and yield misleading inferences because of associated regression-to-the-mean effects, or the *regression fallacy* for short.

The regression fallacy is most evident when job creation for a pair of years is examined and employers are classified by size according to their employment level in the base year. The fallacy arises because of the interaction between the base-year classification methodology and transitory employer-level employment movements. On average, employers classified as large in the base year are more likely to have experienced a recent transitory increase in employment. Since transitory movements reverse themselves, employers that are large in the base year are relatively likely to contract. Likewise, employers classified as small in the base year are more likely to have experienced a recent transitory decrease in employment. Hence, employers that are small in the base year are relatively likely to expand. This regression phenomenon (regression to the employer's own long-run size) creates the illusion that small employers systematically have higher growth rates than large employers.

The magnitude of the bias associated with the regression fallacy depends on several factors: the extent of measurement error in the data, the importance of transitory employment movements for individual employers, the size distribution of employment, and the precise size-class boundaries chosen by the analyst. As a consequence, precisely quantifying the extent of regression-to-the-mean bias in previous studies is impossible without direct access to their longitudinal data. The section on Evidence reports the quantitative significance of this problem for the LRD.

Distinguishing Between Births and Small Establishments

A related problem with the typical analysis of job creation by employer size is the failure to make a careful distinction between the contribution of new establishments and small establishments. This problem is most evident in studies that use the base year to assign establishments to size classes. It is an overwhelming problem in studies that use the base-year method for both new and continuing establishments. By construction in the latter case, all new establishments in year t have zero employment in year $t - 1$. If new establishments in year t are classified in size class according to their size in year $t - 1$, then they will all be classified in the smallest size class. Using this methodology generates enormous growth rates within the smallest size class since all of the job growth due to entry to be associated with small employers.

Many studies that use the base-year method (e.g., Birch, 1979, 1987) avoid this grossly misleading approach by classifying new establishments in year *t* by their size in year *t*. While this would appear to avoid the problem, further consideration raises a series of related concerns. Consider, for example, a new manufacturing establishment that on commencing full-scale production operations will have employment equal to 1,000. However, suppose that in the months prior to full-scale production activity, the plant "opens" with a very small number of employees (such as managerial, maintenance, and security) to prepare the plant for operations. In this example, the plant may appear in the data with the following sequence of employment (0 in year, 0, 5 in year 1, 1,000 in year 2).[8] Using the base-year method yields job growth between years 1 and 2 that all would be attributable to small employers.[9]

This discussion raises a more general underlying issue: the importance of distinguishing the effects of the startup process for new businesses from other effects. The startup process for new businesses is more complex than accounting for the possibility that preoperations staff are being measured in the first time period of observation. Learning by doing and uncertainty can lead to new businesses having an incentive to start small before expanding. According to various theories in the economics literature, there is an ongoing selection process that reflects information about future profitability that the firm acquires over time as a by-product of operating the plant, as a consequence of investing in the plant, or by the simple passage of time. The selection process is apt to exhibit greater intensity early in the life cycle of plants so that younger plants are likely to exhibit greater volatility in outcomes like employment growth rates. All of this highlights the importance of distinguishing between employer size and age effects, which we consider in the next section.

EVIDENCE FROM DATA COVERING THE MANUFACTURING SECTOR IN THE UNITED STATES AND OTHER NATIONS

Measuring Employer Size and Employer Age

There are many related but distinct concepts of employer size and age. The results below consider one definition of employer age—plant age—and three different concepts of employer size: current average plant size, average firm size, and base-year size. Plant age equals the number of years since the plant's construction or conversion to manufacturing use. Current average plant size equals the simple average of the plant's current employment and its employment twelve months earlier. Firm size equals the weighted mean number of manufacturing workers employed by the plant's parent firm computed over all the observations of the firm in a Census of Manufactures.[10] Finally, base-year size indicates the number of employees in the prior year (except for births in which the size is the number of employees in the current year).

A few remarks help clarify the usefulness, strengths, and weaknesses of these alternative measures of employer age and size. As discussed in the Methodological Issues section, plant age is inherently linked to the selection process that, over time, weeds out less successful plants. Plant size is a natural metric for the scale of operations at a geographically distinct production unit. Since demand variation and other factors causes plants' employment to fluctuates from year to year, current average plant size provides a better indication of the scale of operations by mitigating regression-to-the-mean effects. In what follows, comparing the results using base-year size and current average plant size enables us to evaluate the empirical relevance of regression-to-the-mean effects.

Note also that firm size is superior to plant size as an indicator of the overall scale of operations carried out by the plant's parent firm. Firm size corresponds closely to the notion of business size that underlies most public discourse on job creation. In addition, patterns of government regulation and business access to financial markets are more closely associated with firm size than plant size. However, our ability to measure firm size is limited given that we have comprehensive measures of the firm size only in Economic Census years. Thus, we cannot consider the empirical impact of alternative size classification methodologies (such as base year versus current average) using firm size.[11] Moreover, tracking the ownership structure of establishments is a formidable exercise even in Census years so that measurement error is likely to be more of a problem in measures of firm size. It is useful to emphasize that this problem of tracking the ownership structure of the establishments in the U.S. economy is a problem that goes well beyond the LRD. It is a problem for all of the alternative databases that could be used for this type of analysis.

Job Creation and Destruction Rates by Employer Size

Figure 5.1 depicts average annual gross job flow rates by current average plant size and base-year size.[12] Figure 5.2 presents average annual gross job flow rates by firm size. The gross job-creation and job-destruction rates are measured following the methodology described in detail in Davis, Haltiwanger, and Schuh (1996). These figures reveal strong regularities in the relationship between employer size and gross job-flow rates. Consider, first, the average rates of gross job creation. By all size class measures, gross job-creation rates decline monotonically with employer size. Thus, small employers create new jobs at a much higher gross rate than large employers. But gross job-creation measures clearly reveal only part of the story. Figures 5.1 and 5.2 show that gross job destruction rates also decline sharply with employer size. Thus, small employers also destroy jobs at a much higher rate than large employers. The findings in Figures 5.1 and 5.2 suggest that small businesses disproportionately create jobs and disproportionately destroy jobs. This finding is common to many studies in the literature regardless of measurement methodology.

How does net job creation vary by employer size? The discussion in the Methodological Issues section suggests that the regression fallacy and the treatment of births are potentially important factors that interact with the choice of which size measure is used to analyze the relationship between net growth rates and employer size.

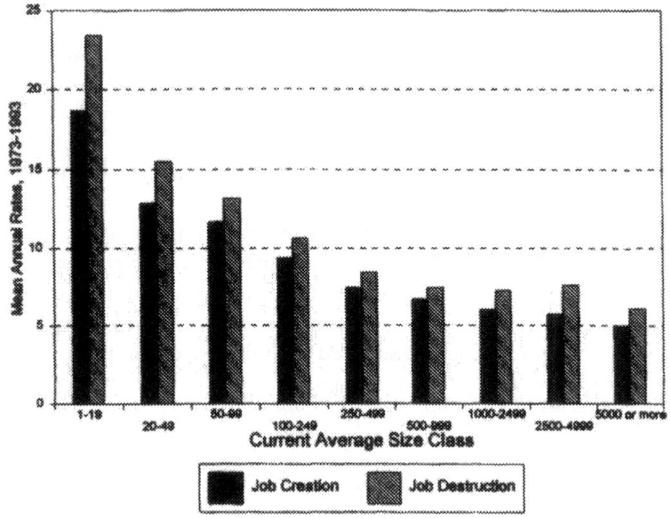
Mean Annual Rates, 1973-1993
0
5
10
15
20
25
1-19
20-49
50-99
100-249
250-499
500-999
1000-2499
2500-4999
5000 or more
Current Average Size Class
Job Creation
Job Destruction

(a)

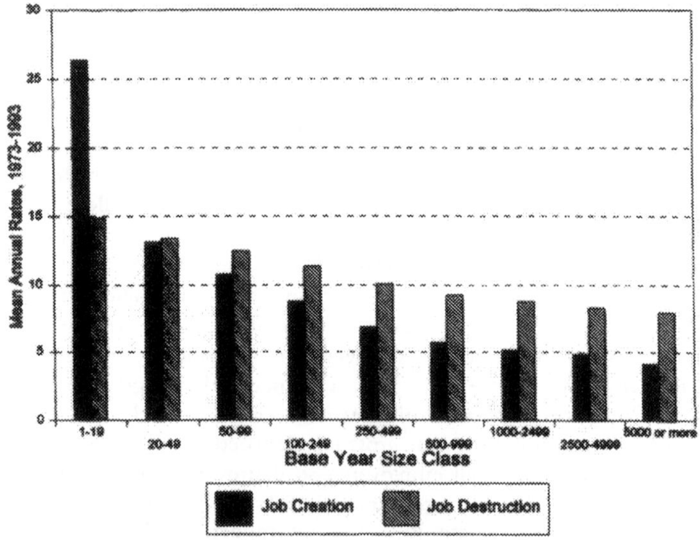
Mean Annual Rates, 1973-1993
0
5
10
15
20
25
30
1-19
20-49
50-99
100-249
250-499
500-999
1000-2499
2500-4999
5000 or more
Base Year Size Class
Job Creation
Job Destruction

(b)

Figure 5.1.

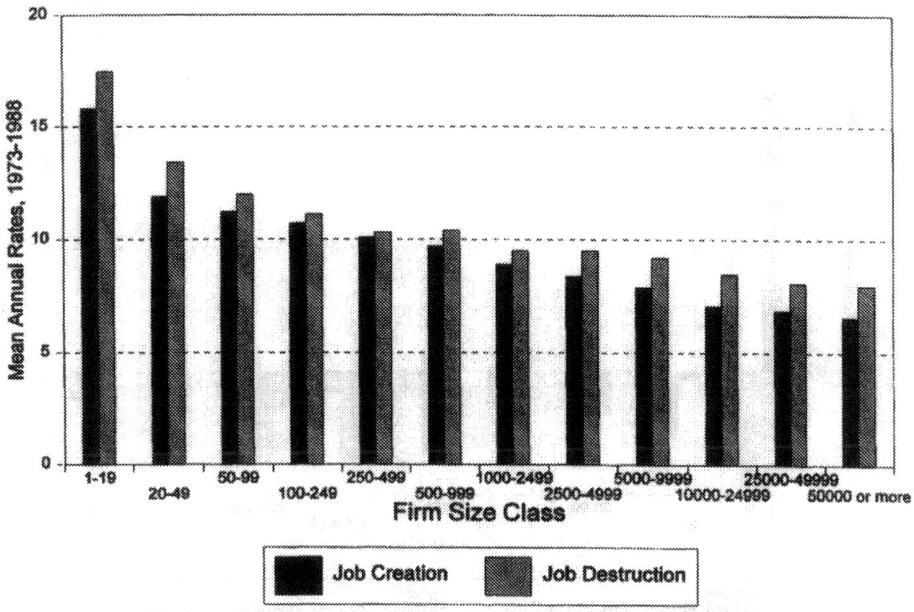

Figure 5.2.

Figure 5.3 reports net growth rates by employer size using the two alternative establishment-level size class measures: base-year size and current-average-plant size. Using the base-year method, the net job-creation rate declines steeply over the first five size-class intervals and then flattens out over the remaining intervals. Using the current-average-plant size, the empirical evidence produces no systematic pattern. That is, there is not a monotonic relationship between employer size and net employment growth rates.

As explained above, the results using the base-year size are especially subject to the regression fallacy. In contrast, the current average plant size results are less subject to the regression fallacy. The contrast between the base-year and current-year average-plant-size results suggests that the regression fallacy operates with powerful effect in the LRD data for the U.S. manufacturing sector. There is good reason to suspect that the regression fallacy operates with even greater effect in the longitudinal data sets used in the widely cited studies by Birch (1979, 1987) and others based on the DMI files. In particular, measurement error is almost certainly more serious in the DMI files than in the LRD. Given the base-year methodology that has been commonly used, the more serious measurement problems suggest greater susceptibility to the regression fallacy.

Interestingly, recent studies from other countries yield evidence that the base-

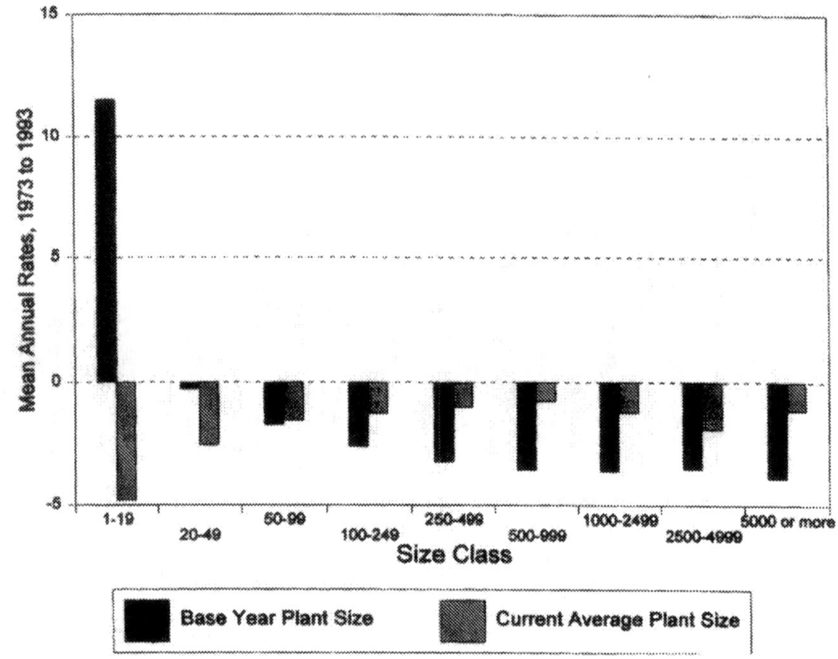

Figure 5.3.

year methodology yields misleading inferences due to the regression fallacy. The top panel of Figure 5.4 depicts the results of the analysis by Baldwin and Picot (1995) using data on Canadian manufacturing. The bottom panel of Figure 5.4 depicts analogous evidence for the Australian manufacturing sector obtained by Borland and Home (1994). An attractive feature of both of these studies is that they mimic the methodology used in Figure 5.3 for the U.S. manufacturing sector. From the Canadian data, we observe that the base-year methodology yields a very large net employment growth rate for the 1 to 19 size class, which mimics the findings for the United States. However, like for the United States, the net growth rate for the 1 to 19 size class is much smaller using the current-year average methodology. More generally, as in the U.S. data, using the base-year methodology for the Canadian data systematically yields higher growth rates for the smaller-size classes and lower growth rates for the larger-size classes relative to the current-average-plant-size methodology. Roughly similar patterns are exhibited for Australia, although additional caution must be used in interpreting these results given the relatively short sample period for this study.

In summary, the standard practice of measuring firm or plant size according to base-year employment leads to a regression fallacy, which in turn paints an overly

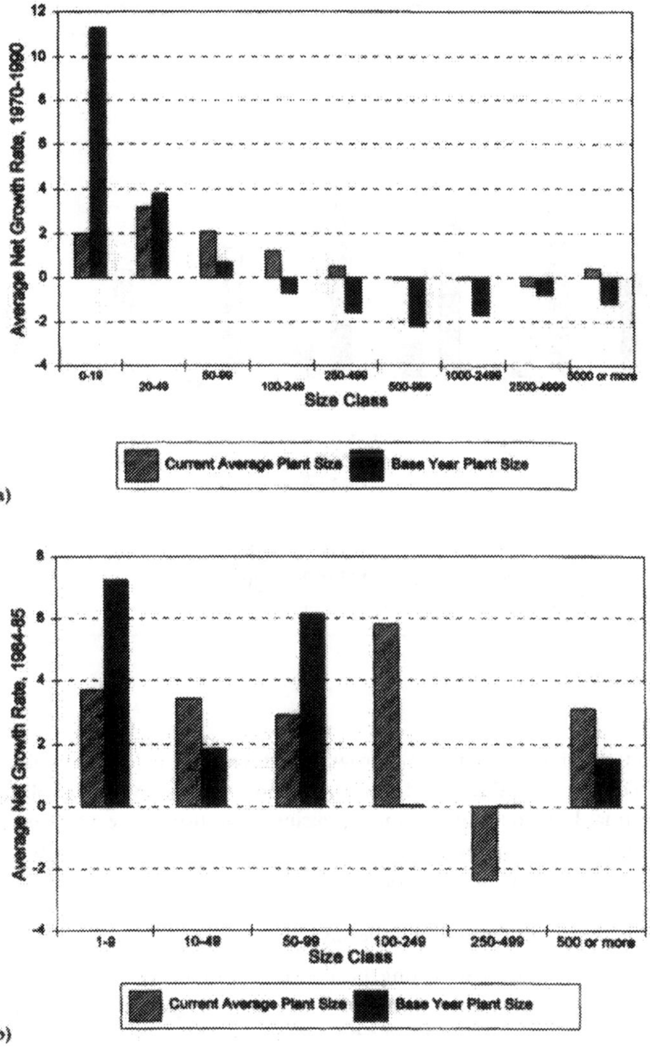
Average Net Growth Rate, 1970-1990
12
10
8
6
4
2
0
-2
-4
0-19
20-49
50-99
100-249
250-499
500-999
1000-2499
2500-4999
5000 or more
Size Class
Current Average Plant Size
Base Year Plant Size
Average Net Growth Rate, 1984-85
8
6
4
2
0
-2
-4
1-9
10-49
50-99
100-249
250-499
500 or more
Size Class
Current Average Plant Size
Base Year Plant Size

(a)

(b)

Figure 5.4.

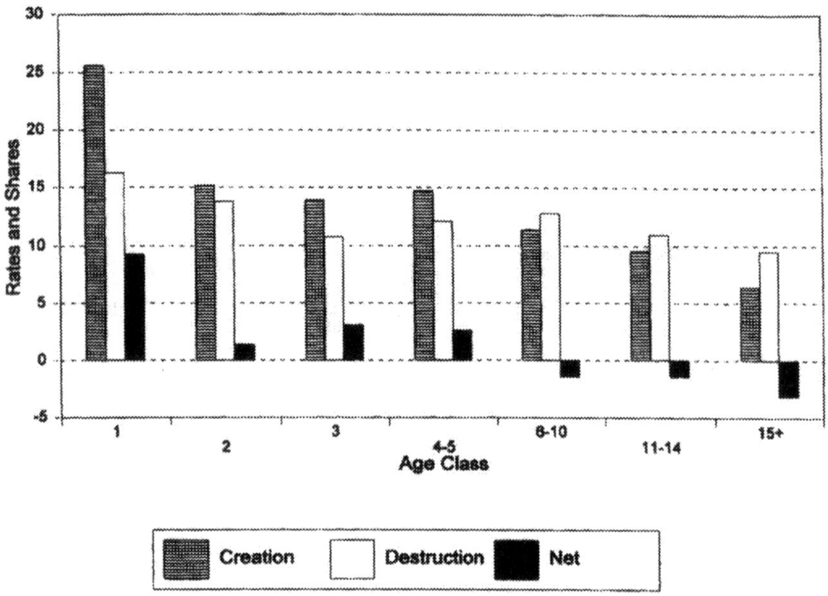

Figure 5.5.

favorable picture of the relative job-growth performance of small employers. Our sensitivity analysis with LRD data finds a substantial bias in favor of small businesses under the standard practice for measuring business size using base-year employment. Results that mimic this methodology for other countries also find a substantial bias from using the base-year methodology.

Distinguishing Between Employer Size and Employer Age

Many small businesses are also young businesses. Further, there are systematic relationships between employer age and both gross and net job growth rates. Chapter 4 of Davis, Haltiwanger, and Schuh (1996) presents evidence of several age-related patterns. We present some of that evidence in Figure 5.5 (which is drawn from Table 4.5 of Davis, Haltiwanger, and Schuh, 1996). One clear pattern that emerges is that net job-creation rates decline with plant age. This pattern brings to mind the replacement of old, outmoded plants by new, technologically superior plants. While this characterization of plant life-cycle dynamics contains a germ of truth, another clear pattern is that gross job-destruction rates decline sharply with plant age. Contrary to an image of insecure jobs in obsolete production facilities, the typical older manufacturing plant offers jobs with unusually good prospects for continued employment.

The strong relationship between net and gross job flows with employer age raise questions about distinguishing between employer size and employer age effects. The high average growth rates of plants in the first few years of existence suggest that classification by employer size is apt to be highly unstable for very young plants. Since the LRD data permit cross-tabulations of job flows by employer size and age simultaneously, one can use the disaggregated tabulations to control directly for age effects in assessing the relationship between employer size and job-flow rates. We investigate these relationships in the following manner. For every year in the LRD, we construct a crude age measure using entry based on the first Census year the plant entered. Using this information, we then construct a measure of job creation and destruction among young plants (less than ten years old) and mature plants (ten years or older) (see Davis, Haltiwanger, and Schuh, 1996, for more discussion of this methodology), respectively. Note that it is not feasible to construct the detailed age measures used in Figure 5.5 for every year in the LRD given the rotating panels of the ASM, but as will become apparent we obtain striking results using even the crude age measure.

Figure 5.6a presents annual average gross and net job-flow rates for young plants for the 1972 to 1993 period while Figure 5.6b presents the analogous rates for mature plants. For young plants, job-creation and job-destruction rates decline monotonically with employer size. However, for young plants, net employment growth rates exhibit no systematic pattern by employer size. In evaluating these results it is useful to note that most of the young plants are also small plants—for example, the employment share of young large plants (more than 5,000 workers) is very small. For mature plants, there is also some tendency for gross job-creation and job-destruction rates to decline by employer size, but the relationship is not monotonic. Moreover, for mature plants, net employment growth rates tend to rise by employer size. Comparing the magnitudes across Figures 5.6a and 5.6b, for an employer of a given size, net employment growth is higher for young plants as are the gross job-creation and job-destruction rates.

Taken together, Figures 5.5 and 5.6 show that employer age is an important determinant of differences across plants in net and gross job-flow rates. Young plants grow faster than mature plants (even holding size constant), and very young plants (such as plants that are one to two years old) grow much faster, on average, than plants that are just a bit older. For young plants, we observe that small plants disproportionately create and destroy jobs, although that pattern is not systematic for mature plants. Moreover, for young plants there is no systematic relationship between net employment growth and size, while the relationship between net growth and size is positive for mature plants. In short, these results indicate that employer age yields systematic effects on net and gross rates, controlling for employer size, but the reverse is not true. The implication is that employer age is the more important factor in accounting for differences in net and gross job flows.

In spite of the large, systematic effects of employer age, several cautions are in order. First, it is useful to recall that a key finding that has emerged from the analysis of establishment-level employment dynamics is that idiosyncratic factors domi-

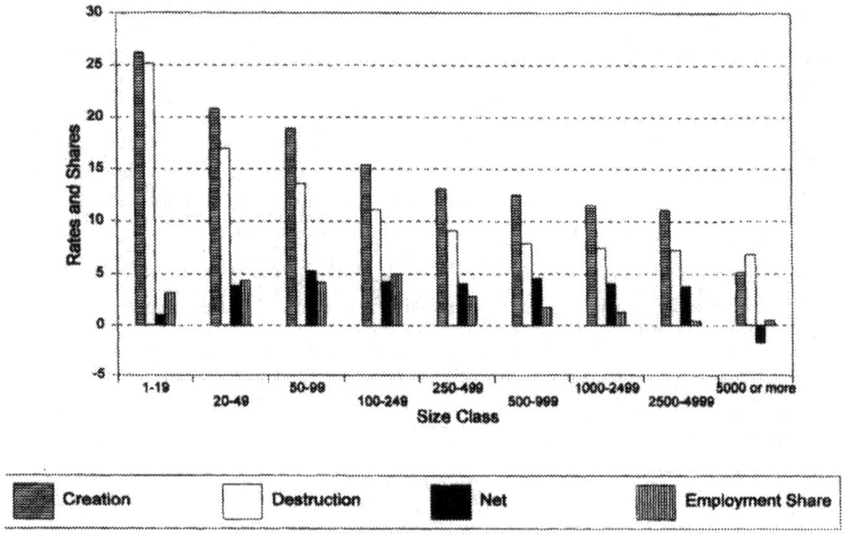
Rates and Shares
Size Class
1-19
20-49
50-99
100-249
250-499
500-999
1000-2499
2500-4999
5000 or more
Creation
Destruction
Net
Employment Share

(a)

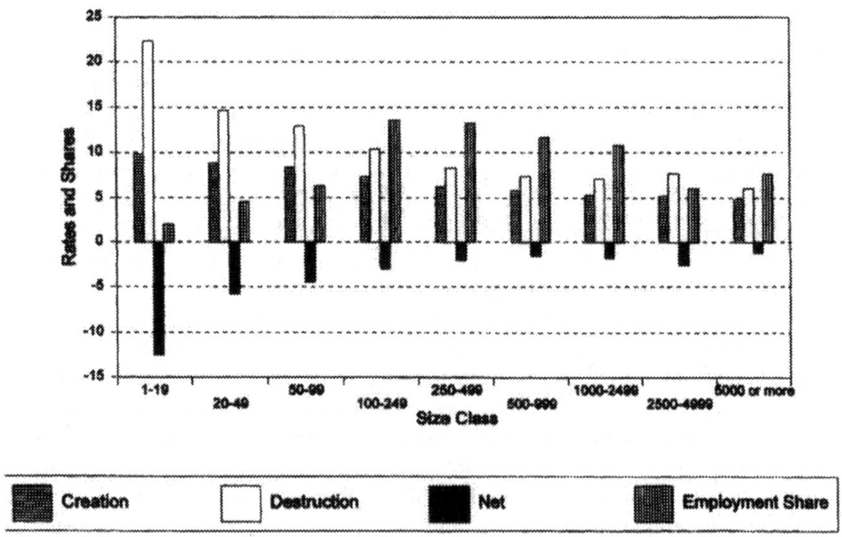
Rates and Shares
Size Class
1-19
20-49
50-99
100-249
250-499
500-999
1000-2499
2500-4999
5000 or more
Creation
Destruction
Net
Employment Share

(b)

Figure 5.6.

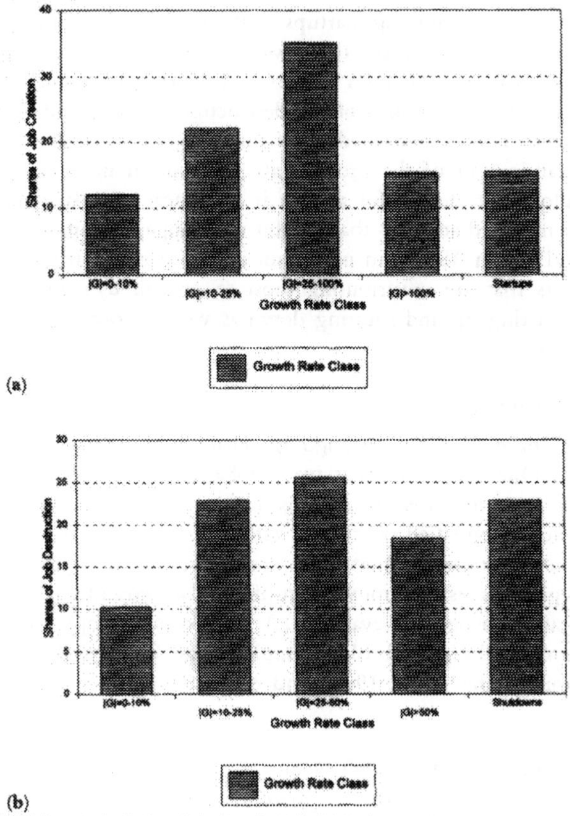

Figure 5.7

nate the determination of establishment growth. Even employer age effects account for little of the heterogeneity of growth rates across establishments. For example, Davis, Haltiwanger, and Schuh (1996) show that employment shifts across employers classified by detailed age and two-digit SIC industry account for only 16 percent of the pace of job reallocation. The dominance of idiosyncratic factors serves as an important caution for attributing net growth to plants classified by any observable plant characteristic.

A related caution is that plants undergoing dramatic changes, such as startups or shutdowns, disproportionately account for the observed patterns of job creation and destruction. Figure 5.7 shows that a large fraction of gross job creation is accounted for by startups and a large fraction of gross job destruction is accounted for by shutdowns. Figure 5.7 also depicts the contributions of continuing establishments by growth-rate class. Combining startups with plants with dramatic increases in employment, we observe that more than two thirds of job creation is accounted for by establishments with growth rates that exceed 25 percent annually. Similarly, we observe that more than two thirds of job destruction is accounted for by establishments with growth rates that exceed more than 25 percent in absolute magnitude annually. An examination of the growth-rate distribution nevertheless reveals that the modal employment change for a plant is at or near zero. Roughly, 18 percent of workers are employed at plants that exhibit no change in employment (see Davis, Haltiwanger, and Schuh, 1996). An important inference is that it is a relatively small number of plants that are contributing most to growth dynamics—in particular, plants that are starting up and shutting down as well as continuing plants that are exhibiting dramatic changes.

CONCLUDING REMARKS

In this study, we have revisited the ongoing debate about the role of small business in job creation. One limitation that we emphasize is the lack of economywide datasets that permit comprehensive analysis of these issues. While this situation is in the process of being remedied by current efforts at the U.S. statistical agencies, the analysis in this chapter stresses that there are important conceptual, measurement, and methodological issues that must be confronted in considering this issue (even once the requisite data become available). A focus of this chapter, in this regard, is the role of births and the related role of employer age. Using data for the U.S. manufacturing sector for the 1970s, 1980s, and early 1990s, we emphasize the following findings:

1. Young establishments exhibit high average net employment growth rates and high volatility of growth rates relative to mature establishments.
2. Among young establishments, net employment growth rates do not exhibit any systematic pattern by employer size. Small, young establishments exhibit greater volatility than larger, young establishments.
3. Among mature establishments, net employment growth rates actually increase with employer size.
4. Establishment-level growth rates are dominated by idiosyncratic factors with plants exhibiting dramatic changes (such as startups and shutdowns) accounting for most of the observed gross job creation and destruction.

These findings raise two related sources of caution regarding the role of employer size. For employment growth, it looks as if the more important factor is age and not size. Put differently, most small establishments are new and young establishments. Thus, the role of small business in job creation may simply reflect the role of births and in turn young establishments. A related caution is the dominance of idiosyncratic factors and the contribution of establishments exhibiting dramatic changes to creation and destruction. These latter results suggest that attributing a dominant role to any observable characteristic like size (or age) is misleading.

These remarks do not deny that small (and young) businesses play important roles in the economy. Young, small businesses are undoubtedly an important part of the continuous renewal process of the U.S. economy. The high pace of reallocation that is dominated by idiosyncratic effects reflects experimentation with new products, technologies, marketing strategies, and business locations with young, small establishments playing an important role. Indeed, the disproportionately high job-creation and job-destruction rates exhibited by young, small businesses may be interpreted as a healthy signal of the trial-and-error process inherent in experimentation.

ACKNOWLEDGMENTS

The analyses and conclusions set forth in this document are those of the authors and do not necessarily reflect the concurrence of the U.S. Bureau of the Census.

NOTES

1. Previous studies include Acs and Audretsch (1988), Baily, Bartelsman, and Haltiwanger (1996), Baily, Hulten, and Campbell (1992), Brown and Medoff (1989), Brown, Hamilton, and Medoff (1990), Davis and Haltiwanger (1991, 1996), Doms, Dunne, and Troske (1996), Dunne (1995), and Hansen (1992).

2. See Davis, Haltiwanger, and Schuh (1994) for a detailed characterization of the nature of the public discourse.

3. Other studies that raise similar concerns include Armington and Odle (1982a) and Brown, Hamilton, and Medoff (1990).

4. Using establishment-level as opposed to firm-level data is desirable for a number of reasons. Changes in ownership structure muddy the ability to track firms over time and the role of entry and exit. Accordingly, growth and decline at the firm level may reflect merger or divestiture activity as opposed to changes in the scale of activity at any given establishment. In addition, large complex firms have many establishments distributed across geographic locations and industries and thus measuring employment change at the establishment is essential to understand the variation in growth rates by region or industry.

5. At Census, part of the development of economywide longitudinal establishment-level databases has been the result of collaboration with the U.S. Small Business Administration.

6. See Aldrich et al. (1988), Armington and Odle (1982a, 1982b), Birch and MacCracken (1983), Birley (1984), Davis, Haltiwanger, and Schuh (1994, 1996), Howland (1988, ch. 2), Evans (1987a, 1987b), and the U.S. Small Business Administration (1983, 1987).

7. Detailed examples of these problems are presented in Davis, Haltiwanger, and Schuh (1994, 1996).

8. Given the manner in which data are collected, this pattern is possible even if the startup period is only a few months. Recall that the data are either point-in-time data (such as March 12 for a given year) or an annual average of monthly or quarterly values. In either case, plants that "opened" up just before the sampling period in the case of point-in-time data or toward the end of the sampling interval for annual average data could easily fit this pattern.

9. Brown, Hamilton, and Medoff (1990) also discuss this phenomenon.

10. Only in Census years can we measure total manufacturing employment for every firm. The Census of Manufactures available in the LRD are 1963, 1967, 1972, 1977, 1982, 1987, and 1992. For our firm-size analysis, we borrow from the results obtained by Davis, Haltiwanger, and Schuh (1996), who exploit the LRD from 1972 to 1988.

11. The size classes for small establishments are dominated by single-unit establishments so that the analysis for these establishment size classes is likely to be similar to that for firm-size classes.

12. Davis, Haltiwanger, and Schuh (1996) base their analysis on the LRD from 1972 and 1988. Where straightforward, we have updated their analysis to include the 1989 to 1993 period. This includes

Figures 5.1, 5.3, and 5.6. Figures 5.2 and 5.5 are drawn directly from Davis, Haltiwanger, and Schuh (1996).

REFERENCES

Acs, Zoltan, and David Audretsch. (1988). "Innovation in Large and Small Firms: An Empirical Analysis." *American Economic Review*, 78(4), 678–690.

Aldrich, Howard, Arne Kallenberg, Peter Marsden, and James Cassell. (1988). "In Pursuit of Evidence: Five Sampling Procedures for Locating New Businesses." Paper prepared for the 1988 Babson College Entrepreneurship Conference, MA.

Anderson, Patricia M., and Bruce D. Meyer. (1994). "The Nature and Extent of Turnover." *Brookings Papers on Economic Activity: Microeconomics*. Washington, DC: Brookings Institution.

Armington, Catherine, and Majorie Odle. (1982a). "Small Business: How Many Jobs?" *Brookings Review* (Winter).

Armington, Catherine, and Majorie Odle. (1982b). "Sources of Employment Growth, 1978–80." Washington, DC: Brookings Institution.

Baily, Martin, Eric J. Bartelsman, and John Haltiwanger. (1996). "Downsizing and Productivity Growth: Myth or Reality?" *Small Business Economics*, 8, 259–278.

Baily, Martin, Charles Hulten, and David Campbell. (1992). "The Distribution of Productivity in Manufacturing Plants." *Brookings Papers on Economic Activity: Microeconomics*. Washington, DC: Brookings Institution, 177–249.

Baldwin, John, and Garnet Picot. (1995). "Employment Generation by Small Producers in the Canadian Manufacturing Sector." *Small Business Economics*, 7(4), 317-331.

Birch, David L. (1979). *The Job-Generation Process*. Cambridge, MA: MIT Program on Neighborhood and Regional Change.

Birch, David L. (1987). *Job Creation in America: How Our Smallest Companies Put the Most People to Work*. New York: Free Press.

Birch, David, and Susan MacCracken. (1983). "The Small Business Share of Job Creation: Lessons Learned from the Use of a Longitudinal File." Unpublished report, MIT Program on Neighborhood and Regional Change.

Birley, Susan. (1984). "Finding the New Firm." *Proceedings of the Academy of Management Meetings*, 47, 64–68.

Borland, Jeff, and Richard Home. (1994). "Establishment-Level Employment in Manufacturing Industry: Is Small Really Beautiful?" Working Paper, University of Melbourne.

Brown, Charles, James Hamilton, and James Medoff. (1990). *Employers Large and Small*. Cambridge, MA: Harvard University Press.

Brown, Charles, and James Medoff. (1989). "The Employer Size Wage Effect." *Journal of Political Economy*, 97(5), 1027–1059.

Davis, Steven J., and John Haltiwanger. (1990). "Gross Job Creation and Destruction: Microeconomic Evidence and Macroeconomic Implications." *NBER Macroeconomics Annual*, 5, 123–168.

Davis, Steve J., and John Haltiwanger. (1991). "Wage Dispersion Between and Within U.S. Manufacturing Plants, 1963–86." *Brookings Papers on Economic Activity: Microeconomics*, Washington, DC: Brookings Institution, 115–200.

Davis, Steven J., and John Haltiwanger. (1992). "Gross Job Creation, Gross Job Destruction, and Employment Reallocation." *Quarterly Journal of Economics*, 107(3), 819–863.

Davis, Steven J., and John Haltiwanger. (1996). "Employer Size and the Wage Structure in U.S. Manufacturing." *Annales d' Economie et de Statistique*. January/July 323–368.

Davis, Steven J., John Haltiwanger, and Scott Schuh. (1994). "Small Business and Job Creation: Dissecting the Myth and Reassessing the Facts." In Lewis Solmon and Alec Leoinson eds *Labor Markets, Employment, and Job Creation*. Boulder, CO: Westview Press., 13–22.

Davis, Steven J., John Haltiwanger, and Scott Schuh. (1996). *Job Creation and Destruction*. Cambridge, MA: MIT Press.

Doms, Mark, Timothy Dunne, and Kenneth Troske. (1996). "Workers, Wages and Technology." *Quarterly Journal of Economics*.

Dunne, Timothy, (1995). "Patterns of Technology Usage in U.S. Manufacturing Plants." *Rand Journal of Economics*. 25(3), 488–499.

Dunne, Timothy, Mark Roberts, and Larry Samuelson. (1989). "The Growth and Failure of U.S. Manufacturing Plants." *Quarterly Journal of Economics*, 104(4), 671–698.

Ericson, Richard, and Ariel Pakes. (1989). "An Alternative Theory of Firm and Industry Dynamics." Working Paper, Yale University.

Evans, David. (1987a). "The Relationship Between Firm Growth, Size and Age: Estimates for One Hundred Manufacturing Industries." *Journal of Industrial Economics*, 35(4), 567–581.

Evans, David. (1987b). "Tests of Alternative Theories of Firm Growth." *Journal of Political Economy*, 95(4), 657–674.

Friedman, Milton. (1992). "Do Old Fallacies Ever Die?" *Journal of Economic Literature*, 30(4), 2129–2132.

Hansen, John A. (1992). "Innovation, Firm Size, and Firm Age." *Small Business Economics*, 4(1), 37–44.

Hopenhayn, Hugo. (1992). "Entry, Exit, and Firm Dynamics in Long-Run Equilibrium." *Econometrica*, 60(5), 1127–1150.

Howland, Marie. (1988). *Plant Closings and Worker Displacements: The Regional Issues*. Kalamazoo: Upjohn Institute for Employment Research.

Jovanovic, Boyan. (1982). "Selection and the Evolution of Industry." *Econometrica*, 50(3), 649–670.

Leonard, Jonathan S. (1986). "On the Size Distribution of Employment and Establishments." NBER Working Paper No. 1951.

Leonard, Jonathan S. (1987). "In the Wrong Place at the Wrong Time: The Extent of Frictional and Structural Unemployment." In Kevin Lang and J. Leonard (eds.), *Unemployment and the Structure of Labor Markets*. New York: Basil Blackwell.

U.S. Bureau of the Census. (1979). "The Standard Statistical Establishment Program." Bureau of the Census Technical Paper No. 44 (January), report prepared by the Economic Surveys Division.

U.S. Small Business Administration. (1983, 1987). *The State of Small Business: A Report of the President*. Washington, DC: U.S. Government Printing Office.

6. SMALL BUSINESS, ENTREPRENEURSHIP, AND INDUSTRIAL DYNAMICS

BO CARLSSON

Case Western Reserve University, Cleveland, OH

INTRODUCTION

Most firms are small and don't grow very much. Small firms have lower productivity and shorter life expectancy, pay lower wages, and provide fewer benefits and less employment security than large firms. They create a lot of new jobs, but they also often fail, so that their role as net creators of employment is unclear. Nevertheless, a strong argument can be made that small firms, especially entrepreneurial ones, are important—indeed, indispensable—for long-term economic growth and economic welfare.

As mentioned in the introduction to this volume, recent studies have shown that the trend toward larger firms that has characterized most lines of economic activity for over 150 years has been broken, and even reversed, in the last two decades in advanced industrial economies as well as in the transition economies of central and eastern Europe.[1] This trend reversal seems to have occurred at about the same time in many countries, even though differences in share of small firms in the economy persist among countries. This suggests that common factor, such as technological and institutional change, are at work, even though the cultural, historical, geographical, and other differences that have given rise to variations in the size structure of firms in different countries continue to exist.

The United States is a case in point. In recent years, small-business-dominated industries have increasd their employment faster than large-business-dominated industries, resulting in smaller business units on average. Average establishment size in most industries increased more or less continually from the beginning of this century until about 1980. Since then, average establishment size has declined substantially in industries with the largest establishments (manufacturing, mining, transportation), as well as in construction, while it has stayed constant or increased in other industries (particularly services) where the establishments are typically smaller (see Figure 6.1). The overall net result in terms of establishment size is a slight decline for the economy as a whole. While the number of establishments has increased in all industries over this entire period, the mechanisms that have led to smaller or larger firm or establishment size vary from industry to industry. For example, a decrease in firm size may be the result of net new entry (presumably of small firms) or net reduction in the number of large firms or in their employment.

As shown in Chapter 1, there is substantial evidence that the share of small firms in output and employment has increased in recent years. But even if this were not true, or if the opposite were true, it could well be argued that small firms are important for economic growth and economic welfare. Their importance is not determined, certainly not solely, by their share in the economy. This is the main argument of this chapter. It is akin to the idea of the role of yeast in making bread: it is only one of several ingredients, but without it the bread does not rise. Similarly, small firms play a unique role in the economy.

There are two main reasons that small firms are important—namely, efficiency and dynamics. The essence of the efficiency argument is that small firms do certain things better than large firms. As a result, through division of labor between small and large firms, the efficiency of the economy is increased. The argument with respect to dynamics is that small firms are needed to provide the entrepreneurship and variety required for macroeconomic growth and stability.

THE CONTRIBUTION OF SMALL FIRMS TO ECONOMIC EFFICIENCY

Division of Labor in Production

Small firms can provide certain goods and services better and more efficiently than large firms. Even in the presence of pervasive scale economies, there is evidence that small firms are able not only to survive but actually to thrive. In industries characterized by large economies of scale, such as automobiles and steel, small firms continue to coexist with large. Small and large firms specialize in different product segments and are more often collaborators than competitors. The recent increase in outsourcing among large U.S. firms is a result of increased specialization (division of labor) among firms. Table 6.1 provides examples of types of activities that large firms once performed in-house but more recently have decided to purchase from smaller, more specialized firms instead. Typically, outsourcing involves special functions, products, or services that are not part of the core competence of large firms and that can be more efficiently performed by smaller, more specialized firms. These small firms usually carry out their operations on at least as large a scale as would the large companies if they performed the same operations in-house. The work may be subcontracted because the processes involved are messy, cannot be carried out alongside the other processes used by the large firms, require different skills or work

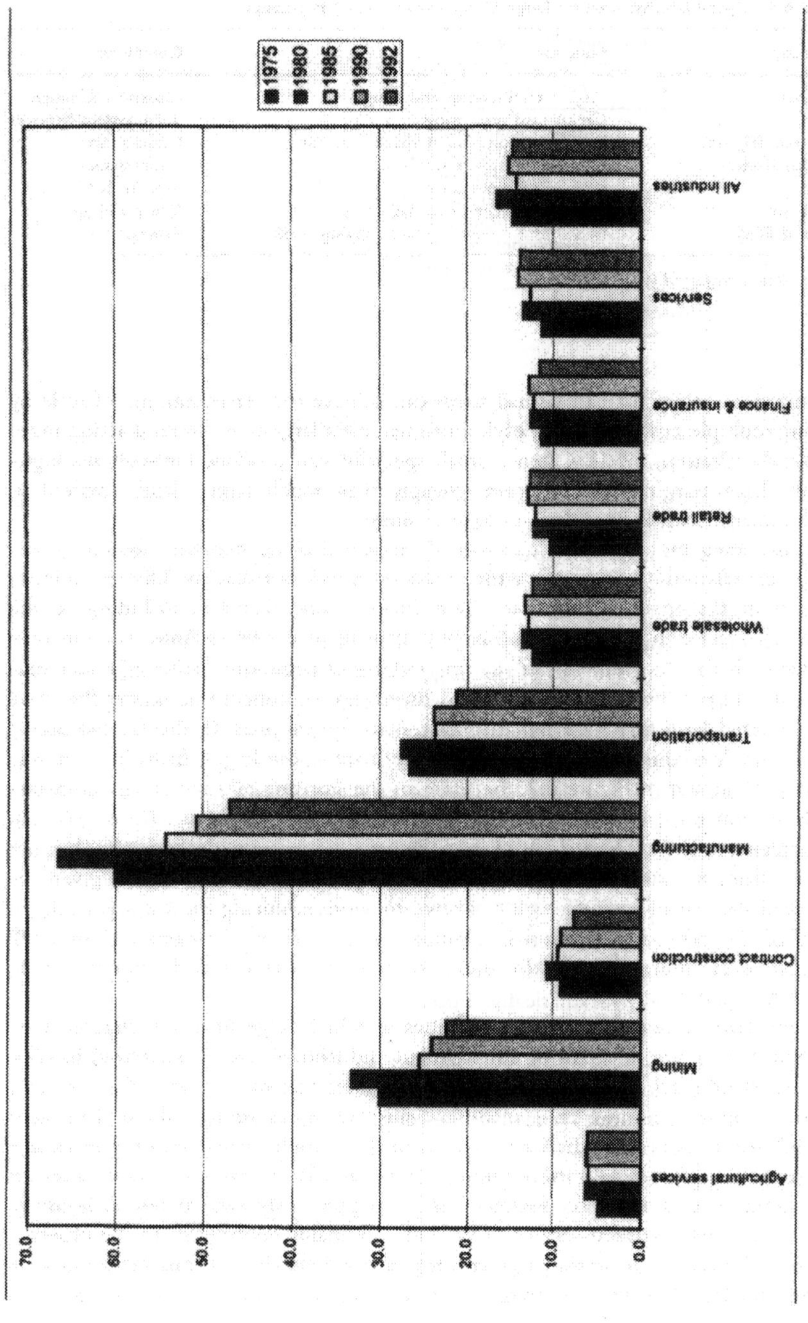
1975
1980
1985
1990
1992
70.0
60.0
50.0
40.0
30.0
20.0
10.0
0.0
Agricultural services
Mining
Contract construction
Manufacturing
Transportation
Wholesale trade
Retail trade
Finance & insurance
Services
All industries

Figure 6.1.

Table 6.1. Operations Assigned by Large Companies to Small Businesses

Company	Function	Contractor
Du Pont	Project engineering and design	Morrison Knudsen
AT&T	Credit-card processing	Total System Services
Northern Telecom	Electronic component manufacturing	Comptronix
Eastman Kodak	Computer support services	Businessland
Mobil	Refinery maintenance	Serv-Tech
Whirlpool	Distribution center management	Kenco Group
National Steel	Mail-room operations and copying work	Ameriscribe

Source: *Wall Street Journal* (1991, p. B1).

organization, or are such that small firms can achieve greater economies of scale by serving multiple customers than each customer, even large ones, could if acting independently (Pratten, 1991). Often a small specialist can produce low-volume, high-quality, high-margin products more cheaply than much larger firms involved in large-volume, standardized, low-margin businesses.

Outsourcing by large firms to small of services that are necessary for companies to operate efficiently and to serve their customers well but that are different in character from the main activities in these firms is one factor contributing to the observed decline in the size of the largest firms in recent years. Another contributing factor is the "deglomeration" or unbundling of economic activities, concentration on core products and activities, and divestiture of noncore businesses that have characterized large firms during the last ten to fifteen years. In the United States, the net result of this is a sharp decline in the share of the largest firms in economic activity. As shown in Figure 6.2, the share of the Fortune 500 industrial companies in manufacturing employment declined from nearly 80 percent in 1975 to less than 60 percent in 1996. Their share of manufacturing shipments declined also, but less steeply: from 83 percent in 1975 to 75 percent in 1996. But of course, given the observed decline of manufacturing relative to services during the same period, the share of the 500 largest industrial companies in total employment and in GDP dropped even more dramatically: from 16.8 to 8.4 percent and from 55 to 37 percent, respectively.

Restructuring and focusing the activities in which large firms are engaged tend to reduce their size in terms of employment and (though less dramatically) in sales. But the divestitures usually involve lines of business that have a better fit in another firm in a similar business. Thus, manufacturing businesses are typically sold to other manufacturing firms and therefore remain in the manufacturing sector. The same is not true with respect to outsourcing of service activities: here the typical pattern is for manufacturing firms to outsource services previously carried out in-house to existing or newly created service firms. This is a major contributor to the observed decline of manufacturing employment. But if the definition of manufacturing were to be broadened to include engineering and management services, legal services,

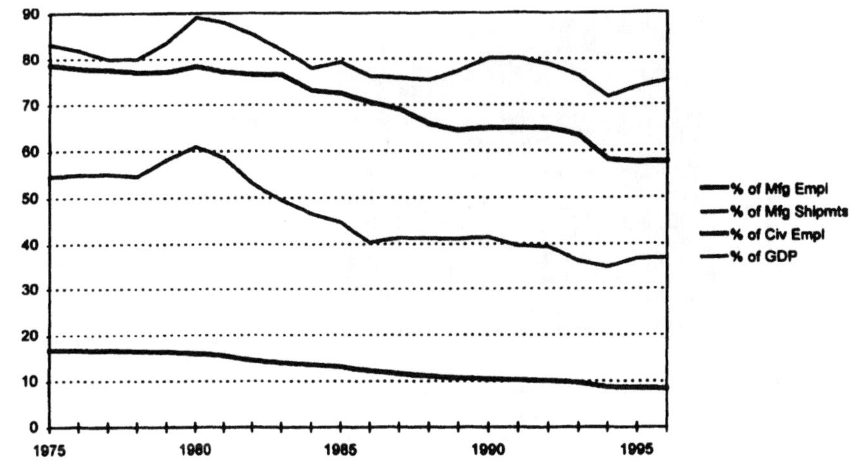

Figure 6.2.

and business services—arthritis that have been involved in outsourcing in recent years—it turns out that the share of manufacturing firms in the total economy has been quite stable over the last twenty years, even if measured in terms of employment (Karaomerlioglu and Carlsson 1997) (see Figure 6.3).

Outsourcing is a good example of the division of labor between large and small firms. Another aspect of the division of labor involves the greater flexibility that can be achieved in smaller operations. By virtue of their small size, absence of bureaucracy, less rigidity in decision-making, and so on, small firms are often quicker than large firms to respond to new opportunities and threats. Examples abound of cases in which small companies can fill a specific order in twenty-four hours but large companies would require a week to fill, the same order. Less formal organization, fewer work rules, better individual incentives, and closer links between individual effort and company performance in small firms than large all contribute to the greater flexibility of small firms.

Division of Labor in Innovation

Another dimension of the efficiency argument runs along the lines of division of labor in innovative activities. There is a large literature and a continuing debate in economics regarding the role of large versus small firms in innovation.[2] On one hand, large firms may be expected to dominate innovative activity by virtue of their

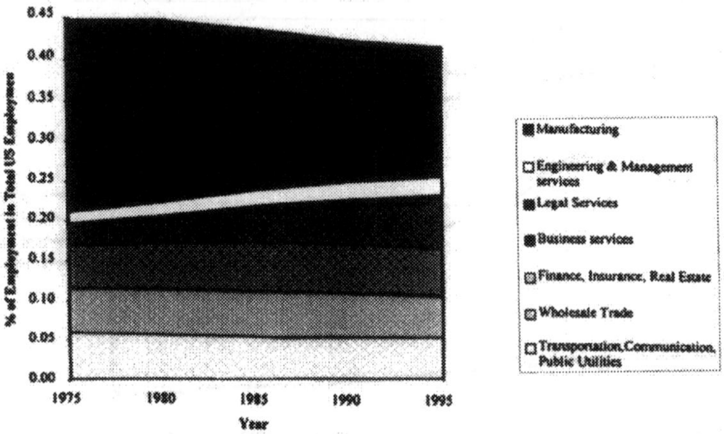

Figure 6.3.

ability to reap economies of scale and scope: spreading fixed costs over larger output and a greater product range, having greater ability to appropriate the results of R&D, and being able to take greater risks (Acs, 1996, pp. 25–27). On the other hand, small firms may have an advantage by being less bureaucratic, being able to exploit innovations that are too modest to interest larger firms, and providing more direct personal incentives (Scherer, 1988, pp. 4–5). On balance, there is a role for both large and small firms, but they are good at different things. Small firms tend to have the innovative advantage in certain industries, and large firms in others. For example, the number of innovations per employee tends to be much higher in small firms than in large in computing equipment, control instruments, scientific instruments, and measuring devices, while the opposite is true in tires, chemicals, and industrial machinery (Acs, 1996, p. 34).

Consider this illustration of the division of labor in innovation. The high rate of technological change in many industries and the shift to more knowledge-based activities increase the degree of specialization, resulting among other things in increased reliance on networks of specialized agents to carry out functions that would be too expensive to accomplish in large, hierarchical organizations. Examples of this are so-called technological systems—networks of actors interacting in a particular field of technology within a particular institutional framework to generate, diffuse, and utilize technology (Carlsson and Stankiewicz, 1991; Carlsson, 1997). These networks comprise not only business firms but also academic institutions, research institutes, industry associations, and government agencies. Some systems are dominated by large firms, especially where innovation is design-driven (such as, for example, in factory automation where the main players have typically been large firms working with suppliers of machinery, equipment, and systems). But where innovation is discovery-driven (experimental), the process is often dominated by small firms. Biotechnology is an obvious case. For example, Losec (marketed as Prilosec in the United States)—the world's best-selling drug in 1997—was developed by a small subsidiary of the Astra pharmaceutical company in Sweden, which had an entrepreneurial culture and lacked the large-scale chemical-process industry tradition characteristic of many large pharmaceutical firms, giving it the freedom to experiment (Eliasson and Eliasson, 1997). In fact, the pattern in the whole biotechnology sector seems to be that new products are developed in small, specialized firms that are then often acquired by large pharmaceutical firms when the capital requirements for large-scale production and marketing escalate. The challenge then is for the large firms to nurture the innovativeness of the acquired entities and not stifle it by imposing large-company bureaucracy.

Another example of the division of labor in innovation is found in the clustering, both geographically and in technology, of firms in high-technology industries such as semiconductors and biotechnology where small firms play an important role in specialist functions. A certain critical mass of activity is required, but given the high degree of uncertainty and consequent risk of failure, it is necessary to have many actors acting independently, operating under different rules, making different assumptions, and thus evaluating uncertain prospects differently. If all these actors were all under the same management, the stakes would be too high, and the chances of progress much smaller.

In addition, it has been shown that startups in some fields, such as semiconductors, are oriented toward exploration of diversity by targeting relatively uncrowded technological fields in peripheral areas with few players, whereas larger companies typically target technological fields with higher density in terms of both the number of actors and number of activities involved (Almeida and Kogut, 1997). This raises the degree of variety, which, as we shall see, is important from a dynamic perspective.

DYNAMICS: THE CONTRIBUTION OF SMALL ENTREPRENEURIAL FIRMS TO ECONOMIC GROWTH AND STABILITY

In addition to the contributions small firms make to the division of labor and hence the efficiency of the economy, they also contribute strongly to economic growth and stability. In fact, it is the connection between entrepreneurship and small business that makes small business interesting in an economic-growth perspective, not the share of small firms in economic activity at a particular point in time. Whereas the static effects of the division of labor between large and small firms may involve the vast majority of firms, the dynamic effects are tied to a small subset of firms—namely, those that are entrepreneurial. That is why there is not necessarily any connection between a large share of small firms in an economy or industry and economic growth; if there is a connection, it depends on the entrepreneurship exercised by small firms.

Small Firms as Entrepreneurs

To the extent that small firms are new entrants into an industry, they serve as carriers of new ideas, particularly with regard to product innovation, less so with respect to process innovation. Although the contribution of small firms to net job creation varies over the business cycle (see Chapters 4 and 5 in this volume), small businesses generate two-thirds of *initial* job opportunities and are responsible for most of the initial, on-the-job training in basic skills (U.S. Small Business Administration, 1997, p. 5).

Small firms provide the lion's share of entrepreneurship: most startups are, of course, small. Small firms are not necessarily more innovative than large firms, but *new* firms (which are typically small) are often the carriers of new ideas. Thus, a high rate of entry is associated with fast economic growth. As shown in Table 6.2, 40 percent or more of all firms in the U.S. office machinery, electronic components, and communications equipment industries in 1986 were firms that had been established in 1980 or later. These are also among the most innovative and highest-growth industries. At the opposite end of the spectrum, new firms accounted for

Table 6.2. Percentage of 1986 Firms and Employment Accounted for by Enterprises Started in 1980 to 1986

	Number of Firms	Percent of Employment
Office machinery	46.41	1.50%
Electronic components	41.72	7.24
Communications equipment	39.60	2.89
Motor vehicles	37.92	1.41
Other transportation equipment	37.68	9.33
Textiles and apparel	37.13	8.26
Radio and TV equipment	36.99	3.58
Scientific and measuring instruments	36.99	5.45
Drugs and medicinals	35.95	1.24
Optical, surgical, and photographic instruments	35.25	4.87
Other manufacturing	34.93	8.25
Other electrical equipment	34.21	4.65
Rubber	33.43	6.68
Total manufacturing	**32.61**	**5.31**
Ferrous metals	32.51	5.62
Industrial chemicals	32.30	2.03
Aircraft	31.80	0.73
Petroleum	31.27	2.51
Lumber and furniture	31.24	11.79
Nonelectrical machinery	29.39	6.42
Food	29.37	3.37
Paper	29.10	3.59
Fabricated metal products	28.96	8.07
Other chemicals	28.66	2.28
Nonferrous metals	27.46	5.43
Stone, clay, and glass	25.76	5.48

Source: Audretsch (1995, pp. 114–115).

less than 29 percent of the firms in the stone, clay and glass, nonferrous metals, other chemicals, and fabricated metal products industries—all among the lowest-growth and least innovative industries. The main function of the new firms is to create new lines of business as well as new competitors for existing firms, thus increasing the competitive pressure. Their primary role is not to provide employment: as shown in the table, the share of new firms in total employment is much lower in all industries than their share of the total number of firms.

Of course, new growth opportunities can be created not only through the vehicle of entrepreneurship (starting new firms) but also through innovative activities in existing firms. As was indicated in the previous section, small firms provide a large share of innovations (more in some industries than others). According to the U.S. Small Business Administration, small firms (those with fewer than 500 employees) are responsible for more than half (about 55 percent) of all innovations, and they produce twice as many product innovations per employee as large firms. They also obtain more patents per sales dollar than large firms, even though the latter are more likely to patent discoveries; this implies that small firms have more discoveries than large (U.S. Small Business Administration, 1997, p. 6, based on data reported in Edwards and Gordon, 1984).

Thus, the role of small firms as innovators can be summed up as that of creating new ideas that may result either in the startup of new firms (entrepreneurship) or in new products and processes. They provide new grist for the economic mill, as it were.

Small Firms as a Source of Macroeconomic Stability

But it isn't just that new (and therefore small) firms provide a disproportionate share of new ideas that generate new business opportunities and hence economic growth. New business opportunities also give rise to what Schumpeter called *creative destruction*. The term itself implies that there are two sides to creative destruction: the positive side involves increased variety, and the negative side involves increased turbulence, and together they result in both the creation and destruction of jobs and firms. In a dynamic perspective, both are essential. Burton Klein (1977), Gunnar Eliasson (1984, 1991), and Paul Reynolds (1997), among others, have demonstrated that stable growth at the macroeconomic level requires a great deal of heterogeneity (and resulting instability) at the micro level.

One way in which small firms contribute to macroeconomic stability is that they increase the range of options available to deal with adversity. Klein argues that "generally speaking, highly structured organizations are inefficient when dealing with changes in their environment" (Klein, 1977, p. 58). Established routines enable them to deal effectively and efficiently with expected challenges but not with unpredicted ones. By contrast, more loosely structured organizations (many of which are small firms) are more flexible and can therefore respond more effectively to new challenges.

Another way small firms contribute to macro stability is that they increase the variety of approaches to innovation. This has nothing to do with whether small firms are more innovative than large. Even if small and large firms are equally capable at R&D, there are nonetheless important social advantages associated with both large and small firm size. Having more firms simply provides more independent approaches to innovation. Hence, industries composed of a greater number of firms will be characterized by a greater amount of technological diversity (Cohen and Klepper, 1992). As Metcalfe (1995) has demonstrated, technology can be treated in terms of knowledge, skills, and artifacts. In each case there are different variety-generating mechanisms, different selection processes, and different institutional structures. This is another reason that a mixture of small and large firms contributes to macro stability.

It has also been suggested that technological diversity itself influences firm R&D expenditures within industries (Cohen and Klepper, 1992). As Burton Klein (1977, p. 30) put it:

> Competition, as defined in dynamic terms, plays a major role in explaining both the regularity and the rate of progress (the degree of macrostability). Because firms cannot predict each other's discoveries, they undertake different approaches toward achieving the same goal. And because not all of the approaches will turn out to be equally successful, the pursuit of parallel paths provides the options required for smooth progress. On the other hand, the rate of advance in an industry will depend upon the degree of competitive interaction. The more unpredictable the discoveries in a particular industry (the greater the diversity of behavior in that industry), the greater will be the rate of advance firms demand from each other. Conversely, if firms could predict each other's advances, they would not have to insure themselves against uncertainty by taking risks. And no smooth progress would occur.

Experience suggests that when firms no longer face genuine challenges, they have only a small chance of remaining dynamic. Therefore, without variety, the economy stagnates or declines. In simulations on the Swedish micro-to-macro model, Eliasson has demonstrated that without steady input of innovative technical change through new investment, entry of new firms, and exit, it is impossible in the long run to sustain micro diversity. In the absence of such diversity, incumbent firms become too much alike, and the economy becomes too vulnerable to sudden changes so that it eventually collapses. Both entry and exit are necessary; if either entry or exit is impeded, the economy becomes unstable and slows down.

Thus, the rate of economic progress is determined by degree of risk taking: the higher the degree of competitive interaction, the more rapid will be the rate of growth. And the easier entry is into an industry, the higher the likely degree of risk taking. The smoothness of progress is mainly determined by the number of firms in an industry. Industries that are made up of only a few large firms exhibit much more volatile behavior over time than those characterized by a large number of entities of varying size. Certainly the experience over the last several decades in the former centrally planned economies confirms this view. The privatization of the huge state-owned enterprises was necessary but not sufficient; without new entry and vigorous competition (partly through breakup of existing entities) privatization has resulted only in the enrichment of a few individuals, not stable macroeconomic growth.

Recently, Reynolds (1997) studied births and deaths of establishments and jobs in 382 U.S. labor market areas over the period 1980 to 1988. He concluded that no matter what measures are utilized, higher levels of business volatility are strongly associated with economic growth. But turbulence, by itself, is not a source of economic growth. It is a necessary but not sufficient condition. This is consistent with the interpretation that unless the new jobs and firms that are created also expand the variety in the economy, they do not create growth. Entry and exit can cancel each other out; only *innovative entry* causes the range of opportunities to expand. Thus, for stable macroeconomic growth to take place, a great deal of micro heterogeneity and instability is necessary.

CONCLUSION

Small firms are important from a variety of points of view, as indicated by the various contributions to this volume. From the perspective of industrial dynamics as presented in the present essay, small firms are important for two main reasons. The first is that small firms contribute to economic efficiency through division of labor. In production, small firms and large specialize in different segments within the same fields, so that there is more often cooperation than competition between firms of different sizes. The outsourcing of certain activities, especially services, in which large firms have been engaged in recent years is a result of this division of labor; its structural consequences were outlined above. In innovation, it was shown that small firms and large are good at different things. In particular, small firms dominate in discovery-driven innovation processes, and large firms dominate in design-driven ones. In cases of a high degree of uncertainty, many small firms acting independently of each other are more likely to make discoveries than large, monolithic organizations. Also, small startups in certain fields tend to target relatively peripheral and less crowded technological fields, thus increasing the variety of new discoveries.

The second, and arguably more important, contribution is made by a subset of small firms—namely, those that are entrepreneurial. Whereas the share of small firms in the economy has no inherent connection to economic growth, the fact that new firms are typically small and that new firms are often carriers of new ideas makes small, entrepreneurial firms essential in economic growth. They are often the vehicles for creating new opportunities and increased variety. As such, they are a source of stable macroeconomic growth. The growth process fundamentally involves creative destruction. Stable growth at the macro level is associated with a fair amount of turmoil—creation and destruction of jobs, births and deaths of firms—at the micro level. But it is not just entry and exit that are important; what is needed is *innovative* entry that opens up new business opportunities and raises the competitive pressure. This results in a great deal of heterogeneity and volatility (entry and exit) at the micro level. Without that, the economy eventually stagnates or even collapses.

NOTES

1. See, for example, Acs (1996), Carlsson(1992), Loveman and Sengenberger (1991), and OECD (1996).

2. See Acs and Audretsch (1990) and Acs (1996) for a summary of the literature.

REFERENCES

Acs, Zoltan J. (1996). "Small Firms and Economic Growth." In P.H. Admiraal (ed.), *Small Business in the Modern Economy*. Oxford: Blackwell.

Acs, Zoltan, J., and David B. Audretsch. (1990). *The Economics of Small Firms: A European Challenge*. Dordrecht: Kluwer Academic.

Almeida, Paul, and Bruce Kogut. (1997). "The Exploration of Technological Diversity and the Geographic Localization of Innovation." *Small Business Economics*, 9(1), 21–31.

Audretsch, David. (1995). *Innovation and Industry Evolution*. Cambridge, MA: MIT Press.

Carlsson, Bo. (1992). "The Rise of Small Business: Causes and Consequences." In W.J. Adams (ed.), *Singular Europe: Economy and Polity of the European Community After 1992*. Ann Arbor: Michigan University Press.

Carlsson, Bo (ed.), (1997). *Technological Systems and Industrial Dynamics*. Dordrecht: Kluwer Academic.

Carlsson, Bo, and Rikard Stankiewicz. (1991). "On the Nature, Function, and Composition of Technological Systems." *Journal of Evolutionary Economics*, 1(2), 93–118.

Cohen, Wesley M., and Steven Klepper. (1992). "The Tradeoff Between Firm Size and Diversity in the Pursuit of Technological Progress." *Small Business Economics*, 4(1), 1–14.

Edwards, Keith L., and Theodore J. Gordon. (1984). "Characterization of Innovations Introduced on the U.S. Market in 1982." The Futures Group, prepared for the U.S. Small Business Administration under Contract No. SBA-6050-0A-82, March.

Eliasson, Gunnar. (1984). "Micro Heterogeneity of Firms and the Stability of Industrial Growth." *Journal of Economic Behavior and Organization*, 5, 249–274.

Eliasson, Gunnar. (1991). "Deregulation, Innovative Entry and Structural Diversity as a Source of Stable and Rapid Economic Growth." *Journal of Evolutionary Economics*, 1(1), 49–63.

Eliasson, Gunnar, and Åsa Eliasson. (1997). "The Pharmaceutical and Biotechnological Competence Bloc and the Development of Losec." In B. Carlsson (ed.), *Technological System and Industrial Dynamics* (pp. 139–168). Dordrecht: Kluwer Academic.

Karaomerlioglu, Dilek C., and Bo Carlsson. (1997). "Manufacturing in Decline? A Matter of Definition." Paper presented at the European Association for Research in Industrial Economics (EARIE) conference, Leuven, Belgium, August 31–September 3.

Klein, Burton H. (1977). *Dynamic Economics*. Boston: Harvard University Press.

Loveman, Gary, and Werner Sengenberger. (1991). "The Re-Emergence of Small-Scale Production: An International Comparison." *Small Business Economics*, 3(1), 1–39.

Metcalfe, J. Stanley. (1995). "Technology Systems and Technology Policy in an Evolutionary Framework." *Cambridge Journal of Economics*, 19(1), 25–46.

Organization for Economic Cooperation and Development (OECD). (1996). *SMEs: Employment, Innovation and Growth*. Paris: OECD.

Pratten, Cliff. (1991). *The Competitiveness of Small Firms*. Cambridge: Cambridge University Press.

Reynolds, Paul D. (1997). "Business Volatility: Source or Symptom of Economic Growth?" In Z.J. Acs, B. Carlsson, and C. Karlsson (eds.), *Entrepreneurship, Small and Medium-Sized Enterprises, and the Macroeconomy*. Cambridge: Cambridge University Press.

Scherer, Fredric M. (1988). Testimony Before the Subcommittee on Monopolies and Commercial Law, Committee of the Judiciary, U.S. House of Representatives, February 24.

U.S. Small Business Administration. (1997). "Facts About Small Business." www.sbaonline.sba.gov/ADVO/stats/fact1.html, p. 5.

Wall Street Journal. (1991). September 11, p. B1.

7. WOMEN-OWNED BUSINESSES: WHY DO THEY MATTER?

CANDIDA BRUSH

Boston University, Boston, MA

ROBERT D. HISRICH

Case Western Reserve University, Cleveland, OH

Elizabeth Arden and her kind, in other words, are not professional women. They are women by profession, and, as such, they do not belong in an enumeration of women industrialists.
—*Fortune* (August 1935)

The role of women in entrepreneurial endeavors has changed dramatically over the past decades. Since 1970, women's share of small businesses increased from 5 percent to 38 percent, growing from 1.5 million to nearly 8 million in number (U.S. Small Business Administration, 1995b). Today, women-owned businesses contribute more than $2.3 trillion in sales and employ one out of every four company workers, a total of 18.5 million employees (National Foundation of Women Business Owners, 1996). Less than three decades ago few women-owned businesses achieved sales of greater than $1 million, but now more than 600,000 boast sales greater than this figure (NFWBO, 1992).

In addition to this growth in numbers, women are now visible in all industrial sectors, including construction, automotive parts, and engineering (U.S. Small Business Administration, 1995a; NFWBO, 1996). Although a majority of women-owned firms are concentrated in services (53 percent), retail trade (18.6 percent), and finance, insurance, and real estate (10.2 percent) (SBA, 1995a, p. 65), there have been significant increases in all sectors. Between 1987 and 1992, women's participation in all sectors grew overall, the largest growth occurring in construction (94 percent),

Table 7.1. Women's Entrepreneurship: Growth

A. Number, 1970 to 1997

Year	Number (millions)	Share (percent)
1970	1.5 million	5%
1980	2.3	26
1990	5.3	32
1997	8.0	38

B. Sector, 1987 to 1992 (percent)

Sector	Women-Owned Businesses	All
Construction	94%	10%
Wholesale	87	23
Transportation	77	17
Agriculture, forestry, fisheries	72	21
Manufacturing	62	20
Mining	41	24
Retail	36	11
Finance, insurance, real estate	38	58
Services	39	31
Total	43%	26%

wholesale (87 percent), and transportation (77 percent) (see Table 7.1). Not only has the number of women-owned businesses risen, but their share has increased across sectors. Their growth outpaces that of their male counterparts, with women-owned firms growing at 43.1 percent compared to all firms at 26.0 percent between 1987 to 1992. Further, the ratio for growth in number of women owned in some sectors—such as construction, transportation, communications, utilities, agricultural services, forestry and fishing firms, and retail trade—is at least three times greater than that for all firms (SBA, 1995a, p. 63). On the other hand, women's share of businesses continues to remain small in certain areas—for instance, in agriculture, forestry, and fishing, mining, and transportation women's share is less than 4 percent of all businesses (NFWBO, 1994, p. I-21). In spite of this, women continue to start and acquire businesses in these areas. For instance, women's shares of businesses in the construction industry and in wholesale trade have increased (SBA, 1995a).

Despite this dramatic growth, the reasons that women-owned businesses differ from their male counterparts are not well understood. In part, this stems from a lack of visibility of women entrepreneurs and their businesses in both academic publications and popular press (Baker, Aldrich, and Liou, 1997). Scholarly research is extremely limited in numbers of studies focusing on or including women business owners, hovering around 7 to 10 percent (Baker, Aldrich, and Liou, 1997). Numbers of government-funded studies focusing on or including women is similarly slim,

Table 7.2. Studies of Women Entrepreneurs and Businesses

	Number of studies of Women	Total Number of studies	Percent
Government funded, 1977–1995	10	360	3%
Research conferences, 1993–1995	6	240	3
Academic journals, 1977–1995	77	1,500	5

numbering 10 of 360 between 1977 and 1995 (3 percent) (see Table 7.2). Compared to the number of women business owners, this is a large discrepancy that leads to unfounded speculations about performance, management characteristics, and style—as well as about the contributions of women-owned businesses.

The role of women-owned businesses can be better understood by taking a broader perspective about their role in society over time and examining the social context influencing women business owners. This chapter presents an historical overview of the role of women in the workforce and discusses the trends that encouraged their entry into business ownership. Following the summary of current research highlighting the state of our knowledge on women-owned businesses is a theoretical discussion of factors influencing differences in women's approach to business ownership. The chapter concludes with a discussion of contributions of women-owned businesses and future considerations.

WOMEN'S ENTREPRENEURSHIP: A HISTORICAL PERSPECTIVE

Less than half a century ago the entire workforce in the United States was composed of less than 26 percent women, who most often were employed as secretaries, nurses, or teachers (Bergman, 1986). Women's entry into and increased presence in the workplace was strongly influenced by several trends and developments, particularly regulatory changes, social trends, and family transitions.

Regulatory events—notably the passage of the Civil Rights Act in 1964 (prohibiting discrimination based on gender), the Equal Credit Opportunity Act in 1975, and the Affirmative Action Act in 1978—helped to remove structural barriers that women faced in business ownership. The first national government study of women business owners, *The Bottom Line* (President's Task Force on Women Business Owners, 1979) documented their participation, barriers, and contributions. Ten years later, the passage of the Women's Business Ownership Act provided set-asides for women business owners, and created the National Women's Business Council—a group of business owners that works with intergovernment agency representatives to advocate and represent issues and concerns of women business owners. This Act also called for data collection on businesses owned by women through studies by the government and developed incentives to decrease barriers and provide funding for startups through U.S. Small Business Administration (SBA) guaranteed loans. While in 1988 women received nearly 10 percent of federal procurement dollars (SBA, 1988), in 1994 women received 14 percent of the $6.4 billion SBA guaranteed loans. These percentages are small compared to procurements and loan guarantees received by men, but it is expected that these amounts will increase given new programs such as the Women's Prequalification Loan Program and Micro-Loan Programs. Additional programs assisting and supporting the development of women-owned businesses are Women's Demonstration Programs, which provide training and counseling, and the Women's Network for Entrepreneurial Training (WNET).

Parallel to regulatory changes, the role of women in society also has changed. One important event was the birth of the feminist movement marked by the publication of Betty Friedan's *Feminine Mystique* in 1963. The National Organization for Women (NOW) was founded with the goal of bringing women into full participation in American society. As more women successfully created, managed, and grew companies, greater recognition of their achievements was recorded by the media and government. Women's networking groups such as the Committee of 200 and national professional associations including the National Association of Women Business Owners (NAWBO) were founded. Organizations providing information and research emerged, notably Catalyst, the National Foundation for Women Business Owners (NFWBO), and the National Education Center for Women in Business (NECWB). Publications directed toward women, such as *Entrepreneurial Women* and *Working Women*, also emerged. These developments helped to provide support, resources, and greater legitimacy for women entrepreneurs.

In addition to these influences, family-life transitions contributed to the increased numbers of women business owners. Increased divorce rates, and consequently a rise in single-parent families, often pushed women into entrepreneurial endeavors. Likewise, trends toward smaller families and longer lifespans all influenced women's participation in business ownership. In some cases, divorced women started businesses out of economic necessity, whereas women starting families later decided to begin home-based enterprises after pursuing corporate careers (Moore and Buttner, 1997).

RESEARCH ON WOMEN BUSINESS OWNERS: WHAT DO WE KNOW?

Comparatively few research studies over the past thirty years have focused on or included women business owners. A comprehensive review of both practitioner and scholarly journals by Baker, Aldrich, and Liou (1997) found the percentage of articles about women business owners has declined from 1980 to 1995 from 44 percent to 14 percent. In the popular press, the proportions were lower—especially for the *Wall Street Journal* and the *New York Times*, where articles about women business owners were around 5 percent of all business articles between 1980 and 1990 (Baker, Aldrich, and Liou, 1997).

Similarly, a 1987 Proceedings of the Babson College Research Conference on Entrepreneurship, *Frontiers of Entrepreneurship*,[1] categorized 227 studies published between 1980 to 1987 by topic and found that only thirteen (6 percent) investigated women and minority business owners. Between 1988 and 1993, 522 studies were identified with summaries published in this proceedings. Of these, seventeen (3 percent) focused on women-owned businesses, and thirty-five (7 percent) included gender as a variable. These reviews provide an indication that women business owners are understudied.

Why are women so "invisible" in the literature? Baker, Aldrich, and Liou (1997) suggests that since few differences are empirically shown, it is not productive to focus on women if they are similar in approaches and practices to business ownership. There is a basis to this argument. Motives for venture creation (independence, achievement, job satisfaction) are shown to be similar for both men and women (Schrier, 1975; Schwartz, 1976; Hisrich and Brush, 1983; Chaganti, 1986), while demographic characteristics including marital status (married), age (thirty to forty-five), and birth order (first-born) are also equivalent by sex (Hisrich and Brush, 1983; Sexton and Kent, 1981; Neider, 1987). Years of work experience and education are also parallel for men and women (Hisrich and Brush, 1983; Stevenson, 1986; Birley, Moss, and Saunders, 1987).

On the other hand, it is important to point out that the bulk of research is seldom comparative, including both men and women. The authors conducted a comprehensive review of eighty-nine entrepreneurship studies and found that although more than 50 percent of studies focus on individual characteristics of women entrepreneurs, less than 29 percent compared men and women entrepreneurs in their samples, the remainder being based on samples of only women (see Table 7.3).

Conclusions about differences may be subject to question because a majority of the instruments employed by researchers to measure entrepreneurial traits are derived from research on samples of male entrepreneurs (Hurley, 1991; Brush, 1992). For instance, McClelland's (1961) work on need for achievement as a motivation for entrepreneurship emerged from research on young men. Collins and Moore (1969) studied motivations of male founders in manufacturing firms and concluded that these individuals had unresolved fears of their fathers motivating them to pursue autonomy through business creation. Measures and instruments rooted in this work were subsequently developed using samples of males (Kent, Sexton, and Vesper, 1982) and therefore may not fully explain the motives and psychological traits of women entrepreneurs. Holmquist and Sundin (1988) support this by noting that a majority of entrepreneurial theories are created by men and for men and applied to men. Furthermore, more recent research using attribution theory shows that women do differ from men in their explanations of personal self-efficacy (Gatewood, Shaver, and Gartner, 1995). Cooper and Artz (1995) found no evidence

Table 7.3. State of Entrepreneurship Research: What We Know

Topics	Number of Entrepreneurship Studies	Percent Comparing Men and Women Eutrepreneurs	Trend
Individual	46	51%	+
Organizations	22	25	+
Process	15	17	+
Environment	6	7	−
Total	89	100%	

that women were satisfied with lower financial results but noted that women may perceive greater levels of satisfaction than men given a certain level of financial performance. Hence the argument reached by Baker, Aldrich, and Liou (1997) that differences between men and women are minimal is based on very few comparative studies, many of which are descriptive in nature and less recent.

Research examining organization characteristics of women-owned businesses is similarly sparse. Only twenty-two (or 25 percent) of the studies reviewed examined organizational aspects of women-owned businesses. Again, descriptive methodologies were used, and fewer than half the studies were comparative. Early studies showed that women-owned firms are predominantly service oriented (Scott, 1986; Neider, 1987; Hisrich and Brush, 1983) and small in terms of revenues and employees (Hisrich and Brush, 1987; Scott, 1986; Johnson and Storey, 1993).

More recent work examines strategies, management, and organizational structures of women-owned businesses. Srinivasan, Woo, and Cooper (1994) found that male-owned businesses were more likely to survive if started with greater initial capital and professional advice, whereas women-owned firms survived if the business was similar to the type of organization where the owner was previously employed. Research on strategies suggests that women emphasize quality orientation more than men (Chaganti and Parasuraman, 1994). Carter, Williams, and Reynolds (1997) examined startup resources and survival in men- and women-owned retail businesses and found that strategic choice for women could enhance survival, whereas for men prior business experience and human capital were more influential. Other studies of performance suggest that women-owned firms are no less likely to fail (Kalleberg and Leicht, 1991; Johnson and Storey, 1993) but may grow more slowly than their male counterparts (Hisrich and Brush, 1987).

Hence, research about differences in men- and women-owned businesses is inconclusive, mainly due to the small numbers of studies that are comparative and comprehensive. In particular, studies controlling for industry sector and systematically analyzing for business age, size, strategy, policies, organizational structure, and other factors comparing men- and women-owned businesses are nearly absent from research; notable exceptions are Kalleberg and Leicht (1991), Johnson and Storey (1993), and Carter, Williams, and Reynolds (1997).

Research about activities involved in identifying opportunities, acquiring resources, and building a business are similarly few, comprising 17 percent of the eighty-nine articles reviewed (see Table 7.3). A majority of this research focused on networks and on associated activities and found that information needs, the process of building contacts, and process are similar regardless of gender (Smeltzer and Fann, 1989; Aldrich, 1989). Support systems and engagement of team members were also studied, but no significant differences were evident regarding composition or impact on survival and success (Smeltzer and Fann, 1989; Carter, Williams, and Reynolds, 1997). Furthermore, studies of opportunity identification, resource acquisition, and business formation are few in the entrepreneurial domain in general, and none have compared men and women in this process.

Environmental influences and impact on entrepreneurial supply of women-owned businesses comprise the smallest area of study. This research focuses almost entirely on access to credit (Riding and Swift, 1990) and the perspectives that loan officers have on success of women-owned firms compared to those owned by men (Buttner and Rosen, 1989). Research on access to technology, supplies of raw materials, or international ports has not compared women- and men-owned businesses and seldom includes women in these samples.

As is evident, academic and government empirical research on women-owned businesses is minimal compared to studies of men-owned businesses and relative to the population of women who own businesses. Previous research has focused on individual characteristics of women and their businesses using descriptive methodologies and instruments developed on samples of men. This research has indicated that demographic characteristics of the women and men are somewhat similar. Little, if any, research has examined the strategies, structures, and policies of women-owned businesses, the processes of venture creation, or environmental factors effecting entrepreneurial supply of women entrepreneurs. And, more significantly, fewer than 20 percent of all studies compare men and women.

Although a beginning, this research base has not developed a broader theoretical understanding of the contextual factors influencing women's participation in business ownership. Yet social structures, work, family, and organized social life influence women's access to entrepreneurial opportunities (Aldrich, 1989; Lerner, Brush, and Hisrich, 1997). An examination of these social structures would provide a basis for discussing the contributions of women-owned businesses.

CONTEXTUAL FACTORS INFLUENCING WOMEN'S ENTREPRENEURSHIP

Social structures—work, family, and organized social life—have a direct influence on development of human and social capital providing the resource base of an entrepreneurial endeavor (Brush, 1997). In new and small ventures, the entrepreneur's resources (money, connections, and experience) are often identical to those of the business. Organizations are comprised of bundles of unique resources (Penrose, 1959; Andrews, 1971) without which the organization cannot produce products and services, develop unique advantages, or design and implement strategies (Wernerfelt, 1984). In new and small ventures, the entrepreneur has a key influential role (Churchill and Lewis, 1983), envisioning the future for the new enterprise, creating strategy, and developing the policies and practices of the organization. The entrepreneur's human capital (achieved attributes, education, experience, and reputation) (Becker, 1964; Cooper, 1981) and social capital (relationship networks, family, race, ethnicity, and political connections) (Bourdieu, 1983; Glade, 1967; Greene and Brown, 1997) provide the starting "endowments" from which entrepreneurs take on their role.

Using their human and social capital, the entrepreneur acquires physical resources (tangible assets, technology, facilities) and financial resources (funds) leading to the formation or development of a new or small enterprise (Greene, Brush, and Hart, 1997). Organizational resources (which include structures, policies, routines, procedures, culture, knowledge, and alliances) (Tomer, 1987; Hofer and Schendel, 1978) are created through the application and combinations of these other basic resources.

The entrepreneur's resources are shaped by his or her experiences in work, family, and organized social life. For instance, previous experience as a chief executive officer in a business provides a solid basis for leadership and strategic decision-making in a new venture. Likewise, membership in a college fraternity can provide a social network of contacts that can be useful for accessing capital or building an entrepreneurial team. For women, social structures differ in their influences on men and women worldwide.

Work

Occupational segregation and underrepresentation of women at upper management levels continue to persist. Although women have made significant progress in non-traditional areas, women still comprise fewer than 16 percent of all undergraduates in engineering, are highly concentrated in services and administrative positions, and are less often employed in production, transportation, or agriculture (United Nations, 1991). Pay differentials by sector range from a low of $12,000 to $13,000 in transportation and retail to more than $30,000 in finance, real estate, and insurance) (U.S. Department of Labor, 1995).

Women's participation in executive, administrative, and managerial occupations averages 36 percent of the total but ranges from a low of 15 percent in construction to a high of 66 percent in social services and health services. Utilities (17 percent), manufacturing (23 percent), and public administration (30 percent) are also male dominated in administrative, executive, and managerial occupations. Moreover, women's work experience is often not continuous, as women leave the workforce to have children and care for dependents (Powell, 1993).

At the upper executive levels, the numbers of women are even smaller. Fewer than 5 percent of all corporate board members of Fortune 1000 companies are women, and fewer than 5 percent of vice-presidents and executives of corporations are female (Sharpe A-1). In some industry sectors the numbers are extremely low; for instance, seven of 1,300 biotechnology executives are female (Gupta, 1994, B-2), while the percentage of women presidents or owners of franchise systems is only 7 percent (Dant, Brush, and Iniesta, 1994).

Family Life

In addition to differential influences of worklife, family life varies for women. Expectations about family roles restrict women in terms of time, acceptance as business owners, and child- or dependent-care responsibilities. Although U.S. women have made significant progress, most women are expected to manage a household and assume a primary role for their family (Aldrich, 1989; Powell, 1993). A recent United Nations report states that "women everywhere retain the primary responsibility for unpaid housework" (United Nations, 1991, p. 83). Post–World War II prevailing family values encouraged women to marry, have children, and stay home to care for them. It was accepted that men were the "heads of the households" and that their responsibilities were to work to support their families (Powell, 1993). Today, while tax credits for dependent care are available, the maximum allowable credit is inadequate to pay for full-time daycare. It was estimated that women spent at least twelve more hour per week in unpaid housework than their male counterparts (29.2 to 17.4) (United Nations, 1991). These rules and laws, as well as societal expectations, have not facilitated the active participation of women in higher-level managerial positions or assisted them in becoming entrepreneurs and forming new ventures.

Organized Social Life

Organized social life is also different for women than for men. While networking behavior or the process does not vary by gender (Aldrich, 1989), the composition of networks does differ for men and women, in that women have a greater proportion of females in their networks. Although there remain institutions that are still male only or 99 percent male in membership (such as service organizations, eating clubs, and country clubs), some of these organizations have admitted women over the years but still do not treat women equally. For instance, in golf clubs, women may not play at certain times or participate in voting on club policies. In essence, women are left out of certain social networks of men. On the other hand, there are several female-only formal and informal groups that provide networking opportunities. The National Association of Women Business Owners and National Association of Female Executives are among the largest. Smaller local groups that are trade oriented (by industry) or general (city breakfast clubs, political or issue-based organizations) provide contact opportunities for women. In the volunteer area, women tend to participate more in school, church, and volunteer fundraising activities (Driscoll and Goldberg, 1993), which often have a social basis.

Differences in social structures directly affect the human and social capital with which many women come to business ownership. Occupational structures may limit incentives (in the form of salary differentials) for women to participate in nontraditional sectors. Furthermore, statistics show that women start businesses with less money than men ($15,000 versus about $36,000 for men) (NFWBO, 1992). This in part can be explained by sectoral differences because women are more likely to start businesses in the service or retail areas, which require less capital. However, salary differentials would suggest that they have less access to funds from previous employment that could be applied to a new business.

Lack of opportunity to gain experience at the chief executive level decreases the leadership experience with which women start companies, as well as the number of social contacts at the top levels with other CEOs and executives of companies. Some women believe they are left out of venture capital networks, which, on the surface, appears to be true: less than 0.1 percent of the $3 billion institutional venture capital was awarded to women-owned businesses in 1993 (Gupta, 1994). On the other hand, women can gain more managerial-level and supervisory experience being in administrative and director positions. They can develop strong social skills leading to unique mutual relationships, trust, and commitment (Johannison, 1996). This may provide an advantage in building entrepreneurial teams and bringing people into a new organizations.

Women's primary responsibility for family responsibilities means that women may have less opportunity to devote to full-time work endeavors, being subject to time fragmentation, career interruption, and consequently lower expectations for success in entrepreneurial endeavors. This appears most prevalent with regard to credit access. Even successful women note they have difficulty obtaining credit despite their having collateral and a track record (Brush, 1997). One study indicated that women comprised the highest proportion of nonrecipients for collateralized loans averaging $250,000 and concluded that women faced greater obstacles in this area (Thornburgh and Callahan, 1994). Hence, the endowments of human and social capital with which women come to business ownership can be different than for men due to social structures and their influence on women's socialization. These social structures also can affect access to financial, physical, and organizational resources. For instance, women may have to search harder and longer to develop contacts or locate information if they have had interrupted careers, are acquiring or starting a business in a different industry, or are located in a region where expectations for women's family roles are more traditional.

With this theoretical foundation indicating why women's entrepreneurship may differ from men's, it is possible to examine the contributions to the U.S. economy that go beyond traditional economic measures, which is the focus of the next section.

TRENDS AFFECTING WOMEN-OWNED BUSINESSES

Contributions of businesses are typically assessed in terms of economic and objective market measures. Historically, objective measures such as product innovations, jobs created, and market share have served well for measuring business performance and contributions to the U.S. economy. However, today and into the future, three major trends suggest that these traditional measures of entrepreneurial contributions need to be broadened. These trends include rapid technological change, sociocultural trends, and demographic shifts.

Rapid Technological Change

American manufacturing firms continue to lose employment, as the economy increasingly moves toward a service-based one. Technology and computerization contribute to shorter production runs. The increase in outsourcing contracts by large companies to small companies influences dynamics of this sector. In addition, service businesses are projected to grow rapidly during the next ten years. Business investment in computers will continue making it easier for companies to internationalize—to sell or import products globally—as well as to seek information, contacts, and business outside U.S. borders. Further, computer technology is expected to make it easier for people to start and run home-based businesses, do work at home, or telecommute. The impact of these rapid technological changes will impact the nature of work and the type of firms doing business, which in turn will require that new measuring instruments be used.

Sociocultural Trends

Increased competition, depersonalization, and complexity created through technology and mobility are expected to create a demand for greater connectivity (person to person) and desire for customization of products (catering to individualism) (Phillips, 1994). Futurists project that these trends will provide opportunities for new entrepreneurs to participate in the economy, using strategies that vary greatly from those of traditional institutions.

Demographic Shifts

Many shifts are occurring in the demographics of the United States, most notably the increasing diversity in the workforce. One element of diversity is the increasing elder population, with projections suggesting that the population of people over the age of sixty-five will increase by almost 15 percent, while people of working age (twenty-five to thirty-four) will decline. With this increase, there will be a significant increase in demand for medical services, housing, and low-cost meals (Phillips, 1994). Further, it is projected that more women will enter the labor force; some projections suggest that women will make up nearly half of the workforce within the next decade. Hispanics will account for more than 25 percent of the additions to the labor force, and blacks and Asians 14 and 15 percent, respectively. The immigrant population is expected to add to the labor force as well, accounting for approximately 24 percent of new additions. In sum, the labor force will be increasingly heterogeneous, where workers will come for a wide variety of cultural and educational backgrounds.

These shifts suggest that traditional objective, discrete measures of business performance and contributions may need to be broadened to better reflect the changing environment. Historically, performance and contributions were based on clear standards with accompanying beliefs about cause and effect. For instance, jobs created or lost were somewhat tangible and measurable, and beliefs about the cause and effect of economic policies on sales or profits were more certain. This caused the measures of firm performance to focus on economic, objective, and efficiency criteria. Today, cause-and-effect relationships between policies and performance are more incomplete, reflecting wide deregulation, open trade policies, and other changes. Similarly, the standards of desirability by which performance is judged are more ambiguous. For example, definitions of what constitutes fraud on the Internet versus clever entrepreneurship widely vary. A framework implied by these changes is rooted in earlier work by Thompson (1967) and is proposed as a sample from which new measures might be organized (see Table 7.4). In the first cell we might have productivity and innovation; in the second, we would have sales growth, profit growth; in the third, beliefs guide the measure, meaning that a social referent or anchor (opinions of others) becomes an important reference group. This sug-

Table 7.4.

PERFORMANCE MEASURES
Belief in Cause and Effect Knowledge

Standards of Desirability	*complete* ←→ *incomplete*	
crystallized ↑	1. efficiency productivity	2. effectiveness goal achievement
ambiguous ↓	3. referent group/ comparative	incomplete

Adapted from Thompson, J.D. (1967) Organizations in Action.

gests that we would want to compare women to other groups; hence, our proposal is, at a minimum, to collect data by gender for all segments of economic activity. Relative measures might also be comparative internationally or across other ethnic or racial groups. Moreover, the problem of ambiguous standards is compounded as new forms of organizations emerge; how does one, for example, compare home-based businesses or virtual companies with cooperatives?

Contributions of Women-Owned Businesses

While this is just one framework of measurement, the trends and new economic and societal issues support consideration of the contributions, using rather different measures of women-owned businesses consistent with the activities of their businesses. Using this perspective, it appears that women will be in a good position to take advantage of and capitalize on societal trends, thereby significantly contributing overall to the U.S. economy and society. Some of the specific contributions of women-owned businesses are in the areas of sector development, employee policies, and family stability.

Sector Development

The presence and growth of women-owned firms in sectors traditionally dominated by men will continue to increase. Increasingly, women are entering the manufacturing, agriculture, transportation, and construction areas. The experiences of women in managerial positions where supervisory experience is obtained as well as in predominantly service and retail backgrounds suggest that women will innovate when they enter these new sectors. Further, business practices of women who are more accepting of diversity and value communitarianism (Adler and Izraeli, 1994) may be more comfortable in international environments where cooperative business arrangements are the norm.

Women entrepreneurs construct their business differently in terms of the organizational forms and structures. Flatter hierarchies, participative decision-making, and more open communications (Chaganti, 1986; Neider, 1987) are common in women-owned firms. In addition, a significant number of self-employed women have home-based enterprises, and internationally there is wide involvement by women in cooperatives (Brush, 1990). Relatedly, both men and women have networks primarily composed of men (Aldrich, 1989), but women will nevertheless turn primarily to other women for information sources (Smeltzer and Fann, 1989). There is emerging evidence that women have a high propensity to engage in informal cooperative arrangements based on emotional and personal aspects of the relationship equally to transactional and professional (Monsted, 1994).

Regina McManus, president of MIDASCO, a construction company, noted that "Women-owned firms are more likely to partner on various levels. Instead of engaging in adversarial relationships, even with competitors, women-owned firms seek out areas where everyone can come together on a project."

Relatedly, international research indicates that women-owned firms produce fewer innovations, mainly because they are predominately in service or retail sectors (Ducheneaut, 1997). These service sectors, however, account for between 50 and 65 percent of technology use, a large majority of which are women-owned firms. Hence, women-owned businesses are the users and implementers of innovations.

The combined effect results in women who are creating new hybrid organizational forms, employing different information networking behaviors, and implementing technological innovations. These approaches create new entrants and strategies for competing industries due to location variations and employment of technology, which ultimately can be developed into a knowledge-based competency in service and retail sectors.

This suggests that contributions will be better measured by including home-based enterprises, which will add new dynamics to business activities in industry sectors. This calls for the establishment of a new measurement system at the federal level—recording business activity by sector and by gender in terms of both domestic and international activity.

Employee Policies

Emerging research indicates that women employ broader social policies for their employees. Pursuing social as well as economic goals (Holmquist and Sundin, 1988; Chaganti, 1986), anecdotal evidence suggests that women will be more likely to hire more diverse workers, institute child-care policies, and pay full benefits. Demographic trends toward more women, minorities, immigrants, and aging workers are consistent with the socialization experiences of women. Some women-owned businesses carry this further.

Preliminary results of a national comparative study of male- and female-owned businesses show that while male-owned businesses are more likely to have family employees, women-owned firms more often have female executives and minority employees (Hisrich and Brush, 1997). In addition, the base salaries of the lowest-paid employees of women-owned firms was on average $10,000 more than for men-owned businesses.

Another woman entrepreneur makes it a practice to hire ex-convicts and provide rehabilitation on the job. These types of contributions also need to be measured by gender, age, and employee background by company and ownership gender.

Family Stability

Technological and telecommunications improvements now, more than ever, make it possible for women to operate businesses from home locations. This, in part, resolves the child- or dependent-care issue, in that women can stay in the workforce and be with their children while working. Moreover, the rise in demand for services and customization has spawned family businesses, while encouraging family values and good work environments.

There is evidence that women spend proportionately more time than men caring for their children, even if they are business owners. Our data indicate that the mean child-care hours for male business owners is ten hours per week, whereas for female owners the mean is thirty hours per week (Hisrich and Brush, 1997). Our research also shows that women more strongly support educational, social, and environmental causes with cash donations and time, whereas men spend time in community service and donate money to charity.

With more women in the workforce and with many women contributing to family stability economically, the profits from women-owned businesses serve to increase the standard of living for sons and daughters of these women, especially if they are single parents. Alternatively, if they were not business owners, they would be in other occupations that arguably would be lower paying and probably suffer some degree of wage discrimination. Average salary from our data indicates women entrepreneurs earn about $50,000 (Hisrich and Brush, 1997); the highest average salary for women managers or directors in any industry is $32,900, while for men it is $58,666. In every sector, women earn one/three to one/two less than their male counterparts (••, 1995, pp. 134–135). In the words While working from home is perceived as a business that will stay small, it offers the flexibility of being virtual yet permits the woman to care for dependents or children and have a business.

CONCLUSION

Given the increasing number and growth of women entrepreneurs, the research level from both academic and trade perspectives needs to be increased to provide a better understanding of women entrepreneurs and their enterprises. Part of this focus needs to be on the contributions of women-owned businesses, which will involve the development of new measurements of entrepreneurial contributions beyond the typical economic and objective market measures now widely used. These new measurements will need to reflect three major trends occurring in the United States today—rapid technological change, sociocultural changes, and demographic shifts. With the development of new measurements and paradigms, women entrepreneurs, their enterprises, and their contributions can be more fully understood.

NOTE

1. The Babson Entrepreneurship Research Conference attracts the top 100 to 150 researchers in the field of entrepreneurship. While the Proceedings of this conference are not comprehensive, they are representative of the current focus of research in this field. As the largest conference requiring an empirical paper as a criterion for admission, it is one of the few forums encouraging cutting-edge empirical research.

REFERENCES

Adler, N. (1994). "Competitive Frontiers: Women Managing Across Borders." In N. Adler and D. Izareli (eds.), *Competitive Frontiers: Women Managers in a Global Economy* (pp. 22–42). Cambridge, MA: Blackwell.

Adler, N., and D. Izareli. (eds.). (1994). *Competitive Frontiers: Women Managers in a Global Economy.* Cambridge, MA: Blackwell.

Aldrich, H. (1989). "Networking Among Woman Entrepreneurs." In O. Hagan, C. Rivchun, and D. Sexton (eds.), *Women-Owned Businesses* (pp. 103–132). New York: Praeger.

Andrews, K. (1971). *The Concept of Corporate Strategy.* Homewood, Il: Irwin.

Baker, T., H. Aldrich, and N. Liou. (1997). "Invisible Entrepreneurs: The Neglect of Women Business Owners by Mass Media and Scholarly Journals in the U.S.A." *Entrepreneurship and Regional Development,* 9, 221–238.

Barney, J. (1991). "Firm Resources and Sustained Competitive Advantage." *Journal of Management,* 17(1), 99–120.

Becker, G.S. (1964). *Human Capital.* New York: Columbia University Press.

Bergman, B. (1986). *The Economic Emergence of Women.* New York: Basic Books.

Birley, S., C. Moss, and P. Saunders. (1987). "Do Women Entrepreneurs Require Different Training?" *American Journal of Small Business,* 12(1), 27–35.

Bourdieu, P. (1983). "Forms of Capital." In J. Richardson (ed.), *Handbook of Theory and Research for the Sociology of Education* (pp. 241–258). New York: Greenwood Press.

Brush, C.G. (1990). "Women's Enterprise Creation." In S. Gould and J. Parzen (eds.), *Enterprising Women* (pp. 39–60). Paris: OECD.

Brush, C.G. (1992). "Research on Women Business Owners: Past Trends, a New Perspective and Future Directions." *Entrepreneurship Theory and Practice,* 16(4), 5–30.

Brush, C.G. (1997). "Women-Owned Businesses: Obstacles and Opportunities." *Journal of Developmental Entrepreneurship,* 2(1), 1–24.

Buttner, E.H., and D.P. Moore. (1997). "Women's Organizational Exodus to Entrepreneurship: Self-Reported Motivations and Correlates with Success." *Journal of Small Business Management,* 35(1), 34–46.

Buttner, H., and B. Rosen. (1989). "Funding New Business Ventures: Are Decision Makers Biased Against Women Entrepreneurs?" *Journal of Business Venturing,* 4(4), 249–261.

Carter, N., M. Williams, and P.D. Reynolds. (1997). "Discontinuance Among New Firms in Retail: The Influence of Initial Resources, Strategy, and Gender." *Journal of Business Venturing,* 12(2), 125–145.

Chaganti, R. (1986). "Management in Women-Owned Enterprises." *Journal of Small Business Management,* 24(4), 18–29.

Chaganti, R., and S. Parasuraman. (1994). "Venture Performance: Gender, Goals, Business Strategies, and Management Practices." Working Paper, Rider College.

Charbonneau, J. (1981). "The women entperoneat." American Demographics, 21–23.

Churchill, N., and J. Hornaday. (1987). "Current Trends in Entrepreneurial Research." In *Proceedings of the Babson Entrepreneurial Research Conference* (1–2).

Churchill, N., and V. Lewis (1983). "The Five Stages of Small Business Growth" *Harvard Business Review,* May–June, 30–50.

Collins, O.F., and D.G. Moore. (1969). *The Enterprising Man*. East Lansing: Michigan State University Press.
Collis, D., and C. Montgomery. (1995). "Competing on Resources: Strategy in the 1990s." *Harvard Business Review* (July-August), 118–128.
Cooper, A. (1981). "Strategic Management: New Ventures and Small Business." *Long Range Planning*, 14(5), 39–45.
Cooper, A., and K. Artz. (1995). "Determinants of Satisfaction for Entrepreneurs." *Journal of Business Venturing*, 10(6), 439–457.
Cooper, A., and Gimeno-Gascon. (1992). "Entrepreneurs, Processes of Founding, and New Firm Performance." In D.L. Sexton and J.D. Kasarda (eds.), *State of the Art of Entrepreneurship*. Boston: PWS Kent.
Dant, R., C. Brush, and J. Niesta. (1994). "Patterns of Participation of Women in Franchising," *Journal of Small Business Management*, 34(2), 14–28.
Ducheneaut, B. (1997). "Women Entrepreneurs in SMEs." Report prepared for the OECD Conference on Women Entrepreneurs in Small and Medium-Sized Enterprises, Paris, France.
Gatewood, E.J., K.G. Shaver, and W.B. Gartner. (1995). "A Longitudinal Study of Cognitive Factors Influencing Start-Up Behaviors and Success at Venture Creation." *Journal of Business Venturing*, 10(5), 371–391.
Glade, W.P. (1967). "Approaches to a Theory of Entrepreneurial Formation." *Explorations in Entrepreneurial History*, 4(3), 245–259.
Good for Business: Making Full use of the Nation's Human Capital, 1995, U.S. Department of Labor, Government Printing Office, Washington, DC.
Grant, R.M. (1991). "The Resource-Based Theory of Competitive Advantage: Implications for Strategy Formulation." *California Management Review* (Spring), 112–135.
Greene, P.G., and T.E. Brown. (1997). "Resource Needs and The Dynamic Capitalism Typology." *Journal of Business Venturing*, 12(3), 161–173.
Greene, P., C. Brush, and M. Hart. (1997). "Resources in New Ventures: Dimensions and a Typology." Working Paper. Boston, MA.
Gupta, Udaynar. (1994). Enterprising Venture Capitalists Target Women Owned Businesses, Wall Street Journal, Th. July 6, 1994, B-2.
Hisrich, R.D., and C.G. Brush. (1983). "The Women Entrepreneur: Implications of Family, Education, and Occupational Characteristics." In *Proceedings Babson Research Conference* (255–270).
Hisrich, R.D., and C.G. Brush. (1987). "Women Entrepreneurs: A Longitudinal Study." In *Proceedings Babson College* (187–199).
Hisrich, R.D., and C.G. Brush. (1997). "Performance in Entrepreneurial Ventures: Does Gender Matter?" *Proceedings Babson Conference*. Boston, MA.
Hofer, C.W., and D.E. Schendel. (1978). *Strategy Formulation: Analysis and Concepts*. St. Paul, MN: West.
Holmquist, C. (1996). "The Female Entrepreneur: Woman and/or Entrepreneur?" In NUTEK, *Aspects of Women's Entrepreneurship* (87–114). Stockholm: Swedish National Board for Industrial and Technical Development.
Holmquist, C., and E. Sundin. (1988). "Women as Entrepreneurs in Sweden: Conclusions from a Survey." *Proceedings Babson Conference* (643–653).
Hurley, A. (1991). "Incorporating Feminist Theories into Sociological Theoretical Entrepreneurship." Paper presented at the Academy of Management Meeting, Miami, Fl.
Izraeli, D., and N. Adler. (1994). "Competitive Frontiers: Women Managers in a Global Economy." In N. Adler and D. Izareli (eds.), *Competitive Frontiers: Women Managers in a Global Economy* (3–21). Cambridge, MA: Blackwell.
Johannisson, B. (1996). "Existential Enterprise and Economic Endeavor: Women's Use of Personal Networks in the Entrepreneurial Career." In NUTEK, *Aspects of Women's Entrepreneurship* (115–142). Stockholm: Swedish National Board for Industrial and Technical Development.
Johnson, S., and D. Storey. (1993). "Male and Female Entrepreneurs and Their Businesses: A Comparative Study." In S. Allen and C. Truman (eds.), *Women in Business: Perspectives on Women Entrepreneur* (70–85). London: Routledge Press.
Kalleberg, A., and K.T. Leicht. (1991). "Gender and Organizational Performance: Determinants of Small Business Survival and Success." *Academy of Management Journal*, 34(1), 136–161.
Kent, C.A., D.L. Sexton, and K.H. Vesper (eds.). (1982). *Encyclopedia of Entrepreneurship*. Englewood Cliffs, NJ: Prentice Hall.
Lerner, M., C. Brush, and R. Hisrich. (1997). "Israeli Women Entrepreneurs: An Examination of Factors Affecting Performance." *Journal of Business Venturing*, 12, 315–339.

McClelland, D.C. (1961). *The Achieving Society.* Princeton, NJ: Van Nostrand.
Moore, D.L., and E.H. Buttner. (1997). "Women's Organizational Exodus to Entrepreneurship: Self-Reported Motivations and Correlates with Success." *Journal of Small Business Management,* 35(1), 34–36.
Monted, M. (1994). "Strategic Networks and Social Control: Dilemmas of Network Export Strategies for Small Firms." *Proceedings of the ICSB Conference, Strasbourg, Germany* (177–188).
National Foundation of Women Business Owners (NFWBO). (1992). *Women Owned Businesses: The New Economic Force.* Data report. Washington, DC: NFWBO.
National Foundation of Women Business Owners (NFWBO). (1996). *Research Findings.* Silver Spring, MD: NFWBO.
Neider, L. (1987). "A Preliminary Investigation of Female Entrepreneurs in Florida." *Journal of Small Business Management,* 25(3), 22–24.
Penrose, E. (1959). *The Theory of Growth of the Firm.* New York: Wiley.
Peteraf, M.A. (1993). "The Cornerstones of Competitive Advantage: A Resource-Based View." *Strategic Management Journal,* 14(3), 179–192.
Phillips, B. (1994). *Small Business in the Year 2005,* Office of Advanly, U.S. Government Printing Office, Washington, DC.
Powell, G.N. (1993). *Women and Men in Management.* Newbury Park, CA: Sage.
President's Task Force on Women Business Owners. (1979). *The Bottom Line: Unequal Enterprises in America.* A Report of the President's Task Force on Women Business Owners. Washington, DC: U.S. Department of Commerce.
Riding, A., and C.S. Swift. (1990). "Women Business Owners and Terms of Credit: Some Empirical Findings from the Canadian Experience." *Journal of Business Venturing,* 5(5), 327–340.
Schrier, J.W. (1975). "The Female Entrepreneur: A Pilot Study." Milwaukee, WI: Center for Venture Management.
Schwartz, E.B. (1976). "Entrepreneurship: A New Female Frontier." *Journal of Contemporary Business,* 5(1), 47–76.
Scott, C.E. (1986). "Why More Women Are Becoming Entrepreneurs." *Journal of Small Business Management,* 24(4), 37–44.
Sexton D.L., and C.A. Kent. (1981). "Female Executives and Entrepreneurs: A Preliminary Comparison." *Frontiers of Entrepreneurship Research* (pp. 40–46). MA: Babson College.
Sharpe, Rochelle. (1994). The Waiting Game: Women make progress but men stay firmly in top corporate jobs, Wall Street Journal, Tues, May 29, 1994, A-1.
Smeltzer, L.R., and G.L. Fann. (1989). "Gender Differences in External Networks of Small Business Owner/Managers." *Journal of Small Business Management,* 27(2), 25–32.
Srinivasan, R., C. Woo, and A.C. Cooper. (1994). "Performance Determinants for Male and Female Entrepreneurs." Working Paper 1053, Purdue University.
Stevenson, L. (1986). "Against All Odds: The Entrepreneurship of Women." *Journal of Small Business Management,* 24(4), 30–36.
Thompson, J.D. (1967). *Organizations in Action.* New York: McGraw Hill.
Thornburgh, D., and C. Callahan, (1994). "Public Policy Aspects of Federal and Statue Small Business Programs," White House Conference of *Small Business and Entrepreneurship,* July, Washington, DC.
Tomer, J.F. (1987). *Organizational Capital.* New York: Praeger Press.
United Nations. (1991). *The World's Women 1970–1990: Trends and Statistics.* New York: United Nations.
U.S. Department of Labor. (1995). *Good for Business: Making Full Use of the Nation's Human Capital, The Environmental Scan.* A Fact-Finding Report of the Federal Glass Ceiling Commission. Washington, DC: U.S. Government Printing Office.
U.S. Small Business Administration. (1988, 1995a). *The State of Small Business.* Washington, DC: U.S. Government Printing Office.
U.S. Small Business Administration. (1995b). *The Third Millenium: Small Business and Entrepreneurship in the Twenty-First Century.* Washington, DC: U.S. Small Business Administration.
Wernerfelt, B. (1984). "A Resource-Based View of the Firm." *Strategic Management Journal,* 5, 171–180.

8. "DON'T CALL ME SMALL": THE CONTRIBUTION OF ETHNIC ENTERPRISES TO THE ECONOMIC AND SOCIAL WELL-BEING OF AMERICA

JOHN SIBLEY BUTLER

The University of Texas, Austin, TX

PATRICIA GENE GREENE

University of Missouri, Kansas City, MO

INTRODUCTION

The source of U.S. entrepreneurs and their contributions to the economic and social well-being of American society are issues that are being addressed in many quarters today. One approach emphasizes the role that immigrant and minority entrepreneurs play in this process. The stereotypical enterprises created by ethnic immigrants evoke certain images: the corner retail establishment, predominately coethnic employees and customers, and a geographically bounded and identifiable section of town. Additional assumptions are also often made that the businesses are tied to the ethnic community and benefit from resources distributed through community ties. In fact, these businesses share many of the same characteristics of small enterprises in general. However, some also do share conditions, perceived as advantageous, that are related to the structure of specific ethnic communities. For these groups business enterprise is an important tool that contributes to the incorporation of ethnic immigrants into American society.

Research on this process therefore has the potential for articulating the relationship between certain groups of ethnic immigrants and the community-based entrepreneurial process. This process can be seen from two perspective—that of the community's effect on the entrepreneur and that of the entrepreneurs' contribution to the community. To illustrate these perspectives we use a metaanalysis approach using previously published research for case studies.

We begin by reviewing the concept of ethnic and minority entrepreneurship, providing conceptual clarification for the phenomenon, and examining the size and

Z.J. Acs (ed.). ARE SMALL FIRMS IMPORTANT? Copyright © 1999. Kluwer Academic Publishers. Boston. All rights reserved.

scope of this phenomenon in the United States. We then present our case studies, which describe three ethnic- or minority-owned business communities. We use the concept of gateway cities and show how waves of immigrants have influenced these cities. Our case studies are drawn from different historical periods to illustrate the dynamics of community entrepreneurship. Because community entrepreneurship has not always been driven by ethnicity or immigration, we take a history page from black America as a test for our ideas on the relationship between entrepreneurship and community building. We conclude by exploring the applicability of issues raised in the ethnic context to U.S. small businesses in general.

CONCEPTUAL CLARITY

Before we can analyze these issues, there is a critical need for conceptual clarity of terms. Discussions of immigrant-owned business, minority business, and ethnic entrepreneurship are related areas of research but require separate theoretical approaches to understand the various phenomena in question. *Immigrant-owned business* is a straightforward term used to describe businesses owned by immigrants to the country. It implies no inherent assumptions about the owners, the creation process, or levels of community involvement. The term *minority business* varies by usage. It is most often used by the government to refer to any business owned by a nonmajority person. Usually the term *minority business* is used in the context of a policy or specific program description. This category sometimes will include women and other times will not. And finally, *ethnic entrepreneurship*, in its purest sense, has a specific meaning that captures the essence of the community dimension of this phenomenon. Ethnic entrepreneurship consists of "a set of connections and regular patterns of interaction among people sharing common national background or migration experiences" (Waldinger, Aldrich, and Ward, 1990, p. 33).[1]

SMALL ENTERPRISES AND THE ECONOMY

Wilson Harrell (1995), the retired president and chief operating officer of *Inc.* magazine, has a chapter in *For Entrepreneurs Only* entitled "Don't Call Me Small." The title is not designed to capture the operational definition of small businesses in America but rather to accentuate statistics that surround these enterprises: 99 percent of all U.S. enterprises have fewer than 500 employees, 50 percent of those in the labor force work for businesses with fewer than 500 employees, and 50 percent of all business assets are held by enterprises with fewer than 500 employees. Wilson's major point is that you cannot call an enterprise small when it has such a significant economic impact on the lives of individuals and communities.

It is, however, difficult to get a handle on statistics on businesses in the United States, especially small, privately held businesses.[2] One of the major sources of such information on ethnic and minority entrepreneurs and the businesses they own is a specialized economic census that the United States conducts to capture firm-level data on businesses owned by African Americans, persons of Hispanic or Latin American ancestry (including Mexican, Puerto Rican, Cuban, Central American,

European Spanish, and other Hispanic), and persons of Asian, Pacific Islander, American Indian, or Alaska Native descent. The *Survey of Minority-Owned Business Enterprises* is performed every five years and categorizes ethnic owners into very broad racial and ethnic categories, providing useful demographics of the businesses and their owners.

The 1992 survey provides the most recent data available and reveals the growth of the small-business sector of the U.S. economy. Between 1987 and 1992 the total number of U.S. businesses reported in the survey increased 26 percent, from approximately 13.7 million to over 17 million.[3] In 1987, 8.86 percent of all U.S. businesses were reported as minority owned. By 1992 that number had increased to 12.5 percent minority-owned businesses. In actual numbers, firms reported as minority-owned increased from 1.2 million to almost 2 million, an increase of 62 percent.

Of equal interest is that the size of these businesses, measured by sales receipts, is also growing. Sales and receipts of all U. S firms increased by 67 percent.[4] Receipts from businesses with minority owners increased at more than twice that rate, 160 percent, from $7.8 billion to a total of $202.0 billion. These increases appear even more striking if examined at the firm level. In 1987 the average per-firm receipt for a minority-owned business was $64,132; by 1992 this number was $97,590. While the increase per minority-owned firm is substantial, it is still only approximately half of the average per firm annual receipts for all U.S. firms, $192,672. However, these increases do demonstrate a general trend, continuing the climb from the 1982 data. It should be noted that the differences in the size of receipts do not correspond to increases in the number of paid employees reported by firms. Only 18 percent of all U.S. firms report having any paid employees. The number reported by minority-owned firms is similar, 16 percent.

While government statistics document the growth rates of these businesses, much remains to be known about how the businesses are actually created and managed and what are the actual success rates. Indeed, much is assumed, and these assumptions fall largely into two camps. The first assumption is that these businesses are indeed fringe enterprises, barely subsisting in inner-city neighborhoods and ethnic enclaves. Under this model the businesses do not provide any means of upward economic or social mobility. The second model is that the businesses are economically lucrative and are indeed a source of wealth creation for the owners. Indeed, both models contain some elements of reality. However, other underlying assumptions are relevant for understanding the motivation and behaviors of the immigrant business owners. We do know that immigrant communities vary greatly in their participation in entrepreneurial behaviors as well as in the activities they are involved in.

SMALL BUSINESS, ETHNIC ENTREPRENEURSHIP, AND THE SHAPING OF COMMUNITIES

The idea that immigrant entrepreneurs influence communities emerged during a debate between Max Weber and Werner Sombart. Weber, noted German scholar and author of *The Protestant Ethnic and the Spirit of Capitalism* (1930 [1904]), was interested in explaining how the Protestant religion was instrumental in providing the philosophical groundwork for the development of capitalism. Unlike Catholicism, Weber argued, Protestantism emerged as a worldly religion—one that stressed the development of economic security while here on earth. Catholicism had always stressed the idea that in order to achieve heavenly goals one must simply be one with the church. The attitudes of Catholic members toward wealth accumulation were desired from the biblical scripture that said that it was easier for a camel to go through the eye of a needle than a rich man to enter the gates of heaven. Although Weber noted that early Protestant thinkers such as Calvin and Luther were devoted to religious concerns, their ideas also became the source for what he called "the Spirit of Capitalism." (Weber, 1930 [1904]).

After analyzing the European economy, Sombart countered Weber's idea that Protestant ideas were responsible for the development of capitalism. He did this by examining the history of the Jewish people in Europe. After noting that the group had been expelled from many cities of that continent, Sombart (1982, p. 13) used the observed patterns to posit the first relationship between ethnicity, business enterprise, and community:

> Cannot we bring into connection the shifting of the economic centre from Southern to Northern Europe with the wandering of the Jews?...It is indeed surprising that the parallelism has not before been observed between Jewish wanderings and settlement on the one hand, and the economic vicissitudes of the different peoples and states on the other. Israel passes over Europe like the sun; at its coming new life bursts forth; at its going all falls into decay.

The questions raised by these two scholars have been carefully explored over the last few decades, largely through community-based studies. In the United States alone studies have been done on Japanese Americans in California (Light, 1972; Bonacich and Modell, 1981), Cubans in Miami (Portes and Bach, 1985), Koreans in Atlanta (Min, 1988), Chinese in New York (Zhou, 1992, 1995), and Pakistanis in Texas (Greene and Butler, 1996), to name a few. However, the phenomenon is certainly worldwide, including Chinese in Singapore (Fallers, 1967), Coptic Christians in Egypt (Hamilton, 1978), Ibo in Nigeria (Waterbury, 1972), Greeks in Egypt (Becker, 1940), and Arabs in China (Hamilton, 1978). The motivation for many of these studies was to better understand how immigrants develop a sense of economic stability.

The research focus on immigration is largely directed through migration networks and the resultant linkages between migrants, former migrants, and nonmigrants. What unites the members of the network is some common element, possibly common origin, whether country, community, family ties, or so on. The migration networks support the continuing migratory flow through the development of autonomous social structures, reducing social, economic, and emotional costs that are associated with immigration.

The idea of ethnic revival through economic behaviors is given broad meaning in Joel Kotkin's work *Tribes* (1992), where he argues that the entire world economy has always been and will be shaped by "ethnic tribes." Kotkin's first tribe is the British, who in the Middle Ages lived in "one of the most backward countries in Europe," but emerged in the seventeenth and eighteenth centuries as the primary force for commerce and the development of a world economy. Kotkin's other tribes are the Jews of Europe, Indians, Chinese, and the Japanese. His argument is that in their diasporas, ethnic tribes utilize trust, business experience, and solidarity as they place business enterprise at the very center of community.

The contribution of such migratory networks in the United States is supported by Thomas Muller in *Immigrants and the American City* (1993). Muller suggests that network connections that skilled immigrants bring with them contribute to raising the technological standing and the standard of living for the American middle class, ultimately facilitating the resurgence of inner cities. This research on immigration contrasts with the view that the process is detrimental to the economic success of America. It points to the fact that the entrepreneurial process that immigrants bring with them must be considered in the overall debate focusing on immigration in advanced countries around the globe.

Muller supports his ideas by drawing on a 1993 President's Commission on Immigration and Naturalization: "The richest regions are those with the highest proportion of immigrants. . . . Their industry, their skills, and their enterprises were major factors in the economic development that made these regions prosperous" (1993, p. 111).

Muller particularly referred to Los Angeles, Miami, New York, and San Francisco, describing these regions as "gateway cities." Since 1970 their population growth has been related directly to immigration. In 1930 about one out of four residents in these cities was foreign born—about two times the national average. About two-fifths of all recent immigrants have settled in these cities, although they account for less than 8 percent of the nation's population. Of all of the foreign bank branches in America, two-thirds are in gateway cities. As early as 1987, foreign investors put more than $12 billion or 60 percent of total overseas investment in office real estate in America, primarily in these cities (Muller, 1993).

COMMUNITY STUDIES OF ETHNIC ENTREPRENEURSHIP

The explanation for why certain immigrant groups create businesses at a greater rate than other groups draws from the following dimensions:

- A group immigrates to a new country or area in which its members are recognizable as a minority, often with the intention of sojourning, earning money, and then returning to their home land.
- Group members are discriminated against in the labor force and are prevented from securing jobs with reasonable wages, benefits, and career opportunities.
- In order to "avoid falling to the bottom of the economic ladder" group members create their own economic activity through self-employment and business creation.

- The businesses created are characterized by low liquidity and low barriers to entry and exit.
- The businesses may or may not be geographically bounded in an ethnic community, serving coethnics as customers and hiring coethnics as employees.

These dimensions are drawn from sociological theories of middleman minority and ethnic enclave theory. Of critical importance is the socially embedded nature of the economic activities, as opposed to strictly economic functions or the characteristics of the entrepreneur.

Given these dimensions, the practice of including the entrepreneurial behaviors of both immigrant groups and African Americans in the same measures of minority entrepreneurship is problematic. African American business owners have been approached under rubrics of black capitalism and black entrepreneurship. The theoretical explanation differs from that of ethnic entrepreneurship along several key dimensions. Historically, while African American entrepreneurs are not immigrants, they meet the criterion of facing discrimination and were originally prohibited from entering the labor market, owning property, or operating independent businesses. The more accurate theoretical description is that of the truncated middleman.[5] This explanation posits that a segment of the African American population did follow an entrepreneurial path and continues to do so.

Studying the impact of entrepreneurship on communities is also confounded by temporal effects. For example, black entrepreneurship in America was strongest between the late 1800s and the 1960s, a long historical period that saw the development of stable entrepreneurial communities, the building of over 120 private schools, and the creation of trade schools. Communities such as Durham, NC, and Tulsa, OK, became renowned for their business neighborhoods. Although blacks are certainly represented in entrepreneurship today, entrepreneurial communities were much stronger during these earlier years (Bulter, 1991). This is also true of early ethnic entrepreneurship, where most immigrant groups developed enterprises in their own communities. One thinks of Little Italy, Little Germany, and Chinatown. Not all groups have maintained an ethnic component to their enterprises or strong business communities such as a Chinatown. As they became assimilated over time into the larger society, sometimes moving to other parts of the country, some communities of enterprises tended to disappear. We consider this historical effect and discuss the impact of entrepreneurship over time and space.

Whether we study ethnic entrepreneurship from a historical perspective or concentrate on ethnic entrepreneurs today, it is clear that "success," and the impact of that success on communities, is very strong. However, it is necessary to consider success not only as financial achievements but also as economic and social mobility, largely seen through the educational attainments of the children. Observing this mobility prompts the question whether entrepreneurial knowledge and know-how can be transplanted to groups that are less economically successful and that may have significant social welfare needs.

THE JAPANESE IN CALIFORNIA 1890S TO WORLD WAR II

By area, Los Angeles is the third-largest city in the country. Once a sleepy Spanish pueblo, the city has a colorful history of developing from a frontier area into a sprawling urban center with a diversity of commerce. Historical highlights of the city include gold discovered just north of the area in the foothills of the Sierra Nevada in 1842, incorporation in 1852, the Southern Pacific Railroad line extended from San Francisco in 1876, and oil discovered within the city limits in 1892.

Despite the discovery of oil, agriculture dominated the economy during the beginning of the twentieth century. Between 1899 and 1908 large numbers of Japanese immigrated from Japan (often by way of Hawaii) in search of a "decent" wage. These immigrants filled the labor needs in agriculture, mining, and the railroads until a 1908 Agreement with Japan temporarily cut off all immigration. Although the Japanese entered the country as laborers, within a short period of time they established themselves in city trades and agriculture and became major contributors to the economic well-being of Los Angeles (Bonacich and Modell, 1981).

By 1929 Los Angeles had a population of approximately 30,000 Japanese Americans, representing the largest settlement of this group on the West Coast. Concentrating on the service sector, this population developed several thousand businesses that focused on the Japanese community but also served the entire community of Los Angeles (Bonacich and Modell, 1981).

The development of small enterprises in Los Angeles by the first-generation Japanese (Issei) was directly related to the development of community economic institutions. The first significant institution was the "money pool" or rotating credit system. Since estabilshed bankers would not finance their enterprises, community members placed their money in a central location to give loans with few stipulations. Debts were repaid with a money gift for each contributor to the pool. Financing individual enterprises was therefore a collective obligation that further grounded people to the ethnic community (Levine and Rhodes, 1981). Additional capital was also raised outside the community from suppliers and distributors.

The community ties for this group were supported by networks that sometimes were based on the prefecture in Japan from where the immigrant came. Prefectural associations were thus the basis of the level of the trust that supported certain business activities. Another example of shared business activities was partnerships, particularly in agricultural endeavors. Mutual responsibility for undertakings reassured landowners that their interests were protected and allowed the Japanese partners to obtain the necessary leases (Bonacich and Modell, 1981).

The community also operated a form of business apprenticeships. Newly arrived immigrants worked in businesses owned by more established relatives. Although working long hours for little pay, the new immigrant benefited from the arrangement by learning about the particular business and business ownership. The sponsoring relative might also assist in eventually providing a startup loan for a new business.

One interesting finding in the literature on ethnic entrepreneurship is the impact that it has on the education of children and the social mobility of future generations. Enterprises provide economic stability and create jobs, but in addition, the children of those who own enterprises are more likely to obtain higher education and advance in the professions. This pattern was noticeable with Japanese Americans. Research has found that, "As a group, the Japanese Americans are one of the most highly educated ethnic elements in the United States population, both sexes enjoying a longer median period of education than blacks, whites, Chinese, Filipinos, and Native Americans. Their educational excellence has been demonstrated qualitatively as well as quantitatively. . . . Japanese American pupils in Los Angeles scored much higher on performance than any other minority group and somewhat higher than native whites as well" (Bonacich and Modell, 1981, p. 142). By the second and third generations, many Japanese moved into the professions.

The development of Los Angeles as a city was enhanced by the entrepreneurial spirit of the Japanese at the turn of the century. Like all immigrants in gateway cities, the Japanese enhanced the development of major industries (agriculture) and contributed to the overall educational level of the city. Today in Los Angeles, Japanese Americans represent an economically stable group that is enjoying the fruits that were planted by past generations.

MIAMI, FLORIDA: THE CUBAN EXPERIENCE

The Japanese in Los Angeles actually grew up with the city and enhanced both themselves and the city. The Cubans in Miami were newcomers who revitalized a city.

The drama of rebuilding and redeeming the city of Miami did not start in that city but rather ninety miles away on the island of Cuba. Cuba was acquired by America in 1898 as a result of the Spanish American War. After two years of military occupation, the island emerged as an independent country. Given its physical proximity, there has always been some degree of migration from Cuba to the United States. In 1930, an estimated 18,000 Cubans lived in America. When Fidel Castro came to power, the mass migration started, and the political nature of the mass migration made Cuban Americans refugees as well as immigrants. By 1973, 273,000 Cubans lived in the United States (Butler, 1991).

In the early 1960s the city of Miami was struggling with massive economic problems and was not ready for a mass migration from Cuba. According to Gilder (1984, p. ••),

> The city did not seem ready for them. For the economy of central Miami, 1961 was a grim year. In the inner-city area . . . more than 1,000 homes, with FHA mortgages, had been vacated, and many were vandalized for their copper pipe and electrical fixtures. The Little League baseball field had become *el parque de la marijuana*; local shops gasped for customers and went broke; forty-year-old Burdine's, the chief downtown department store, was languishing helplessly, as its clientele moved toward the suburbs. Even Miami Beach, the supreme American resort across the Bay of Biscayne, was slipping perceptibly past its prime, as wealthy northern tourists increasingly passed it by for mellower island shores to the south. . . . To

many observers, the arrival of the Cubans seemed a deadly blow to the city's hope for recovery.

City officials were so concerned about the imminent arrival of the refugees that they brought in experts to project the coming crisis. All statistical predictions pointed to disaster; medical facilities, social disorders, need for housing, welfare, and simple hygiene were all seen as major concerns as the Cubans flocked to the city (Gilder, 1984).

Reality proved to be quite different from the projections. Between 1959 and 1962 approximately 215,000 Cuban refugees arrived in the United States, many of them landowners, industrialists, managers, professionals, and small-business owners. After a number of years during which Cubans were prohibited by Castro from leaving the island, a new wave of 340,000 refugees arrived in the United States. Although the average level of occupational and educational attainments of the migrants was decreasing, overall it was still above the average for the Cuban population. In other words, at this point the people who were arriving in the United States were those with the highest levels of human capital in both education and profession (Portes and Bach, 1985).

The reception given to this group was organized through a U.S. program called the Cuban Refugee Program. Many of the refugees were resettled in areas other than Miami; however, a significant number (27.4 percent of the Cubans in Miami) had been returned from other U.S. settlements. In 1967, at the start of the refugee movement, Cubans owned 919 enterprises in the Miami area. By 1978 that number was 8,000, and by 1985 it was estimated to be 13,000. In 1979, 21.2 percent of a sample of Cuban refugees were self-employed (Portes and Bach, 1985).

Instead of entering as laborers, the Cubans quickly developed one of the strongest minority business enclaves in America since African Americans thrived in Durham in the 1940s. Turning inward, within a short period of time, they developed enterprises that served as the basis for the revitalization of the city of Miami Gilder (1984, p. 96),

> with restaurants and cafeterias galore, twenty-four hours a day of thick *café cubano* and the long hard loaves of Cuban bread; all comprising in a once ghostly three and a half square miles what the Latin Chamber of Commerce catalogues as 97 restaurants and cafeterias, 81 groceries and supermarkets, 49 gas stations, 48 clothing stores, 46 barber and beauty shops, 46 jewelry stores, 34 *farmacias*, 33 furniture outlets, 21 bakeries, 20 cigar factores, 20 law and real estate firms, 17 florerias, 17 photo studios, 13 optical shops, 13 hardware stores, 10 private clinics and hospitals, 10 bookstores, 10 tailors, 8 travel agencies, 7 funeral parlors, and 5 banks. The Chamber . . . overlooked several theaters, nightclubs, import/export companies, auto repair shops, discotheques, driving schools, doctors' offices, and vendors of *articulos religiosos*, not to mention the numerous *botanicos* and ten more Cuban banks. In the continuing eruptions of Cuban business in the city, reaching out to the north and south, and by 1980 comprising some 10,000 Cuban-owned companies in Dade County.

Most of the Cuban refugees had friends and family waiting for them in the United States. A community network already existed that facilitated access to resources and opportunities. New arrivals were seen to supplement the Cuban private business sector in South Florida (Portes and Bach, 1985). The community additionally was seen as "a source of emotional support, protection against external pressures, and . . . economic gain. The dense networks of contact within the immigrant community function as sources of employment, information about events in the host and home countries, and social support" (Portes and Bach, 1985, p. 299).

The Cuban migrants showed a strong tendency toward moving into self-employment, expedited by a ladder of opportunities within the ethnic enclave. A recent arrival may start at the bottom of that ladder, depending largely on individual characteristics, but through wage labor positions may obtain skills and contacts conducive to starting his or her own business. In addition, the wages received allow the migrant to accumulate at least some part of the startup capital.

The transformation of Miami was accomplished by immigrants who utilized the tools of small enterprise in order to revitalize an American city. As noted earlier, immigrants have used this method before to ensure the continued rebirth of the American spirit. Research has documented the continuing experiences of Cubans in Miami—how they enhanced the overall educational structure and how they created jobs for people who sometimes could not speak English but were able to find a degree of economic stability in the Cuban community (Wilson and Martin, 1982; Portes and Bach, 1985).

DURHAM NORTH CAROLINA: THE NEGRO WALL STREET

During the early part of this century the literature on entrepreneurship and community was dominated by the experiences of African Americans. Cut off from opportunities in the larger society, this group turned inward and created some of the most dynamic business communities in the history of immigrant and minority enterprise. As Margaret Levenstein (1995) notes in *Journal of Business and Economic History*, statistics generated from community data show that in 1910 black Americans were just as likely to be self-employed as white Americans and just as likely to employ community residents. Durham, North Carolina, is an excellent example of this community building and allows us to test our ideas on a group that has been the recipient of intense discrimination.

Durham caught the attention of several noted scholars. In 1911 Booker T. Washington documented the presence of manufacturing companies, large- and small-scale service enterprises, and community institutions. This work was followed by a more in-depth treatment of the city by E. Franklin Frazier (1925, p. ••) in his comparison of Durham and New York City:

> Durham offers none of the color and creative life we find among Negroes in New York City. It is a city of fine homes . . . and middle-class respectability. It is not the place where men write and dream; but a place where black men calculate and work. ... As we read the lives of the men in Durham who have established the enterprises there, we find stories paralleling the most amazing accounts of the building of American fortunes. We find them beginning their careers without much formal education and practicing the old-fashioned virtues

of the old middle class. . . . These men have mastered the technique of modern business and acquired the spirit of modern enterprise.

When the eminent historian William Boyd wrote *The Story of Durham* (1927), which celebrated the South's development from agriculture to industrial enterprise, he included a chapter on the African American community. He noted that "the increase in wealth, the rise of institutions of public welfare, and the spirit of cooperation have not only been confined to one race. The progress of whites has been accompanied by corresponding progress among the Negroes" (p. 227).

The discussion of Durham went beyond academic analysis and into the trade press. In a Richmond, Virginia, newspaper the following was noted (Weare, 1973, pp. 4–5):

Go to Durham . . . you need the inspiration. Go to Durham and see the industrious Negro at his best. Go to Durham and see the cooperative spirit among Negroes at its best. Go to Durham and see Negro business with an aggregate capital of millions. Go to Durham and see twenty-two Negro men whose honesty and business sagacity are making modern history. Among your New Year's resolves, resolve to go to Durham.

The roots of early Durham were planted when the North Carolina Mutual Life Insurance Company was founded in 1898. Today this is still the largest black-owned insurance company in the world. Founded by free blacks, the company organized in the tradition of benevolent societies, assessing monthly membership dues in order to pay out sick and death benefits. From the very beginning the founders planned to make their company a catalyst for black economic growth by accumulating capital and reinvesting it in black-owned enterprises such as real estate, training, and educational institutions. This insurance company also capitalized the Mechanics and Farmers Bank in 1908 to provide home, commercial property, and business loans. It further invested in the community by placing its own funds in black higher-education institutions such as Durham's North Carolina Central College (Butler and Wilson, 1988).

By 1920 there was a thriving African American entrepreneurial enclave of mutually supporting enterprises. The diversity of goods and services was so wide-ranging that black residents could meet most of their needs by patronizing enterprises within their neighborhoods. In the tradition of ethnic enterprises, these businesses included restaurants, hotels, grocery stores, appliance shops, florists, tailors, haberdasheries, shoe repair ships, movie houses, dry cleaning, and manufacturing. However, the approach to meeting the domestic and business financial needs of the community differed from approaches described in many discussions of ethnic entrepreneurship. Instead of relying on informal or quasi-formal network-based sources of funds, members of the Durham community established formal financial institutions including the Bankers Fire Insurance Company, the Union Insurance and Realty Company, the Southern Fidelity Mutual Insurance Company, the Home Modernization and Supply Company, and the T.P. Parham and Associates Brokerage Corporation (Butler, 1991).

Like most early African American enclaves, Durham provided opportunities (educational and business) for black Americans within a hostile racial atmosphere. Early blacks who completed college were more likely to come from families that were self-employed. This fact is noted in the literature as early as 1911, when W.E.B. Dubois published *The College Bred Negro* (Dubois, 1911). It was supported by Charles Johnson's 1938 work *The Negro College Graduate* (Johnson, 1938). It is also instructive to note that the North Carolina region has the highest number of black private schools, testimony to the vision and dedication of early self-employed people, especially those in Durham.

The Durham black business community of the 1920s provided a community foundation still evident today despite a major setback incurred by urban renewal of the 1960s. An expressway was located through the black business section, obliterating more than 100 enterprises and 600 homes. However, many of the institutions are still at work providing glue for the community. In 1986 the Farmers and Mechanics bank was voted the most efficient bank in America, and the North Carolina Mutual Life Insurance Company consistently sits atop *Black Enterprises'* list of insurance companies. The number of small-scale enterprises also continues to grow as children and grandchildren of the original entrepreneurs return to the community. Indeed, many of the old and new enterprises remain linked by the fifty-eight-year old Durham Business and Professional Chain.

DON'T CALL ME SMALL

These three case studies, which describe the contribution of immigrant entrepreneurship to the constant rebuilding of American cities and the same process in an African American, nonimmigrant context, illustrate several recurring themes that emphasize the robust relationship between entrepreneurial economic behaviors and community membership. These themes center around flows from the community to the entrepreneur as well as from the entrepreneur to the community.

First, the community can be seen as a source of both resources and opportunities that are necessary but not sufficient for the undertaking of entrepreneurial activities. In our first case, Japanese immigrants arrived with very little financial capital and entered an environment in which they needed to create not only their enterprises but also a community itself. Their initial role as laborers placed them at the proverbial bottom of the economic barrel. Their rapid entry into business ownership was based on their taking opportunities that did not require large amounts of financial or physical capital but instead could be met with other types of resources—human capital applied in long hours of work and social capital in the form of family and friends. As the community developed and grew, it became a source of capital, labor, patronage, credit, goods, services, jobs, various types of social assistance, information, and training through apprenticeshiplike programs (Bonacich and Modell, 1980). In addition, the community provided an organizing medium not only for business activities but also for activities that contributed to the social betterment of community members.

The entrepreneurial endeavors of this group need to be viewed from the perspective of what the group was trying to achieve. The business owners worked hard for grueling hours, and not all businesses thrived or even survived (Bonacich and Modell, 1981). Even as individual business owners and their families struggled, however, the group as a whole thrived. The economic mobility of the group can be seen in the economic activities of the post–World War II second and third generations in largely professional occupations based on high levels of educational attainment (Bonacich and Modell, 1981).

The recurring themes of the relationship between the entrepreneur and the community can be examined in the context of our second case study, that of the Cuban refugees. In this case, environmental elements were different, but outcomes were similar. The success of the Cuban community in Miami is largely attributed to the development of an ethnic enclave. Again, this community offers both resources and opportunities that foster entrepreneurship (Portes and Bach, 1985, p. 203):

> Entrepreneurial activities can thrive in this situation because they are able to reproduce, on a local scale, some of the features of monopolistic control that account for successful firms in the wider economy. For example subsequent mass arrivals from the home country provide immigrant entrepreneurs with privileged access to a source of low-wage labor and new consumer markets. As exemplified by the histories of early Jewish and Japanese immigrants, ... there are definite advantages to invoking the principle of ethnic solidarity. Ethnic entrepreneurs have repeatedly used it to inhibit unionization and fight opposition among their workers. Ethnic solidarity also provides the basis for effective forms of capital accumulation through pooled savings and rotating credit systems.

In this situation, the same type of resources are seen as available through community ties, the socially embedded nature of the community (Portes and Sensenbrunner, 1993; Granovetter, 1985). The community provides sources of capital, labor, skills, and contacts. Indeed, in this illustration the recreation of a labor market, with both primary and secondary jobs, is clear.

And finally, our third case does not illustrate immigrant entrepreneurship but an ethnic group's community-based effects to support entrepreneurial economic behaviors, as well as the critical necessity of considering the historical context of the activities. The African American community in Durham developed enterprises that were similar to those developed in the Japanese and Cuban immigrant communities as seen in the other two cases but formalized business relationships through the creation of financial institutions.

As we think about and do research on small business, we need to develop a strong research tradition that connects not only the contributions of ethnic enterprises but also the contributions of small business in general to the well-being of American communities. Who can measure the impact that these enterprises have had on institutions such as youth leagues (Little League baseball, soccer, basketball, and so on), educational institutions, the education of the professional class in America, and overall job creation? The interconnected nature of the social bottom line and the economic bottom line is crucial as we continue to understand the relationship between small enterprises and their contributions to the well-being of American society.

LESSONS TO BE LEARNED?

A close examination of the phenomenon of ethnic entrepreneurship provides the context for practitioner implications. The dimensions related to the success of the ethnic entrepreneurial behaviors are tied to the bounded solidarity and embedded trust resulting from community networks, albeit communities determined by various definitions, such as country of origin, region of origin, and extended family. This sense of community permeates more of ethnic life than the business arena, affecting social relationships, religious practices, educational achievements, and occupations.

Instrumental Networks

One of the components of ethnic entrepreneurship that is most discussed and seems most attractive to outsiders, particularly those interested in promoting entrepreneurship, is the development of social networks as a viaduct for business resources. What is often less carefully considered is that ethnic entrepreneurship is based on a premise of bounded solidarity and enforceable trust. Group membership is predicated on shared beliefs, values, and norms. Members of the group know who is in the group and who it not. Enforceable trust is a tool that artificially created networks lack and cannot easily reproduce. If an ethnic group member breaks trust—for instance, does not pay back a loan—the consequences are significantly more far reaching than their business life. Since the business arena is so entirely integrated into other life arenas, breaking trust in a business sense may mean the breakdown of social, religious, and other family-based ties. Loss of group membership is a severe price to pay.

This is not to say that all members of ethnic groups engaged in entrepreneurial behaviors are trustworthy and enjoy sterling reputations. Even within the group reputations for business skills, trustworthiness, and so on will vary.

Business assistance obtained through networks based on group membership can take many forms, both instrumental and expressive. The lesson derived from the ethnic entrepreneurial communities is the value of these relationships over the long term. Formal business incubators and programs such as incubators without walls currently offer various forms of tangible and intangible business assistance to start-ups and early stage ventures. For the majority of these programs there is a *graduation point* where the firm moves into a more mature state and leaves the physical environment of the incubator or the nurturing environment of the launching program. The ethnic community continues its business mentoring program over the long term, providing a source of shared business information and advice at every stage of the business.

Several organizations have adopted this type of program for other groups. The Young President's Organization (YPO) allows individuals at certain career points to join in a mutual mentoring program. Several other CEO groups have been formed to perform similar functions. A mentoring group in which business owners form a cohort for long-term business and personal development offers the chance for relationships potentially helpful to both the owner and the firm to develop. The advice comes from a group of individuals who know the business and owner from the business's very early stages. The longevity of the relationship allows for an added depth to the types of knowledge shared among the members.

Entrepreneurial Apprenticeships

Entrepreneurial activities within migrant communities are a means of economic survival, undertaken at a point where career or occupational choices are perceived as limited, at least for the immediate future. Many of these communities develop quasi-formal apprenticeship programs for the creation of business (Greene and Butler, 1996). Similar programs are being established around the United States, but as with formal incubators and business-assistance programs, the development of these programs is driven by different motivations, and they are sponsored by different groups, organized in different forms, targeted to different audiences, and used for promote different outcomes. What is shared is an underlying assumption that entrepreneurship—or the creation of new firms—can and should be taught. The programs are increasingly seen in programs for children and teenagers, economically disadvantaged individuals, and groups historically discriminated against, including by race, ethnicity, and gender.

The Eternal Search for Funds

One of the most popular topics in the study of ethnic entrepreneurship is the creation of sources of capital that are unique to the group. These sources are generally some version of a rotating credit system. An example is that each member of the group puts a designated amount into the pot. Access to the total pot then is chosen by some designated scheme, sometimes based on chance. The first individual selected uses the total funds. On repayment—which is virtually guaranteed since it is based on group solidarity and enforceable trust—the next individual takes a turn at the use of the money. The use of the funds generally entails no interest, and the amount of the fund depends on the circumstances of the group. The type, size, and organization of these types of funds vary considerably. What remains the same is that access to the fund is predicated on trust and limited to members of the group.

Recently, a related type of program has received growing attention internationally as well as in the United States. The purpose of the rotating credit system was to provide small sums of money that were not available elsewhere for small-business owners. An offshoot of this practice is that of microlending. Microlending is the current answer to filling the capital gap found in microbusinessed and has proven to be successful in third-world countries, particularly with women starting subsistence-level businesses. These programs provide the small sums of money that aspiring entrepreneurs may need to launch their business. While often targeted at specific groups, such as the economically disadvantaged or women, other programs are open to participation by a wider population.

Microlending is often associated with block grants sponsored by a governmental entity or foundation source that provides the money to some mediating unit, which then actually disperses the funds to much smaller borrowers. These units are often economic-development organizations dedicated to the creation of new businessed and the growth of existing businesses in a specific geographic area. The challenges associated with such programs include the establishment of lending criteria and the potential default rate.

The potential for combining these types of lending programs with other resources inherent in an ethnic entrepreneurial relationship is appealing, but questions remain about limitations predicated on the lack of group solidarity and enforceable trust. The defining question is whether artificially created business cohorts can develop the types of relationships that genuinely support (both instrumentally and effectively) the maintenance and growth of the businesses.

CONCLUSION

The statistics available on ethnic- and minority-owned businesses, despite the ambiguity in the data collection, illustrate the increase in the number of ethnic- and minority-owned businesses in the United States. However, and perhaps more important, the recognition of the increased business success. both in terms of survival and profitability, of these firms prompts us to ask what we can learn from the ethnic business community that can be transferred to the U.S. economic system at large.

As a cautionary note, the interest of the majority population in recreating some of the perceived benefits in the ethnic business community demands a recognition of potential costs of this type of participation. These costs include an intensified level of accountability to members of the community *in all arenas of life*, decreased flexibility regarding professional and personal decisions, and an increased degree of scrutiny in both professional and personal lives. The phenomenon itself calls for continued analysis as to potential benefits and costs to those involved in the business-creation process.

NOTES

1. For a more in-depth discussion of the relevant concepts, see Greene (1996).
2. For a review of small-business data sources on firm births and deaths, as well as an explanation of measurement concerns, see Kirchhoff (1994).
3. The total number of businesses in the United States is estimated to be approximately 20.5 million. The numbers reported here are from the U.S. Census Bureau sampling universe and include those legally organized as individual proprietorships, partnerships, or subchapter S corporations. Only firms with receipts of $500 or more are included. The statistics do not include regular (1120C) corporations.
4. The statistics reported here are calculated from data available in U.S. Department of the Census (1996) and U.S. Small Business Administration (1994).
5. For a detailed description of truncated middleman minority theory, see Butler (1991).

REFERENCES

Becker, H. (1940). "Constructive Typology in the Social Sciences." In H.D. Barnes, H. Becker, and F.B. Becker (eds.), *Contemporary Social Theory*. New York: Applegate-Century-Crofts.

Bonacich, E., and J. Modell. (1981). *The Economic Basis of Ethnic Solidarity: Small Business in the Japanese American Community*. Berkeley: University of California Press.

Boyd, W.K. (1927). *The Story of Durham: City of the New South*. Durham, NC: Duke University Press.

Butler, J.S. (1991). *Entrepreneurship and Self-Help Among Black Americans: A Reconstruction of Race and Economics*. New York: State University of New York Press.

Butler, J.S., and K.L. Wilson. (1988). "Entrepreneurial Enclaves in the African American Experience." *National Journal of Sociology*, 2, 128–166.

Dubois, W.E.B. (1911). *The College Bred Negro*. Atlanta: Atlanta University Press.

Fallers, L.A. (1967). *Immigrants and Associations*. The Hague: Mouton.

Frazier, E.F. (1925). "Durham: Capital of the Black Middle Class." In W. Reiss (ed.), *The New Negro*. New York: Boni.

Gilder, G. (1984). *The Spirit of Enterprise*. New York: Simon and Schuster.

Granovetter, M.S. (1985). "Economic Action and Social Structure: The Problem of Embeddedness." *American Journal of Sociology*, 91, 481–510.

Greene, P. (1996). "A Call for Conceptual Unity." *National Journal of Sociology*, 10(2), 49–56.

Greene, P.G., and J.S. Butler. (1996). "The Ethnic Community as a Natural Business Incubator." *Journal of Business Research*, 36, 51–59.

Hamilton, G. (1978). "Pariah Capitalism: A Paradox of Power and Dependence." *Ethnic Groups*, 2, 1–15.

Harrell, W. (1995). *For Entrepreneurs Only*. Career Press.

Johnson, C. (1938). *The Negro College Graduate*. Chapel Hill: University of North Carolina Press.

Kirchhoff, B. (1994). *Entrepreneurship and Dynamic Capitalism*. Boston: Kluwer.

Kotkin, J. (1992). *Tribes: How Race, Religion, and Identity Determine Success in the New Global Economy*. New York: Random House.

Levenstein, M. (1995). "African American Entrepreneurship: The View from the 1910 Census." *Business and Economic History*, 24, 106–121.

Levine, G.N., and C. Levine. (1981). *The Japanese American Community: A Three-Generation Study*. New York: Praeger.

Light, I. (1972). *Ethnic Enterprise in America: Business Welfare Among Chinese, Japanese, and Blacks*. Berkeley: University of California Press.

Min, P.G. (1988). *Ethnic Business Enterprise: Korean Small Business in Atlanta*. New York: Center for Migration Studies.

Muller, T. (1993). *Immigrants and the American City*. New York: New York University Press.

Portes, A., and R.L. Bach. (1985). *Latin Journey*. Berkeley: University of California Press.

Portes, A., and J. Sensenbrenner. (1993). "Embeddedness and Immigration: Notes on the Social Determinants of Economic Action. "*American Journal of Sociology*, 98, 1320–1350.

Sombart, W. (1982). *The Jews and Modern Capitalism*. New Brunswick, NJ: Transaction.

U.S. Bureau of the Census. (1996). *Survey of Minority-Owned Business Enterprises: Summary*. Washington, DC: U.S. Government Printing Office.

U.S. Small Business Administration. (1994). *Handbook of Small Business Data*. Washington, DC: U.S. Government Printing Office.

Waldinger, R., H. Aldrich, R. Ward, et al. (1990). *Ethnic Entrepreneurs*. Newburg Park, CA: Sage.

Washington, B.T. (1911). "Durham North Carolina: A City of Enterprises". *Independent* 70, 642–651.

Waterbury, J. (1972). *North for the Trade: The Life and Times of a Berber Merchant*. Berkeley: University of California Press.

Weare, W.B. (1973). *Black Business in the New South: A Social History of the North Carolina Mutual Life Insurance Company*. Chicage: University of Illinois Press.

Weber, M. (1930, 1904).*The Protestant Ethic and the Spirit of Capitalism*. Boston: Unwin Hyman.

Wilson, K.L., and W.A. Martin. (1982). "Ethnic Enclaves: A Comparison of the Cuban and Black Economies in Miami. "*American Journal of Sociology*, 86, 295–319.

Zhou, M. (1992). *Chinatown: The Socioeconomic Potential of an Urban Enclave*. Philadelphia: Temple University Press.

Zhou, M. (1995). "Low Wage Employment and Social Mobility: The Experience of Immigrant Chinese Women in New York City. *National Journal of Sociology*, 9, 1–30.

9. EVOLUTION, COMMUNITY, AND THE GLOBAL ECONOMY

ZOLTAN J. ACS

U.S. Bureau of the Census, University of Baltimore, Baltimore, MD

RANDALL MORCK

University of Alberta, Edmonton, Alberta, Canada

BERNARD YEUNG

University of Michigan, Ann Arbor, MI

INTRODUCTION

The world economy at the end of the twentieth century is characterized by increasing cross-border awareness and interdependence among nations. Both international trade and investment have had manifold increases. Total world trade increased from $629 billion (in 1995 dollars) in 1960 by eight times to $5 trillion by 1995 (world output grew only by 3.6 times) (*U.S. Economic Report of the President,* 1997, p. 243). Total world foreign direct investment went up from $48 billion in 1981 to $204 billion in 1994 (United Nations, 1994). Small firms at the end of the century show an increasing degree of importance. Their share of sales, value-added, and employment went up in the European Union era, and smaller firms in the 1990s increased their share in exports and in outward foreign direct investment in the OECD countries and in many Asian countries (OECD, 1996).

This codevelopment is not a coincidence. In the following we first argue that globalization is an Austrian process relying on entrepreneurial discovery (Kirzner, 1997). In the Austrian process, the driving force of the market process is provided neither by the consumers nor by the owners of the means of production, but by the promoting and speculating entrepreneurs. Profit seeking speculation created by market disequilibrium is the driving force of the market. Second, in this new competitive Austrian world the demand on efficiency changes firm boundaries. Previously integrated firms become groups of related firms competing consciously or unconsciously together as a team against other teams. The additional task of large multinational firms is to coordinate and utilize separate firms' assets and capabilities on a global scale. In this light, small firms play several important roles in globalization:

- Small firms may become indispensable partners in team competition. Large and small firms can create synergies to globalize their market reach and mutually enhance their respective firm value.
- Small firms are more likely than large firms to create radical innovations. They are more inclined to search in uncovered corners of the technology landscape. Therefore, small and large firms together provide a more comprehensive coverage in the supply of innovations.
- Smaller firms equipped with niche technological innovations are motivated to internationalize on their own. The successful ones become large multinational firms possessing the coordination skills and become team leaders in globalization.

GLOBALIZATION IS AN AUSTRIAN EVOLUTION PROCESS

The modern business world is characterized by globalization, by which we mean international connectedness and interdependence of firms. Walking into an English toy store, one is bound to find toys that are featured in some Japanese cartoons or U.S. movies, are manufactured by Chinese or Thai manufacturers (who buy supply from U.S. chemical companies), are shipped by Taiwan shippers with insurance coverage underwritten by European firms, are advertised by British companies, have accounting and related data processed by Irish workers, have property rights protected by U.S., Hong Kong, and even Chinese lawyers, and are marketed by one U.S. distributor, who oversees the whole chain of processes. Even identical activities within a company can be internationalized. For example, some firms have around-the-clock engineering design by coordinating electronically the work of their engineers in India, Europe, and the United States.

Three developments probably stand out as the driving force behind globalization: explosive growth in the technology that connects people and locations, creation of a freer environment for international trade and investment, and massive economic restructuring and liberalization. Explosive technological improvements in information processing create awareness of international economic opportunities. They also create the possibility for unbundling activities—for example, a clothing designer and a manufacturer can be a continent apart but only one email away from each other. The creation of a freer trade and investment environment in the form of the Eurpean Community, the North American Free Trade Agreement, Asian Pacific Economic Cooperation, World Trade Organization, and so on gives more freedom for international trade and investment. It also creates a better sense of policy stability and thus encourages investment. Large-scale economic reforms and liberalization in hitherto closed areas, such as China and Eastern Europe, provide incredibly many new economic opportunities and attract a tremendous amount of investments.

Profit-seeking firms and investors identify cross-border economic opportunities created by the three changes and act on them. These are the underlying activities in globalization.

In the above light, globalization is actually an Austrian evolution process on a global scale. Let us visualize the globalization process in the following way. Imagine that the world is cut up into disconnected nations. Formidable natural and artificial barriers have existed in information flow, trade, and investment among nations. Then the world changes: isolated localities are now physically connected, and artificial barriers to information flow, trade, and investment are broken down. The old equilibrium, which is composed of autarky equilibrium in each locality, is not sustainable. The new environment has profitable trade and real investment opportunities that were previously unavailable because of natural and artificial barriers. As firms and individuals actualize these opportunities, there will be international reallocation of production and factor inputs. Individual nations and the world undergo structural adjustments.

The shift from the old equilibrium to the new equilibrium is not automatic. It relies on the discovery and the appropriation of profit opportunities, which Kirzner (1997) refers to as *entrepreneurial discovery*. Entrepreneurial firms seek opportunities as doing cross-border business becomes a possibility. They find that some of their local goods and services may have hitherto unexplored profits in other locations. Firms more able to spot and capture international expansion opportunities prosper and become multinationals that sell their goods and services in multiple locations. In the process, trade and international investment go up, productivity increases, factor and goods prices change, consumption patterns adjust, and the world shifts from the old equilibrium to the new globally efficient equilibrium. Globalization clearly is an Austrian dynamic process. A rigorous process of entrepreneurial discovery on a global scale is the driver of globalization.

There is a positive feedback effect. Globalization by itself speeds up the rate of entrepreneurial discovery and thus the dynamic evolution of the global economy. First, globalization gives innovations a wider scope of application and therefore a much greater reward than they commenced in the old autarky equilibrium. As a consequence, new ideas are created and implemented more often. Second, practice makes perfect: firms learn over time to better spot and capture international economic opportunities. Finally, because of rapid information flow and convenience in cross-border business, globalization increases the number of profit seekers, and innovation profits disappear fast. Firms race to be more innovative and to bring innovations onto markets fast. Less innovative firms are more likely to be outcompeted than in the past. Hence, product cycle time is shortened, and discontinuous changes are more frequent. Overall, globalization leads to a faster pace of creative destruction.

MULTINATIONAL FIRMS AND THE CHANGING COMPETITION BOUNDARIES

We usually consider competition as conducted by value-maximizing firms each being an axiomatic player converting inputs into output. In this consideration, we are tempted to consider that multinational firms are successful competitors and the key to globalization because of their international trade and investment activities. We would like to point out in this section that while multinational firms are indeed key players in globalization, smaller firms play an integral role too. Globalization, as driven by invigorated entrepreneurial discovery on a global scale, adds to the nature of cross-border business the emphasis on efficient coordination of value chain activities. As a consequence, the landscape of global competition is not characterized by axiomatic firms competing against one another. Instead, competition is among groups of firms. In this view, small firms have a naturally important presence because they are indispensable components in the group competition.

Multinationals Are Making Entrepreneurial Discoveries

There is a presumption that large multinational firms are the key suppliers of entrepreneurial discoveries. Multinationals have a proven record of implementing innovations on a global scale. Multinational firms get handsome profits because they possess unique skills that enable them to sell goods and services in multiple countries. Indigenous firms usually have an advantage over outsiders because they know more about the local environment and already have established relationships with vertically related businesses, ranging from intermediate good suppliers to local governments to local consumers. Indigenous firms with a home-court advantage can easily imitate foreign entrants' ordinary goods and services and then drive the entrants out. The outsiders must possess unique and difficult-to-imitate skills to overcome the home-court advantage of indigenous firms. These are information-based capabilities in technology, production, marketing, and management. The internationalization of the application of these capabilities is by itself an entrepreneurial discovery process.

Morck and Yeung (1991, 1992) test the idea using financial economic methods. In their 1991 article, they regress Tobin's *q* on dummies capturing a firm's multinational structure, on proxies capturing production and marketing intangibles, and on the cross-terms between the multinational dummies and intangible proxies. They find that the multinational structure dummies indeed significantly augment firm value. But they become insignificant in the presence of the cross-terms. The cross-terms have positive and significant regression coefficients. The interpretation is that a multinational structure enhances firm value because a firm expands the application of its intangible assets internationally. In their 1992 article, they retest the idea by regressing stock price reactions to news on foreign acquisition on proxies capturing production, marketing, and management intangibles. They find that foreign acquisition increases firm value only when an acquirer possesses intangibles. Otherwise, foreign acquisition reduces firm value.

Multinational firms, once established, have three additional advantages in supplying entrepreneurial discovery. First, their past successes lead to handsome current financial resources that are vitally important in financing the development and commercialization of new innovations. Second, multinational firms' networks of affiliates give them an advantage in spotting innovations and associated international profit opportunities. Third, their secured multinational networks of affiliates allow them to quickly implement viable innovations on a global scale at low risk and cost. Their larger size and greater resources strengthen their ability to overcome entry barriers.

The Changing Means of Competition Boundaries

Undeniably, multinationals are key players in globalization: they are the conduit of changes, and they are the chief beneficiaries of globalization. Their presumed dominance, however, can easily be pushed too far to suggest that small firms have withering survivorship. For example, one may argue that small firms with no global market access will find that their factor inputs generate less return than when employed by multinational firms. How would anyone then be interested in investing and in working for small firms? Certainly that is incorrect. In spite of the presumed dominance of multinational firms in a globalized world, there is growing evidence that small-firm vitality grows in the globalization era. The latest OECD study on small firms finds that they have increased their share in sales, value added, trade, and innovation in both OECD and many developing countries.

To understand the phenomenon, we must change our concept of firm competition. Dunning (1995) suggests in the context of globalization that firm boundaries are changing. Dunning argues that the traditional firm boundaries are defined by ownership-conferred decision rights. Globalization, however, has changed the nature of firm activities substantially. Firm focus is no longer purely on production; it becomes the coordination of value-chain activities ranging from R&D to design to sourcing to production and to marketing.

This view is certainly in concordance with our early point at the end of the section on Globalization. In an Austrian Evolution Process that globalization strives on and drives up entrepreneurial discovery. Globalization is to search globally for more efficient and profitable ways to serve as many customers in as many locations as possible. The latest advancements in communication technology and economic liberalization allow firms more freedom to go anywhere a component of the value chain is most efficiently supplied. Firms are also driven by profit incentives and competition to seek as many assets and capabilities as possible that are complementary to their existing assets and capabilities. Firms are drawn together by the complementarity of their assets and skills in efficiently and profitably generating goods and services for consumers on a global scale.

In the new competitive landscape, firm boundaries are replaced by team boundaries. Firms can now be thought of as coordinated transaction units rather than merely integrated production units. The traditional perception of a firm is that it is an integrated hierarchy transforming inputs to outputs. However, why would hierarchical integration always be optimal? It is not the only means for organizing the transformation of inputs to output. Global competition demands efficiency in arranging these activities. For example, GM has long been wrestling with the questions of when to outsource and which units of GM should become independent.

The transactional relationship between transaction units is a prominent issue in the era of globalization.

Williamson (1991) points out that the governance structure of transactions can be broadly categorized into three modes: market, hierarchy, and the hybrids in between. The comparison of the advantage of the various modes of governance depends on the needs the governance structure serves. The market transaction mode promotes incentive to perform and the ability to adjust to exogenous market changes (such as price changes) that call for autonomy. The hierarchical mode promotes administrative controls and the ability to adapt to changes that call for coordinated responses (such as mutual adjustments in investment and in interaction frequencies). Williamson also points out that judiciary efficiency and effectiveness increases most extensively the effectiveness in the market mode of transactions. Hybrid relationships always score in the middle in the aforementioned comparisons.

Williamson's analytical result suggests that the chosen mode of transactional governance depends on the institutional environment, including commercial risks, political risks, contract laws, and property-rights protection. It also depends on the nature of the transactions. For example, an arm's-length relationship is less preferred when asset specificity is presence, it is also less preferred when independent performance incentives and adjustments to exogenous shock are less important. Global competition probably forces firms to intelligently adopt the optimal transaction governance. Thus, GM has to reduce its extent of integration. The garment industry is now characterized by vertically cooperating but legally separated firm units, each specializing in design, distribution and promotion, and actual manufacturing.

One probably wants to add to Williamson's consideration some simple economic changes. For example, changes in tax laws and government coverage on welfare raise the cost of employment. Larger firms are often required to pay handsome fringe employment benefits. Turning a subunit into an smaller independent firm probably saves employment cost.

Recall that one of multinationals' core assignments in globalization is to coordinate efforts to bring goods and services to consumers globally. Williamson's perspective clearly leads to the conclusion that vertical integration is not necessarily the chosen mode of governance. It will often be the case that *independent* small firms are a part of a team competing globally; their affiliation may be in the form of hybrid dependence or simply at arm's length. In other words, they are partners in a joint effort to conduct entrepreneurial discovery. Large multinational firms will own (integrate) a unit and its production assets when a transaction node in the value chain calls for specific assets, administrative controls, and tight internal coordination. In these cases, the coordinating multinational firm absorbs a smaller firm as an integrated (merged) unit. The perspective suggests that small firms are often part of an orchestrated global effort coordinated by a large firm for the purpose of maintaining its global competitiveness.

Globalization changes the competition landscape: the competitive pressure is higher while specialization and agglomeration are up, the means of competition is more multidimensional, the competition contact points between firms are multiple location, and so on. Globalization also changes the institutional environment of transactions: increase in the size of potential participants reduces the threats of opportunistic behavior, improvement in judicial efficiency and property rights protection are obvious, and so on. Adopting Williamson's (1991) perspective, and indeed an earlier one by Stigler (1951), one would naturally come to the prediction that there ought to be large-scale restructuring of the transaction relationship between firm units. Observed active acquisition, formation of alliances, divestiture, and splitting of companies collaborate on the relevancy of the theoretical perspective.

SMALL AND LARGE FIRMS ARE SYNERGISTIC PARTNERS IN GLOBAL COMPETITION

In accordance with the above perspective, Acs, Morck, Shaver, and Yeung (1997) explicitly suggest that smaller and larger firms have a synergistic relationship in the globalization effort. If the leader of entrepreneurial discovery (a multinational firm) sees value in a small firm's capability, the small firm will be a component of its coordinated globalization effort. The small firm's value to the multinational firm may stem from the complementarity between their respective assets and capability (such an the match between an auto components firm and an autoassembler). It may also stem from the intrinsic and independent value of the small firm's innovation (such as the value of a unique patent of a small pharmaceutical firm to a multinational pharmaceutical giant). The small firm's contribution will be globalized indirectly in the form of acquisition, arm's-length transaction, or hybrid dependence. From the small firm's perspective, it benefits from having an access to the multinational firm's global market reach. In this arrangement, the large firms' contribution is the coordination of profitable globalization, while small firms provide efficient support for the endeavor.

The consequence is not only that smaller firms' contribution is globalized but that their reward is increased because of the larger scope of applications of their capabilities. However, the world is now a volatile one. A small firm faces hidden competition. Global competition will force larger firms to search for more efficient partners everywhere in the world. Nonperforming small firms, and subunits alike, can lose their business to another small firm in a country it may not even know exists. Globalization increases both the returns and risks for small firms.

Acs et al. (1997) recognize that smaller firms can conduct international expansion on their own. They compare the two modes of international expansion: direct versus intermediated by a multinational firm. They argue that when a small firm conducts direct expansion, it has to pay for the internationalization costs, which include market-entry costs and property-rights protection costs. In the intermediated mode, the small firm saves the internationalization costs but has to absorb some deadweight transactions costs and rent extraction by the intermediator. They argue that when competition among qualified intermediators bid away rent extraction, the private choice between the two modes of international expansion is socially efficient in the sense that the small firm's contribution is maximized. (We shall discuss later which types of small firms are more likely to internationalize directly.)

There are certainly ample examples of small firms that use large firms' global access to internationalize their market reach. Gomes-Casseres (1997) reports that small electronic firms form alliances with large firms to increase their capability to exploit their niche on a grander scale. Many garment factories in developing countries benefit from such intermediated internationalization.

SMALL FIRMS ARE RADICAL INNOVATORS

Some small firms possess radical innovations and are therefore key contributors to an international Schumpeterian process. Acs et al. (1997) suggest that smaller firms are more likely to make radical innovations than larger firms. Innovations arise only when property rights are properly aligned. Ace et al. argue that property rights may be less properly aligned in larger corporation than in smaller companies and among individual innovators, An innovator in a large company has only very limited property rights protection. The innovation result generally belong to the corporation and not for the employee who invented it. This creates the tendency to free-ride on others' innovative efforts in a large company. Some may argue that the agency problem can be alleviated by incentive contracts. However, a proper incentive contract has to depend on ex post innovation results. This creates the tendency for established innovators to entrench and stifle the emergence of radical innovations that undermine the value of old innovations. All these concerns reduce creativity within a large company.

In contrast to innovative employees in large corporations, independent innovators can hold clear property rights, can have every incentive to undertake radical innovation, and can be largely free of red tape. Thus, smaller firms are better at creating radical innovations. As such, they are often valuable contributors in the entrepreneurial discovery process.

Almeida and Kogut (1997) argue further that small firms may take a different approach to innovating than large firms take. Their first theoretical argument hinges on the difference in organization incentives between large and small firms, which leads to a deduction as in Acs et al. (1997). They further argue that small firms have fewer resources than large firms and thus rely more on localized knowledge networks for important inputs to the innovation process. They then use patent citation data to examine the innovation in the semiconductor industry regarding firms' exploration of technological diversity and their integration within local knowledge networks. Comparing the innovative activity of startup firms and larger firms, they find that small firms do explore new technological areas by innovating in less crowded areas and are tied into regional knowledge networks to a greater extent than large firms.

Note that the Acs et al. article and the Almeida and Kogut article together suggest that small and large firms complement each other in generating technological innovations. The Almeida and Kogut results imply that small and large firms will together give a more comprehensive search for innovations in the technological opportunity set. The Acs et al. article suggests that small and large firms play complementary roles: small firms form radical innovations, while large firms pursue the deepening of existing innovations. We speculate that small firms are chiefly responsible for the initiation of radical innovations, while large firms are chiefly responsible for the massive commercialization of innovations.

SMALL FIRMS WITH NICHE TECHNOLOGICAL INNOVATIONS INTERNATIONALIZE ALONE

Small firms with radical technological innovations are inclined to internationalize on their own. Morck and Yeung (1992) find that large and small firms depend on different types of intangibles: smaller multinational firms' foreign acquisition gains derive from the possession of production-related intangibles (proxied by R&D spending), while larger firms' foreign acquisition gains depend on marketing related intangibles (Morck and Yeung, 1992, table 4, regressions 4.3 and 4.4). The result implies that the possession of unique innovations of the production type is crucial for small firms' direct international expansion. As the firm gains international management experiences and establishes a larger network of international affiliates, softer skills like marketing and coordination assume their dominance. These firms become the "team" coordination leaders in Dunning's world.

Kohn (1997) reports results corroborating the point that smaller firms' direct internationalization effort relies on production-related skills. Kohn finds that smaller firms do internationalize on their own. These are small firms possessing R&D-related capabilities and often reside in less mature industries than other smaller firms. (On the other hand, larger firms that conduct foreign direct investment often reside in more mature industries than other larger firms.) One explanation for these smaller firms' tendency to conduct wholly owned internationalization is that hierarchical control of their property rights is important for them to claim the first-mover advantage of their innovations.[1] In terms of the argument in Acs et al. (1997), smaller firms equipped with production-related intangibles find that expanding the international application of these skills via intermediation by larger firms leads to high transactions and rent extraction costs and thus is inferior to direct international expansion.

Collaborative evidence for the firm life-cycle idea is found in Harris, Morck, Slemrod, and Yeung (1993), which reports a study on income-shifting behavior. They find that smaller firms do not seem to conduct much income shifting to reduce taxes while larger multinational firms do. Hence, a firm relies on hard intangible capabilities in the young stage and makes uses of soft intangibles like income shifting (a kind of coordination) only in a more mature stage.

CONCLUSION

In this chapter, we have discussed the contributions of small firms and how those contributions relation to large firms in the global economy. We see globalization as an Austrian evolution process based on entrepreneurial discovery. The process involves creating innovations, discovering profitable application of the innovations across borders, and actually capturing the profit opportunities. The process is invigorated by technological progress in communication, by liberalization of economies, and by opening up of trade and investment. Small firms with production innovations internationalize on their own. The successful ones become the large multinationals that have learned global coordination skills. Their softer skills then equip them to search and appropriate other unexplored profit (and efficiency-improving) opportunities, which include internationalizing some smaller firms' worthy innovations and skills.

In this light, small and large firms have a synergistic relationship in globalization. Smaller firms' earnings from innovations increase because larger firms intermediate the international diffusion of their innovations. In turn, large firms' competitiveness and earnings are increased by intermediating small firms' worthy innovations. Thence, small and large firms provide each other with mutual stimulation in terms of innovation creation and tendency to expand internationally. There is also mutual dependence in terms of profits between large and small firms.

We also argue that based on property-rights protection within firms small firms are more likely to be radical innovators than large firms. Their approach in searching for innovations is also fundamentally different from large firms' approach. These differences between large and small firms allow our search for innovation to have a more complete coverage. We suggest that small firms form radical innovations while larger firms conduct a commercial deepening of innovations.

Our argument suggests that small and large firms are playing complementary roles in today's rigorous, globalized Austrian evolution. Besides the complementary efforts in searching for innovation opportunities, one can hardly overlook the efficiency stimulation that small and large firms interactively provide. The stimulation comes in several ways. As we have pointed out, multinational firms can intermediate the internationalization of small firms' innovations and thus increase the speed of their international diffusion. The channel of internationalization increases the reward for innovation and thus elicits innovation efforts (see also Morck and Yeung, (1995, p. 440). Multinationals serve as information-gathering and processing machines for nonmultinational firms. Aitken, Hanson, and Harrison (1997) show empirically that multinationals stimulate exports behavior. Bailey and Gersbach (1995) argue that multinationals transmit back home global best practices. The higher incidence of vertical linkage between firms (domestic and multinational, large and small) undoubtedly raises the speed of international technology transfer and the diffusion of innovations. Finally, rigorous global competition hastens the demise of inefficient and noninnovative firms. It also renders rigid and protective economic policies more impractical.

NOTE

1. One should not conclude that smaller firms possessing other types of innovations do not internationalize. As we have pointed out already, they may internationalize via larger firms' intermediation, including being acquired by larger firms.

REFERENCES

Acs, Zoltan, Randall Morck, Myles Shaver, and Bernard Yeung. (1997). "Small and Medium-Size Enterprises in the Global Economy." *Small Business Economics*, 9(1), 7–20.

Aitken, Brian, Gordon H. Hanson, and Ann E. Harrison. (1997). "Spillovers, Foreign Investment, and Export Behavior." *Journal of International Economics*, 43(1–2), 103–132.

Almeida, Paul, and Bruce Kogut. (1997). "The Exploration of Technological Diversity and Geographic Localization in Start-up Firms in the Semiconductor Industry." *Small Business Economy*, 9(1), 21–31.

Bailey, Martin, and Hans Gersbach. (1995). "Efficiency in Manufacturing and the Need for Global Competition." *Brookings Papers on Economic Activity*, 307–347.

Dunning, John H. (1995). "Reconfiguring the Boundaries of International Business Activities." Paper presented at the Conference on Euro-Pacific Investment and Trade, Halifax, Nova Scotia.

Economic Report of the President. (1997). Washington, DC: U.S. Government Printing Office.

Gomes-Casseres, Benjamin. (1997). "Alliance Strategies of Small Firms." *Small Business Economics*, 9(1), 33–99.

Harris, David, Randall Morck, Joel Slemrod, and Bernard Yeung. (1993) ."Income Shifting in U.S. Multinational Corporations." In Alberto Giovinnini, Glen Hubbard, and Joel Slemrod (eds.), *Studies in International Taxation Chicago*: University of Chicago Press.

Kirzner, Isreal M. (1997). "Enterpreneurial Discovery and the Competitive Market Process: An Austrian Approach." *Journal of Economics Literature*, 35(1)(March), 60–85.

Kohn, Tomas O. (1997). "Small Firms as International Players." *Small Business Economics*, 9(1), 45–51.

Morck, Randall, and Bernard Yeung. (1991). "Why Investors Value Multinationality." *Journal of Business*, 64(2), 165–187.

Morck, Randall, and Bernard Yeung. (1992). "Internalization: An Event Study Test." *Journal of International Economics*, 33, 41–56.

Morck, Randall, and Bernard Yeung. (1995). "The Corporate Governance of Multinationals." In Ronald Daniels and Randall Morck (eds.), *Corporate Decision-Making in Canada. Calgary, Alberta*: Industry Canada Research Series, University of Calgary Press.

OECD. (1996). *SMEs Employment, Innovation, and Growth: The Washington Workshop*. Paris: OECD.

Stigler, George. (1951). "The Division of Labor Is Limited by the Extent of the Market." *Journal of Political Economy*, 59(June), 185–193.

Williamson, Oliver. (1991). "Comparative Economic Organization: The Analysis of Discrete Structure Alternatives." *Administrative Science Quarterly*, 36, 269–296.

United Nations. (1994). *World Investment Report*. Geneva S.W.

10. SMALL BUSINESSES, INNOVATION, AND PUBLIC POLICY

JOSHUA LERNER

National Bureau of Economic Research and Harvard University, Boston, MA

This chapter examines the question of the contribution of small businesses to the process of technological innovation. This complex issue has been one of the most researched topics in the empirical industrial organization literature. To summarize these discussions in a few pages in thus a daunting challenge.

Consequently, this essay takes a selective approach to these issues. First, I briefly summarize the academic literature on the relationship between firm size and innovation. This work suggests that there appears to be a weak relationship between firm size, the tendency to undertake R&D, and the effectiveness of research spending. Small businesses, in aggregate, do not appear to be particularly research intensive or innovative.

I then turn to examining one subset of small businesses that do appear to excel at innovation: venture-capital-backed startups. I highlight some of the venture-backed firms' contributions. I also discuss why the success of such firms is not accidental. In particular, I highlight the key problems that the financing of small innovative companies pose, as well as some of the key mechanisms that venture investors employ to guide the innovation process.

Finally, I consider one set of policy issues related to small firms and innovation. In particular, I discuss some recent changes in the intellectual property protection system that appear to favor larger firms. I then argue that this may be an area that would reward increased attention by policymakers interested in helping innovative small businesses.

SMALL BUSINESS AND INNOVATION

A substantial but largely inconclusive literature examines the relationship between firm size and innovation. These studies have been handicapped by the difficulty of measuring innovative inputs and outputs, as well as by the challenges of creating a sample that is free of selection biases and other estimation problems. Although a detailed review of this literature is beyond the scope of this piece, the interested reader can turn to surveys by Baldwin and Scott (1987) and Cohen and Levin (1989).

Much of the work in this literature has sought to relate measures of innovative discoveries—whether R&D expenditures, patents, inventions, or other measures—to firm size. Initial studies were undertaken using the largest manufacturing firms; more recent work have employed larger samples and more disaggregated data (such as studies employing data on firms' specific lines of business). Despite the improved methodology of recent studies, the results have remained inconclusive: even when a significant relationship between firm size and innovation has been found, it has had little economic significance. For instance, Cohen, Levin, and Mowery (1987) concluded that a doubling of firm size increased the ratio of R&D to sales by only 0.2 percent.

One of the relatively few empirical regularities emerging from studies of technological innovation is the critical role played by small firms and new entrants in certain industries. The role of entrants—typically *de novo* startups—in emerging industries was highlighted, for instance, in the pioneering case-study-based research of Jewkes, Sawers, and Stillerman (1958).

Acs and Audretsch (1988) examined this question more systematically. They documented that the contribution of small firms to innovation was a function that was sensitive to industry conditions: the contribution was greatest in immature industries that were relatively unconcentrated. These findings suggested that entrepreneurs and small firms often played a key role in observing where new technologies could be applied to meet customer needs and in rapidly introducing products. These patterns are also predicted in several models of technological competition, many of which were reviewed in Reinganum (1989), as well in several analyses in the organizational behavior literature (several are discussed in Henderson, 1993).

The 1990s have seen several dramatic illustrations of this patterns. Two potentially revolutionary areas of technological innovation—biotechnology and the Internet—were pioneered by smaller entrants. Neither established drug companies nor mainframe computer manufacturers were pioneers in developing these technologies. By and large, small firms did not invent the key genetic engineering techniques or Internet protocols. Rather, most of the enabling technologies were developed with federal funds at academic institutions and research laboratories. It was the small entrants, however, who were the first to seize on the commercial opportunities.

VENTURE CAPITAL AND INNOVATION[1]

One set of small firms, however, appears to have had a disproportionate effect on innovation: those backed by venture capitalists. (*Venture capital* can be defined as equity or equity-linked investments in young, privately held companies, where the investor is a financial intermediary who is typically acting as a director, advisor, or even manager of the firm.) While venture capitalists fund only a few hundred of the nearly 1 million businesses begun in the United States each year, these firms have a disproportionate impact on technological innovation.[2]

This claim is supported by a variety of evidence. One measure, while crude, is provided by the firms that "graduate" to the public marketplace. In the past two decades, more than one-third of the companies going public (weighted by value) have been backed by venture investors. (Venture-backed IPOs have included such firms as Microsoft, Cisco Systems, Genentech, and Intel.)

A second way to assess these claims is to examine *which* firms have been funded. Venture capitalists, while contributing a relatively modest share of the total financing, provided critical early capital and guidance to many of the new firms in such emerging industries as biotechnology, computer networking, and the Internet. In some cases, these new firms—utilizing the capital, expertise, and contacts provided by their venture-capital investors—established themselves as market leaders. In other instances, they were acquired by larger corporations or entered into licensing arrangements with such concerns. Consider, for instance, the biotechnology industry. Venture capitalists provided only a small fraction of the external financing raised in the industry,[3] and only 450 out of 1,500 firms have received venture financing through 1995. These venture-backed firms, however, accounted for over 85 percent of the patents awarded and drugs approved for marketing.

A final way to assess the impact of the venture industry is to consider the impact of venture-backed firms. While systematic evidence is scant—and its interpretation is hampered by difficult measurement issues—survey results suggest that these investments have powerful impacts. For instance, a mid-1996 survey by the venture organization Kleiner, Perkins, Caufield, and Byers found that the firms that the partnership had financed since its inception in 1971 had created 131,000 jobs, generated $44 billion in annual revenues, and had $84 billion in market capitalization (Peltz, 1996). While Kleiner, Perkins is one of the most successful venture-capital groups, the results are suggestive of the impact of the industry.

Lending particular relevance to an examination of these firms is the tremendous boom in the U.S. venture-capital industry in recent years. The pool of venture partnerships has grown tenfold, from under $4 billion in 1978 to about $40 billion at the end of 1995. Venture capital's recent growth has outstripped that of almost every class of financial product.

It is worth underscoring that the tremendous success of venture-backed firms has not happened by accident. The interactions between venture capitalists and the entrepreneurs that they finance are often complex. They can be understood, however, as a response to the challenges that the financing of emerging-growth companies pose. Entrepreneurs rarely have the capital to see their ideas to fruition and must rely on outside financiers. Meanwhile, those who control capital—for instance, pension-fund trustees and university overseers—are unlikely to have the time or expertise to invest directly in young or restructuring firms. Some entrepreneurs might turn to other financing sources, such as bank loans or the issuance of public stock, to meet their needs. But because of four key factors, some of the most potentially profitable and exciting firms would be unable to access financing if venture capital did not exist.

The first factor, uncertainty, is a measure of the array of potential outcomes for a company or project. The wider the dispersion of potential outcomes, the greater the uncertainty. By their very nature, young companies are associated with significant levels of uncertainty. Uncertainty surrounds whether the research program or new product will succeed. The response of a firm's rivals may also be uncertain. High uncertainty means that investors and entrepreneurs cannot confidently predict what the company will look like in the future.

Uncertainty affects the willingness of investors to contribute capital, the desire of suppliers to extend credit, and the decisions of a firm's managers. If managers are adverse to taking risks, it may be difficult to induce them to make the right decisions. Conversely, if entrepreneurs are overoptimistic, then investors want to curtail various actions. Uncertainty also affects the timing of investment. Should an investor contribute all the capital at the beginning, or should he stage the investment through time? Investors need to know how information-gathering activities can address these concerns and when they should be undertaken.

The second factor, asymmetric information (or information disparities), is distinct from uncertainty. Because of his day-to-day involvement with the firm, an entrepreneur knows more about his company's prospects than investors, suppliers, or strategic partners. Various problems develop in settings where asymmetric information is prevalent. For instance, the entrepreneur may take detrimental actions that investors cannot observe: perhaps undertaking a riskier strategy than initially suggested or not working as hard as the investor expects. The entrepreneur might also invest in projects that build up his reputation at the investors' expense.

Asymmetric information can also lead to selection problems. The entrepreneur may exploit the fact that he knows more about the project or his abilities than investors do. Investors may find it difficult to distinguish between competent entrepreneurs and incompetent ones. Without the ability to screen out unacceptable projects and entrepreneurs, investors are unable to make efficient and appropriate decisions.

The third factor affecting a firm's corporate and financial strategy is the nature of its assets. Firms that have tangible assets—such as machines, buildings, land, or physical inventory—may find financing easier to obtain or may be able to obtain more favorable terms. The ability to abscond with the firm's source of value is more difficult when it relies on physical assets. When the most important assets are intangible, such as trade secrets, raising outside financing from traditional sources may be more challenging.

Market conditions also play a key role in determining the difficulty of financing firms. Both the capital and product markets may be subject to substantial variations. The supply of capital from public investors and the price at which this capital is available may vary dramatically. These changes may be a response to regulatory edicts or shifts in investors' perceptions of future profitability. Similarly, the nature of product markets may vary dramatically, whether due to shifts in the intensity of competition with rivals or in the nature of the customers. If there is exceedingly intense competition or a great deal of uncertainty about the size of the potential market, firms may find it very difficult to raise capital from traditional sources.

Venture capitalists have a variety of mechanisms at their disposal to address these changing factors. They will invest in stages, often at increasing valuations. Each refinancing is tied to a reevaluation of the company and its prospects. In these financings, they will employ complex financing mechanisms, often hybrid securities like convertible preferred equity or convertible debt. These financial structures can potentially screen out overconfident or underqualified entrepreneurs and reduce the venture capitalists' risks. They will also shift the mixture of investors *from whom* a firm acquires capital. Each source—private equity investors, corporations, and the public markets—may be appropriate for a firm at different points in its life. Venture capitalists provide not only introductions to these other sources of capital but certification—a "stamp of approval" that addresses the concerns of other investors. Finally, once the investment is made, they monitor and work with the entrepreneurs to ensure that the right operational and strategic decisions are made and implemented.

INNOVATION, SMALL BUSINESS, AND PUBLIC POLICY[4]

If small firms—or even some subsets of small firms—are playing an important role in the innovation process, one policy goal should be to address threats to their future development. This is particularly true of threats that have been created by misguided government policies, however good the intentions of their designers. The area that I believe deserves particular attention relates to the key mechanism for protecting intellectual property—namely, patents.

The U.S. patent system has undergone a profound shift over the past fifteen years. The strength of patent protection has been dramatically bolstered, and both large and small firms are devoting considerably more effort to seeking patent protection and defending their patents in the courts. Many in the patent community—U.S. Patent and Trademark Office officials, the patent bar, and corporate patent staff—have welcomed these changes. But viewed more broadly, the reforms of the patent system and the consequent growth of patent litigation have created a substantial "innovation tax" that afflicts some of America's most important and creative small firms.[5]

Almost all formal disputes involving issued patents are tried in the federal judicial system. The initial litigation must be undertaken in a district court. Prior to 1982, appeals of patent cases were heard in the appellate courts of the various circuits. These differed considerably in their interpretation of patent law. Because few appeals of patent cases were heard by the U.S. Supreme Court, substantial differences persisted, leading to widespread "forum shopping" by litigants.

In 1982, the U.S. Congress established a centralized appellate court for patent cases—the Court of Appeals for the Federal Circuit (CAFC). As Robert Merges (1992) observes,

While the CAFC was ostensibly formed strictly to unify patent doctrine, it was no doubt hoped by some (and expected by others) that the new court would make subtle alterations in the doctrinal fabric, with an eye to enhancing the patent system. To judge by results, that is exactly what happened.

The CAFC's rulings have been more "pro-patent" than the previous courts. For instance, the circuit courts had affirmed 62 percent of district court findings of patent infringement in the three decades prior to the creation of the CAFC, while the CAFC in its first eight years affirmed 90 percent of such decisions (Koenig, 1980; Harmon, 1991).

The strengthening of patent law has not gone unnoticed by corporations. Over the past decade, patents awarded to U.S. corporations have increased by 50 percent. Furthermore, the willingness of firms to litigate patents has increased considerably. The number of patent suits instituted in the federal courts has increased from 795 in 1981 to 1,553 in 1993; adversarial proceedings within the U.S. Patent and Trademark Office have increased from 246 in 1980 to 684 in 1992 (Administrative Office of the United States Courts, various years; U.S. Patent and Trademark Office, various years). My recent analysis of litigation by firms based in Middlesex County, Massachusetts, suggests that six intellectual-property-related suits are filed for every 100 patent awards to corporations. These suits lead to significant expenditures by firms. Based on historical costs, I estimate that patent litigation begun in 1991 will lead to total legal expenditures (in 1991 dollars) of over $1 billion, a substantial amount relative to the $3.7 billion spent by U.S. firms on basic research in 1991 (these findings are summarized in Lerner, 1995). Litigation also leads to substantial indirect costs. The discovery process is likely to require the alleged infringer to produce extensive documentation and time-consuming depositions from employees and may generate unfavorable publicity. Its officers and directors may also be held individually liable.

As firms have realized the value of their patent positions, they have begun reviewing their stockpiles of issued patents. Several companies, including Texas Instruments, Intel, Wang Laboratories, and Digital Equipment, have established groups that approach rivals to demand royalties on old patent awards. In many cases, they have been successful in extracting license agreements or past royalties. For instance, Texas Instruments is estimated to have netted $257 million in 1991 from patent licenses and settlements resulting from their general counsel's aggressive enforcement policy (Rosen, 1992).

Particularly striking, practitioner accounts suggest, has been the growth of litigation—and threats of litigation—between large and small firms.[6] This trend is disturbing. While litigation is clearly a necessary mechanism to defend property rights, the proliferation of such suits may be leading to transfers of financial resources from some of the youngest and most innovative firms to more established, better-capitalized concerns. Even if the target firm feels that it does not infringe, it may choose to settle rather than fight. It either may be unable to raise the capital to finance a protracted court battle or else may believe that the publicity associated with the litigation will depress the valuation of its equity.

In addition, these small firms may reduce or alter their investment in R&D. For instance, a 1990 survey of 376 firms found that the time and expense of intellectual property litigation was a major factor in the decision to pursue an innovation for almost twice as many firms with under 500 employees than for larger businesses (Koen, 1990). These claims are also supported by my study (Lerner, 1995) of the patenting behavior of new biotechnology firms that have different litigation costs. I showed that firms with high litigation costs are less likely to patent in subclasses with many other awards, particularly those of firms with low litigation costs.

These effects have been particularly pernicious in emerging industries. Chronically strained for resources, USPTO officials are unlikely to assign many patent examiners to emerging technologies in advance of a wave of applications. As patent applications begin flowing in, the USPTO frequently finds the retention of the few examiners skilled in the new technologies difficult. Companies are likely to hire away all but the least able examiners. These examiners are valuable not only for their knowledge of the USPTO examination procedure in the new technology but also for their understanding of what other patent applications are in process but not awarded. (U.S. patent applications are held confidential until time of award.) Many of the examinations in emerging technologies are as a result performed under severe time pressures by inexperienced examiners. Consequently, awards of patents in several critical new technologies have been delayed and highly inconsistent. These ambiguities have created ample opportunities for firms that seek to aggressively litigate their patent awards. The clearest examples of this problem are the biotechnology and software industries.

It might be asked why policymakers have not addressed the deleterious effects of patent policy changes. The difficulties that federal officials have faced in reforming the patent system are perhaps best illustrated by the efforts to simplify one of the most arcane aspects of our patent system, the first-to-invent policy. With the exception of the Philippines and Jordan, all other nations award patents to firms that are the first to file for patent protection. The United States, however, has clung to the first-to-invent system. In the United States, a patent will be awarded to the party who can demonstrate (through laboratory notebooks and other evidence) that he was the initial discoverer of a new invention, even if he did not file for patent protection until after others did (within certain limits). A frequently invoked argument for the first-to-invent system is that this provides protection for small inventors, who may take longer to translate a discovery into a completed patent application.

While this argument is initially compelling, the reality is quite different. Disputes over priority of invention are resolved through a proceeding—known as an *interference*—before the USPTO's Board of Patent Appeals and Interferences. The Board will hold a hearing to determine which inventor first made the discovery.

The interference process has been characterized as "an archaic procedure, replete with traps for the unwary" (Calvert, 1980). These interferences consume a considerable amount of resources: the adjudication of the average interference is estimated to cost over $100,000 (Kingston, 1992). Yet in recent years, in only about fifty-five cases annually has the party that was second to file been determined to have been the first to invent (Calvert and Sofocleous, 1992). Thus, the United States persists in this complex, costly, and idiosyncratic system in order to reverse the priority of 0.03 percent of the patent applications filed each year.

But this system has proved very resistant to change. At least since 1967, proposals have been unsuccessfully offered to shift the United States to a first-to-file system. As recently as January 1994, USPTO Commissioner Bruce Lehman was forced to withdraw such a proposal. While the voices raised in protest over his initiative—as those opposing earlier reform attempts—were led by advocates for small inventors, it is difficult not to conclude that the greatest beneficiary from the first-to-file system is the small subset of the patent bar that specializes in interference law.

It may be thought puzzling that independent inventors, who are generally unable to afford costly litigation, have been so active in supporting the retention of a first-to-invent policy. A frequently voiced complaint is that small inventors take longer to prepare patent applications and hence would lose out to better-financed rivals in a first-to-file world. This argument appears to be specious for several reasons. First, economically important discoveries are typically the subject of patent filings in a number of countries. Thus, there is already an enormous pressure to file quickly. Second, the recent reforms of the U.S. system have created a new provisional patent application, which is much simpler to file than a full-fledged application. Finally, Commissioner of Patents and Trademark Bruce Lehman notes that many most vocal independent inventors opposing patent reform are "weekend lobbyists . . . [rather than representatives of] knowledge-based industries" (Chartrand, 1995).

As this case study suggests, the failure of federal reform efforts is due to several factors. First, the issues are complex and sometimes difficult to understand. Simplistic claims frequently cloud these discussions. For instance, because firms use patents to protect innovations, it is frequently argued that a stronger patent system will lead to more innovation. Second, the people with the greatest economic stake in retaining a litigious and complex patent system—the patent bar—have proven to be a powerful lobby. The efforts of the highly specialized interference bar to retain a first-to-invent system is a prime example. Finally, the top executives of technology-intensive firms have not mounted an effective campaign around these issues. The reason may be that the companies that are most adversely affected are small, capital-constrained firms that do not have time for major lobbying efforts.

Thus, an important policy concern is that we avoid taking steps in the name of increasing competitiveness that actually interfere with the workings of innovative small businesses. The 1982 reforms of the patent litigation process appear to have had exactly this sort of unintended consequence.

ACKNOWLEDGMENTS

I thank Paul Gompers and Jenny Lanjouw for helpful discussions.

NOTES

1. This section is based in part on Gompers and Lerner (1997).

2. Unless cited, empirical data in this section is found in Fenn, Liang, and Prowse's (1995) overview of the venture-capital industry.

3. Expressed in 1995 dollars, venture capitalists provided approximately $7 billion to biotechnology firms between 1978 and 1995. The total financing raised from other sources was about $30 billion (again in 1995 dollars) (drawn from Lerner and Merges, 1997).

4. This section is based in part on Lerner (1997).

5. One question raised by this argument is, IF these obstacles are important, why has the share of R&D expenditures being undertaken by small firms substantially increased in recent years? The rapid pace of change in many facets of information and communications technology may have created more opportunities for newer organizations. Many observers have noted the difficulties that established organizations have had in responding to rapid technological change: for one example, see Michael Jensen's (1993) discussion of the "major inefficiencies [that exist] in the R&D spending decisions of a substantial number of firms."

6. Several examples are discussed in Chu (1992). Examples include the dispute between Cetus Corporation and New England Biolabs regarding the taq DNA polymerase and that between Texas Instruments and LSI Logic regarding semiconductor technology.

REFERENCES

Acs, Zoltan J., and David B. Audretsch. (1988). "Innovation in Large and Small Firms: An Empirical Analysis." *American Economic Review*, 78, 678–690.

Administrative Office of the United States Courts. (Various years). *Annual Report of the Director.* Washington, DC: U.S. Government Printing Office.

Baldwin, William L., and John T. Scott. (1987). *Market Structure and Technological Change*. Chur, Switzerland: Harwood Academic.

Calvert, Ian A. (1980). "An Overview of Interference Practice. "*Journal of the Patent Office Society*, 62, 290–308.

Calvert, Ian A., and Michael Sofocleous. (1992). "Interference Statistics for Fiscal Years 1989 to 1991." *Journal of the Patent and Trademark Office Society*, 74, 822–826.

Chartrand, Sabra. (1995). "Facing High-Tech Issues, New Patents Chief in Reinventing a Staid Agency." *New York Times*, July 14, p. 17.

Chu, Michael P. (1992). "An Antitrust Solution to the New Wave of Predatory Patent Infringement Litigation." *William and Mary Law Review*, 33, 1341–1368.

Cohen, Wesley M., and Richard C. Levin. (1989). "Empirical Studies of Innovation and Market Structure." In Richard Schmalensee and Robert D. Willig (eds.), *Handbook of Industrial Organization* (vol. 2, ch. 18). New York: North-Holland.

Cohen, Wesley M., Richard C. Levin, and David C. Mowery. (1987). "Firm Size and R&D Intensity: A Re-Examination." *Journal of Industrial Economics*, 35, 543–563.

Fenn, George, Nellie Liang, and Steven Prowse. (1995). *The Economics of the Private Equity Industry*. Washington, DC: Federal Reserve Board.

Gompers, Paul A., and Josh Lerner. (1997). "Venture Capital." In Elias Carayannis and Eric von Hippel (eds.), *Handbook of Technology Management*. New York: CRC Press.

Harmon, Robert L. (1991). *Patents and the Federal Circuit*. Washington, DC: Bureau of National Affairs.

Henderson, Rebecca. (1993). "Underinvestment and Incompetence as Responses to Radical Innovation: Evidence from the Photolithographic Alignment Equipment Industry." *Rand Journal of Economic*, 24, 248–270.

Jensen, Michael C. (1993). "Presidential Address: The Modern Industrial Revolution, Exit, and the Failure of Internal Control Systems." *Journal of Finance*, 48, 831–880.

Jewkes, John, David Sawers, and Richard Stillerman. (1958). *The Sources of Invention*. London: St. Martins Press.

Kingston, William. (1992). "Is the United States Right About 'First-to-Invent'?" *European Intellectual Property Review*, 7, 223–262.

Koen, Mary S. (1990). *Survey of Small Business Use of Intellectual Property Protection: Report of a Survey Conducted by MO-SCI Corporation for the Small Business Administration*. Rolla, MO: MO-SCI Corp.

Koenig, Gloria K. (1980). *Patent Invalidity: A Statistical and Substantive Analysis.* New York: Clark Boardman.

Lerner, Josh. (1995). "Patenting in the Shadow of Competitors." *Journal of Law and Economic,* 38, 563–595.

Lerner, Josh. (1997). "Discussion." In *Technology and Growth: Proceeding of the Fortieth Economic Conference* (pp. 208–213). Boston: Federal Reserve Bank of Boston.

Lerner, Josh, and Robert Merges. (1997). "The Control of Strategic Alliances: An Empirical Analysis of Biotechnology Collaborations." Working Paper, Harvard University and University of California at Berkeley.

Merges, Robert P. (1992). *Patent Law and Policy.* Charlottesville, NC: Michie.

Peltz, Michael. (1996). "High Tech's Premier Venture Capitalist." *Institutional Investor,* 30 (June), 89–98.

Reinganum, Jennifer R. (1989). "The Timing of Innovation: Research, Development and Diffusion." In Richard Schmalensee and Robert D. Willig (eds.), *Handbook of Industrial Organization* (vol. 1, ch. 14). New York: North-Holland.

Rosen, Miriam. (1992). "Texas Instruments' $250 Million-a-Year Profit Center." *American Lawyer,* 14 (March), 56–63.

U.S. Patent and Trademark Office. (Various years). *Annual Report of the Commissioner.* Washington, DC: U.S. Government Printing Office.

INDEX

Page numbers in *italics* indicate figures. Page numbers followed by "t" indicate tables.

The U.S. Small Business Administration's Office of Advocacy was created by an act of Congress in 1976 to protect, strengthen and effectively represent the nation's small businesses within the federal government's rulemaking processes. As part of this mandate, the office conducts policy studies on issues of concern to small businesses and also compiles and publishes data on small businesses' characteristics and contributions.

For instant access to small business resources, statistics and research visit the Office of Advocacy's home page at ***http://www.sba.gov/ADVO/stats/***. Or call the office at (202) 205-6533.

If you would like to be included on our economic research mailing list, please complete the form below and mail it to:

U.S. Small Business Administration
Office of Advocacy
Mail Code: 3114
409 Third Street, SW
Washington, DC 20416
Attn: Darlene Moye-Mahmoud

Name: ________________
Title: ________________
Company or Organization: ____________________________
Address: ______________________________________
City: __________ State: __________ Zip Code: __________
Phone Number: __________ Fax Number: ____________
E-mail Address: ______________

Would you like to receive requests for research proposals (RFP) from the Office of Advocacy?

Yes ☐ No ☐

Would you like to receive the Office of Advocacy's monthly newsletter, *The Small Business Advocate?*

Yes ☐ No ☐

MIX
Papier aus verantwortungsvollen Quellen
Paper from responsible sources
FSC® C105338

If you have any concerns about our products,
you can contact us on
ProductSafety@springernature.com

In case Publisher is established outside the EU,
the EU authorized representative is:
Springer Nature Customer Service Center GmbH
Europaplatz 3, 69115 Heidelberg, Germany

Printed by Libri Plureos GmbH
in Hamburg, Germany